TM

References for the Rest of Us!™

BESTSELLING BOOK SERIES

Do you find that traditional reference books are overloaded with technical details and advice you'll never use? Do you postpone important life decisions because you just don't want to deal with them? Then our *For Dummies®* business and general reference book series is for you.

For Dummies business and general reference books are written for those frustrated and hard-working souls who know they aren't dumb, but find that the myriad of personal and business issues and the accompanying horror stories make them feel helpless. *For Dummies* books use a lighthearted approach, a down-to-earth style, and even cartoons and humorous icons to dispel fears and build confidence. Lighthearted but not lightweight, these books are perfect survival guides to solve your everyday personal and business problems.

"More than a publishing phenomenon, 'Dummies' is a sign of the times."

— The New York Times

"A world of detailed and authoritative information is packed into them…"

— U.S. News and World Report

"…you won't go wrong buying them."

— Walter Mossberg, Wall Street Journal, on For Dummies books

Already, millions of satisfied readers agree. They have made For Dummies the #1 introductory level computer book series and a best-selling business book series. They have written asking for more. So, if you're looking for the best and easiest way to learn about business and other general reference topics, look to For Dummies to give you a helping hand.

6/01

Business Plans Kit For Dummies®

Understanding the Elements of a Great Business Idea

Got a great idea? Not sure if it's worth pursuing? Consider the following criteria that great business ideas possess:

- The idea is something you really want to spend time doing
- The idea meets a need or solves a problem
- The idea takes advantage of new opportunities
- The idea has a good chance of making money
- You have the skills, talents, and education to make the idea a reality

Recognizing Why You Need a Business Plan

Consider the following reasons you need a business plan, no matter what sort of business you're in:

- To describe who you are and what you do
- To scope out your customers and competitors
- To decide exactly what steps you need to take to succeed
- To set goals and objectives
- To create a timeline for when tasks need to happen
- To make sure your finances are in order
- To plan for the unexpected
- To gauge your progress

Making a Fantastic Business Plan

Besides including the seven standard components, a great business plan also includes the following:

- A concise executive summary that hits all the key points
- A mission statement that describes and inspires
- A set of measurable goals and objectives
- A complete financial analysis
- An action plan that's both ambitious and doable
- A written document that's clear and well organized
- A schedule for reviewing and revising the plan
- A commitment to using the plan as a blueprint

Business Plans Kit For Dummies®

Avoiding Business-Planning Pitfalls

Your business plan — and your business — can fail for any of the following reasons:

- **Failing to plan in the first place:** Not having a formal business plan is the number-one reason businesses fail.
- **Leaving out values and vision:** Both can be powerful tools to inspire and motivate everyone involved with your company.
- **Misreading your customers:** Companies that fail to understand what their customers want or need soon find themselves in big trouble.
- **Underestimating your competition:** To stay ahead of the pack, you have to know what the rest of the pack is doing.
- **Ignoring your own strengths:** Effective business plans leverage the key strengths of the company and its people.
- **Overlooking your weaknesses:** Failing to recognize and improve weak areas in the company can threaten the health of your entire business.
- **Keeping your plan a secret:** A business plan can guide and inspire only if people at all levels know about it.
- **Failing to organize around the plan:** To be useful, a business plan must act as a blueprint for how to manage and operate your company.

Identifying the Key Components of a Business Plan

When creating you business plan, make sure it contains the following components:

- Executive summary
- Company overview
- Business environment
- Company strategy
- Company description
- Financial review
- Action plan

Succeeding in Business

Taking any of the following steps can create a successful business:

- Offer unbeatable prices
- Provide the best service around
- Offer a unique product or service
- Focus on the needs of specific customer groups

Cheat Sheet $2.95 value. Item 5365-8.
For more information about Hungry Minds, call 1-800-762-2974.

For Dummies: Bestselling Book Series for Beginners

Business Plans Kit FOR DUMMIES®

by Steven Peterson, PhD and Peter E. Jaret

Best-Selling Books • Digital Downloads • e-Books • Answer Networks • e-Newsletters • Branded Web Sites • e-Learning

New York, NY ◆ Cleveland, OH ◆ Indianapolis, IN

Business Plans Kit For Dummies®

Published by:
Hungry Minds, Inc.
909 Third Avenue
New York, NY 10022
www.hungryminds.com
www.dummies.com

Library of Congress Control Number: 2001091994

ISBN: 0-7645-5365-8

Printed in the United States of America

10 9 8 7 6 5 4 3 2

1O/TR/RS/QR/IN

Distributed in the United States by Hungry Minds, Inc.

Distributed by CDG Books Canada Inc. for Canada; by Transworld Publishers Limited in the United Kingdom; by IDG Norge Books for Norway; by IDG Sweden Books for Sweden; by IDG Books Australia Publishing Corporation Pty. Ltd. for Australia and New Zealand; by TransQuest Publishers Pte Ltd. for Singapore, Malaysia, Thailand, Indonesia, and Hong Kong; by Gotop Information Inc. for Taiwan; by ICG Muse, Inc. for Japan; by Intersoft for South Africa; by Eyrolles for France; by International Thomson Publishing for Germany, Austria and Switzerland; by Distribuidora Cuspide for Argentina; by LR International for Brazil; by Galileo Libros for Chile; by Ediciones ZETA S.C.R. Ltda. for Peru; by WS Computer Publishing Corporation, Inc., for the Philippines; by Contemporanea de Ediciones for Venezuela; by Express Computer Distributors for the Caribbean and West Indies; by Micronesia Media Distributor, Inc. for Micronesia; by Chips Computadoras S.A. de C.V. for Mexico; by Editorial Norma de Panama S.A. for Panama; by American Bookshops for Finland.

For general information on Hungry Minds' products and services please contact our Customer Care department; within the U.S. at 800-762-2974, outside the U.S. at 317-572-3993 or fax 317-572-4002.

For sales inquiries and resellers information, including discounts, premium and bulk quantity sales and foreign language translations please contact our Customer Care department at 800-434-3422, fax 317-572-4002 or write to Hungry Minds, Inc., Attn: Customer Care department, 10475 Crosspoint Boulevard, Indianapolis, IN 46256.

For information on licensing foreign or domestic rights, please contact our Sub-Rights Customer Care department at 212-884-5000.

For information on using Hungry Minds' products and services in the classroom or for ordering examination copies, please contact our Educational Sales department at 800-434-2086 or fax 317-572-4005.

Please contact our Public Relations department at 212-884-5163 for press review copies or 212-884-5000 for author interviews and other publicity information or fax 212-884-5400.

For authorization to photocopy items for corporate, personal, or educational use, please contact Copyright Clearance Center, 222 Rosewood Drive, Danvers, MA 01923, or fax 978-750-4470.

About the Authors

Steven Peterson is founder and CEO of Strategic Play, a management training company specializing in hands-on software tools designed to enhance business strategy, business planning, and general management skills. He is the creator and developer of the Protean Strategist, a business simulation that reproduces a dynamic business environment where participant teams run companies and compete against each other in a fast-changing marketplace. Each team is responsible for developing a business plan along with the strategies and programs to put it to work. For more information, check out the Web site at `www.StrategicPlay.com`.

Steven has worked with both large and small companies around the world on strategy and business planning, strategic marketing, new product development, and product management. He uses the Protean Strategist simulation to help managers improve their skills in teamwork and collaboration across functional areas and even across cultures. Prior to founding Strategic Play, Steven served for many years as a consultant to companies in the United States and abroad. He holds advanced degrees in mathematics and physics and received his doctorate from Cornell University.

Peter Jaret is an award-winning writer whose work has appeared in *Newsweek, National Geographic, Health, Men's Journal, Reader's Digest,* and dozens of other magazines. He is the author of *In Self-Defense: The Human Immune System* and *Active Living Every Day.* Over the past 15 years, Peter has also consulted with a wide variety of companies to develop marketing brochures, informational white papers, and annual reports. His clients include the Electric Power Research Institute, Lucas Arts, The California Endowment, WebMD, BabyCenter, Stanford University, Collabria, and Home Planet Technologies.

In 1992, Peter received the American Medical Association's first-place award for medical reporting, and in 1997, he won the prestigious James Beard Award for food and nutrition writing. Peter holds degrees from Northwestern University and the University of Virginia.

Authors' Acknowledgments

Many people helped us in the writing of this book. We especially want to thank Tere Drenth, Heather Gregory, Jill Alexander, Holly McGuire, Carmen Krikorian, Travis Silvers, Cindy Kitchel, and Rick Oliver for all the time, effort, and hard work they put in to making this project such a success.

Publisher's Acknowledgments

We're proud of this book; please send us your comments through our Online Registration Form located at www.dummies.com.

Some of the people who helped bring this book to market include the following:

Acquisitions, Editorial, and Media Development

Project Editors: Heather Gregory, Tere Drenth

Acquisitions Editors: Jill Alexander, Holly McGuire

General Reviewer: Richard Oliver

Senior Permissions Editor: Carmen Krikorian

Media Development Specialist: Travis Silvers

Editorial Manager: Pamela Mourouzis

Media Development Manager: Laura VanWinkle

Editorial Administrator: Michelle Hacker

Editorial Assistant: Carol Strickland

Cover Photo: © David de Lossy/Image Bank

Production

Project Coordinator: Dale White

Layout and Graphics: Amy Adrian, Jackie Nicholas, Jill Piscitelli, Jacque Schneider, Brian Torwelle, Jeremey Unger

Proofreaders: Susan Moritz, Dwight Ramsey, Marianne Santy, TECHBOOKS Production Services

Indexer: TECHBOOKS Production Services

Hungry Minds Consumer Reference Group

Business: Kathleen A. Welton, Vice President and Publisher; Kevin Thornton, Acquisitions Manager

Cooking/Gardening: Jennifer Feldman, Associate Vice President and Publisher

Education/Reference: Diane Graves Steele, Vice President and Publisher

Lifestyles/Pets: Kathleen Nebenhaus, Vice President and Publisher; Tracy Boggier, Managing Editor

Travel: Michael Spring, Vice President and Publisher; Suzanne Jannetta, Editorial Director; Brice Gosnell, Publishing Director

Hungry Minds Consumer Editorial Services: Kathleen Nebenhaus, Vice President and Publisher; Kristin A. Cocks, Editorial Director; Cindy Kitchel, Editorial Director

Hungry Minds Consumer Production: Debbie Stailey, Production Director

Contents at a Glance

Introduction 1

Part I: Doing Your Planning Homework 5

Chapter 1: Beginning with a Brainstorm 7
Chapter 2: Starting Your Planning Engine 25
Chapter 3: Laying Down the Ground Rules 47

Part II: Building Your Plan's Components 71

Chapter 4: Assessing the Business Environment 73
Chapter 5: Explaining Your Strategy 103
Chapter 6: Describing Your Company 127
Chapter 7: Examining Your Financial Situation 145

Part III: Adjusting Your Plan to Fit Your Needs 173

Chapter 8: Planning for the Self-Employed 175
Chapter 9: Planning for a Small Business 191
Chapter 10: Planning in the New Economy 203
Chapter 11: Planning a Not-for-Profit Organization 219

Part IV: Making the Most of Your Plan 235

Chapter 12: Putting Your Plan Together 237
Chapter 13: Putting Your Plan to Work 261

Part V: The Part of Tens 289

Chapter 14: Ten Ways to Evaluate a New Business Idea 291
Chapter 15: Ten Things a Business Plan Does for You 295
Chapter 16: Ten Ways to Fund Your Business Plan 299
Chapter 17: Ten Possible Signs That Your Plan Needs An Overhaul 303

Appendix: About the CD 307

Index 317

Hungry Minds End-User License Agreement 334

Installation Instructions 336

Cartoons at a Glance

By Rich Tennant

"I appreciate your sharing your dreams and wishes for starting your own pool and spa business, but maybe I should explain more fully what we at the Make-A-Wish Foundation are all about."

page 289

"My business plan has changed a little this year."

page 5

"You bought what? You know we're on a budget. Now take Hughes Electric back to General Motors and see if you can get your money back."

page 235

"You can become a 'corporation' or a 'sole proprietor,' Mr. Holk. But there's simply no legal way of filing yourself as a 'formidable presence'."

page 71

"This is a 'dot-com' company, Stacey. Risk-taking is a given. If you're not comfortable running with scissors, cleaning your ear with a darning needle, or swimming right after a big meal, this might not be the place for you."

page 173

Cartoon Information:
Fax: 978-546-7747
E-Mail: richtennant@the5thwave.com
World Wide Web: www.the5thwave.com

Table of Contents

Introduction 1

About This Book 1
Foolish Assumptions 1
How This Book Is Organized 2
Part I: Doing Your Planning Homework 2
Part II: Building Your Plan's Components 2
Part III: Adjusting Your Plan to Fit Your Needs 3
Part IV: Making the Most of Your Plan 3
Part V: The Part of Tens 3
Icons Used in This Book 3
Where to Go from Here 4

Part I: Doing Your Planning Homework 5

Chapter 1: Beginning with a Brainstorm 7

Snaring that Great Idea 7
Being creative alone 8
Being creative together 12
Identifying a Business Opportunity 14
Selecting the finalists 14
Choosing a winner 16
Doing Your First Reality Check 19
Getting a little help from a friend 19
Relying on yourself 20
Forms on the CD-ROM 24

Chapter 2: Starting Your Planning Engine 25

Convincing Yourself that a Plan Is Important 25
Identifying Who Your Plan Is for 27
Your audience 27
Your message 30
Understanding What's in a Business Plan 33
Reviewing plans from top to bottom 33
One step at a time 35
Planning Your Time Frame 37
Start to finish 37
Milestones in between 38

Preparing for the Real World 40
Locating information resources 40
Expert advice 41
Helping hands 42
Forms on the CD-ROM 44

Chapter 3: Laying Down the Ground Rules 47

Giving Your Company its Mission 48
Asking basic questions 48
Framing your mission 50
Crafting your statement 50
Putting your mission statement to work 52
Setting Goals and Objectives 55
Revisiting your mission 56
Goal-setting ACES 57
Covering all bases 58
Making final choices 59
Exploring Values and Vision 61
Understanding why values matter 61
Uncovering values you already hold 63
Writing a values statement 63
Writing a vision statement 66
Forms on the CD-ROM 68

Part II: Building Your Plan's Components 71

Chapter 4: Assessing the Business Environment 73

Taking a Close Look at Your Industry 74
Understanding the business you're really in 74
Looking at your industry's big picture 76
Paying the price of admission 78
Sizing Up Your Customers 81
Describing the ideal customer 81
Doing business with business customers 85
Discovering more about all your customers 88
Grouping your customers together 90
Checking Out the Competition 93
Identifying your stealth competitors 94
Using cloak-and-dagger methods 95
Staying a step ahead 98
Forms on the CD-ROM 100

Chapter 5: Explaining Your Strategy 103

Putting Together Your SWOT Team 104
Sizing up strengths and weaknesses 104
Looking for opportunities and threats 109
Conducting a SWOT analysis 110
Defining Your Business Model 112
Considering where the money comes from 113
Staying in the black 113
Understanding that timing is everything 115
Knowing how customers pay 116
Creating a business model of your own 117
Charting Ways to Grow 117
Understanding your options 117
Planning for growth 119
Outlining an Exit Strategy 120
Forms on the CD-ROM 124

Chapter 6: Describing Your Company 127

Introducing Your Company 128
Hitting the high points 128
Describing exactly what you do 129
Examining Your Business Capabilities 131
Research and development 132
Operations 133
Sales and marketing 134
Distribution and delivery 135
Customer service 136
Management 139
Organization 139
Focusing On What You Do Best 142
Forms on the CD-ROM 144

Chapter 7: Examining Your Financial Situation 145

Putting Together an Income Statement 146
Creating a Balance Sheet 151
Constructing a Cash Flow Statement 159
Forecasting and Budgeting 167
Your financial forecast 167
The master budget 170
Forms on the CD-ROM 171

Part III: Adjusting Your Plan to Fit Your Needs 173

Chapter 8: Planning for the Self-Employed 175

Understanding the Benefits of a Written Plan 175
Knowing What Your Plan Is For 177
Reviewing the Essential Parts of Your Plan 178
Company overview 179
Business environment 179
Company description and strategy 181
Financial review 182
Action plan 182
Putting a Price on What You Do 182
Knowing how to charge 183
Knowing what to charge 184
Getting paid 188
Forms on the CD-ROM 190

Chapter 9: Planning for a Small Business 191

Recognizing the Importance of a Plan 192
Knowing What to Focus on in Your Plan 192
Business environment 193
Company description 195
Company strategy 195
Financial review 196
Action plan 196
Growing Your Small Business 197
Making a name for yourself 198
Managing change 199
Growing or not growing 200
Forms on the CD-ROM 202

Chapter 10: Planning in the New Economy 203

Planning at Internet Speed 204
Reviewing four lessons from the wild west 205
Zeroing in on what matters most 206
Building a Stand-Alone Internet business 208
Fine-tuning your value proposition 209
Putting together a workable business model 212
Adding an Internet Extension to Bricks and Mortar 214
Keeping the Faith 216
Forms on the CD-ROM 218

Chapter 11: Planning a Not-for-Profit Organization 219

Running Your Not-for-Profit Like a Business 220
Fine-tuning your mission and vision 221
Creating the appropriate structure 223
Setting clear goals and objectives 224
Explaining How You'll Get the Job Done 226
Describing what you do 227
Keeping the books 231
Forms on the CD-ROM 234

Part IV: Making the Most of Your Plan 235

Chapter 12: Putting Your Plan Together 237

Doing Your Homework 238
Locating Additional Resources 240
Your local bookstore 240
The Web 241
Business software 243
Expert advice 244
Self help 245
Putting Your Planning Team Together 246
Delegating responsibilities 246
Setting the ground rules 248
Putting first things last 248
Keeping track of it all 249
Targeting Your Plan to Key Audiences 252
Identifying your stakeholders 252
Addressing more than one audience 253
Creating alternate versions of your plan 256
Making Sure All the Pieces Fit 257
Forms on the CD-ROM 260

Chapter 13: Putting Your Plan to Work 261

Organizing Your Company around the Business Plan 262
Form meets function 262
Duties and responsibilities 263
Systems and procedures 265
Making the Most of Your People 266
Distributing your plan 268
Starting at the top 270
Creating the vision thing 272

Leading from within 272
Encouraging pride of ownership 274
Investing in skills 275
Using Your Plan in Times of Trouble 277
Recognizing the warning signs 278
Analyzing your current situation 280
Charting your turnaround 281
Keeping Your Plan Fresh 284
Reviewing the situation 284
Encouraging feedback 285
Forms on the CD-ROM 287

Part V: The Part of Tens 289

Chapter 14: Ten Ways to Evaluate a New Business Idea 291

Is This Something I Really Want to Do? 291
Is This Something I am Capable of Doing? 292
Does This Tap My Personal Strengths? 292
Can I Describe it in 25 Words or Less? 292
What's the Closest Thing to This in the Marketplace? 293
Does it Solve a Customer Problem or Meet a Real Need? 293
Does it Take Advantage of a New Opportunity? 293
What's its Biggest Drawback or Limitation? 294
Will it Make Money — and How Fast? 294
Am I Willing to Re-mortgage my House? 294

Chapter 15: Ten Things a Business Plan Does for You 295

Put Your Business Idea to the Test 295
Turn a Good Idea into a Viable Business 296
Show You What You're Up Against 296
Specify What You Need to Start Your Business 296
. . . and How Much It's Likely to Cost 297
Help Get You Get Funding 297
Tell the World Who You Are 297
Inspire Your Employees 297
Gauge Your Progress 298
Prepare You for the Unexpected 298

Chapter 16: Ten Ways to Fund Your Business Plan 299

Your Own Pocket 299
Friends and Family 299
Bank Loan 300

Commercial Line of Credit 300
Equipment Leasing 300
An SBA Loan 301
Deep-Pocket Partners 301
Venture Capital 301
Angel Money 302
Prospective Customers 302

Chapter 17: Ten Possible Signs That Your Plan Needs An Overhaul 303

Costs Rise, Revenues Fall 303
Sales Figures Head South 304
Employee Morale Sags 304
Key Projects Fall Behind 304
Financials Fall Short 305
New Competitors Appear 305
Technology Shakes Up Your World 305
Important Customers Defect 305
Business Strategy Does a 180 306
You're Growing too Fast 306

Appendix: About the CD 307

System Requirements 307
Using the CD with Microsoft Windows 308
Using the CD with Mac OS 309
What You'll Find on the CD 309
Business plan forms 310
Business plan software 314
Other software 315
Troubleshooting 316

Index....................317

Hungry Minds End-User License Agreement 334

Installation Instructions....................336

Introduction

So you're interested in starting a business? Well, you've come to the right place. The best way to start a business is with a solid business plan. And as almost every successful entrepreneur will tell you, the better your plan, the more likely you are to succeed.

The idea of putting together a business plan can seem a little daunting, especially if you've never done it before. You can probably think of all sorts of basic questions right off the top of your head: What's a business plan supposed to include? What are all the other things you need to think about? Do I really have what it takes to start a new business venture? What if something goes wrong?

Relax. In this book, we walk you through all the steps involved in putting together a business plan — and a new business. In particular, we help you avoid the pitfalls that sometimes knock new companies off track. We also give you plenty of tips on how to get the most out of your business plan. And hey, we even promise to make the whole process not only easy, but even kind of fun.

About This Book

You can find plenty of books on the theories and principles of business planning. This one's different. We've cut through all the fancy talk to provide a no-nonsense, step-by-step approach to putting a business plan together. We've created dozens of simple forms to make your job easier. And we've included examples from all kinds of businesses, everything from freelance contractors and local bookshops to online retailers and small not-for-profit organizations.

Foolish Assumptions

We figure it's a pretty safe bet that you're interested in either starting or improving your own business. Maybe you have nothing more than the glimmer of a good idea for a company. Or maybe you've already started a business and have finally decided it's high time to write a plan. Either way, we assume you're like a lot of entrepreneurs: excited, ambitious, and a little nervous at the thought of creating a business plan. Being excited and ambitious is good, but you don't need to be nervous. With a little bit of effort, anyone can put together a solid business plan. You don't need any previous experience in business to make your way through this book. And if you do have some experience, you'll still find plenty of useful advice.

We also assume you're interested in starting a small- or medium-sized business. Why? Because that's how most businesses begin. After all, it takes a few years to grow up to become the next Microsoft or General Motors. So to fit right in, the examples we include are also mostly from small- and medium-sized businesses.

How This Book Is Organized

We've set out to offer a simple, step-by-step approach to business planning. At the same time, we know that not everyone begins at the same starting point. So we've also organized this book in such a way that you can find exactly what you need and put that information to use right away. The following sections describe the basic layout of the book.

Part I: Doing Your Planning Homework

To get you started, Chapter 1 offers advice on how to brainstorm about and refine your business idea to make sure it stands a serious chance of success. Chapter 2 introduces the basic components of a business plan. In Chapter 3, we help you create a mission and vision for your company, and then help you set some important business goals.

Part II: Building Your Plan's Components

In this part of the book, we get down to the nitty-gritty details of business planning. Chapter 4 helps you assess your business environment so that you have a clear idea of exactly what you're up against in terms of competition and the marketplace. Chapter 5 guides you in shaping a strategy that's based on your own strengths as well as the opportunities out there. In Chapter 6, we help you analyze all aspects of your company in order to make sure you concentrate on what you do best. Finally, in Chapter 7, we pull out a pocket calculator and help you make sense out of the financial reports and projections you need to start and run a business.

Part III: Adjusting Your Plan to Fit Your Needs

In this part, we zero in on four different kinds of businesses and the special planning issues they face. Chapter 8 looks at planning for the self-employed, Chapter 9 focuses on small-business planning, Chapter 10 considers planning in the new economy, and in Chapter 11, we tackle the special issues involved in putting together a not-for-profit business. Chances are, you'll recognize your own business venture in one of these chapters, but because different kinds of businesses face many of the same issues, we recommend browsing through all of the chapters in this part to find general advice and information.

Part IV: Making the Most of Your Plan

In Part IV, we tackle the nuts and bolts of putting your written plan together and then putting it to work for you. Chapter 12 offers advice on assembling a planning team, gathering all the components of your business plan together, and writing up a concise and reader-friendly document. In Chapter 13, we show you how to get the most out of your business plan by making it an integral part of your company's organization and operations.

Part V: The Part of Tens

Don't you find top ten lists irresistible? The ten secrets of successful entrepreneurs, ten dating no-nos, or ten tips to a slimmer, trimmer you.

In this part of the book, we offer our own top tens — including ten ways to evaluate a business idea and ten great ways to get your business plan funded. In fact, you won't want to miss out on any of the lists we've come up with.

Icons Used in This Book

What would a *For Dummies* book be without these perky little icons alerting you to all sorts of useful stuff? Here are the icons you'll find between our covers:

Expert tidbits designed to help save you time or trouble.

Business planning essentials you don't want to forget.

Common problems or pitfalls to avoid.

Real-life examples that provide useful lessons on business planning.

A "heads-up" that the form or resource we're talking about also appears on the CD-ROM.

Advice about research, analysis, strategy, and business decisions that will definitely show up in your written business plan.

Where to Go from Here

You can start anywhere you want in this book, but we'd like to offer a bit of advice: Chapter 1 isn't a bad place to begin, because it's designed to help you fine-tune your business idea. Then again, if your idea is already polished up and ready to go, the chapters in Part II will help you shape your great idea into an even better business plan. If you're planning a freelance business, a small business, a not-for-profit, or an e-business, don't forget to check out the chapters in Part III that are devoted to each of these types of business. Of course, you're welcome to jump around (using the index) to find exactly what you need at any time.

Part I

Doing Your Planning Homework

"My business plan has changed a little this year."

In this part . . .

Why write a business plan? Because it's the best way anyone's ever invented to turn a good idea into a thriving company. By doing the homework involved in business planning, you take the first steps toward creating a company with a long and prosperous future.

In this part, we help you get started by offering useful tips on how to come up with a great business idea — and how to do a reality check to make sure it's worth pursuing. We help you kick off the planning process by reviewing the main components of a business plan. Finally, we plunge right in and guide you through the steps involved in creating a company mission and vision, along with a set of business goals and objectives that enable you to achieve that vision.

Chapter 1

Beginning with a Brainstorm

In This Chapter

- Developing great ideas
- Deciding which ideas are worth pursuing

Chances are, a business plan is near the top of your to-do list. How do we know? Well, you're reading this book, for one thing. You're also probably aware that writing a plan is an important step in making your new business venture a reality. And you're absolutely right. But it's not necessarily the first step.

What comes before a business plan? The *idea* behind the business. Maybe you've already taken your first step and not quite realized it yet, or maybe you're still struggling to find a really great business idea. Either way, your idea doesn't have to be one of a kind, and it doesn't have to be the biggest thing since MTV. But it does have to be solid enough to stand a good chance of making it out in the cold, cruel business world.

In this chapter, we look at different ways to come up with a great business idea. We also look at how you can turn that great idea into a real business opportunity, showing you how to decide whether you have a business proposition that other people — investors, customers, clients, even your colleagues — will want to buy into. Then we help you with your first reality check. Finally, we give you some suggestions about how to ask for advice, and we give you some tools you can use to take stock of your own personal resources.

Snaring that Great Idea

We're in an age when almost everything is changing faster than it's ever changed before — from technologies to people's tastes, from careers to the business challenges we face. You may not like the changes around you, because they come with so much uncertainty and risk. But change can also lead to big opportunities.

If you're like us, you probably come across great new business ideas all the time. And you ask yourself, "Why didn't I think of that? And just how did they come up with it?" Maybe a light bulb simply goes on in somebody's head. Or maybe they're just plain lucky. But look a little closer at any great business idea out there, and you're likely to find that a lot of time and effort went into making it happen. This section considers ways to make some of your own time and efforts pay off.

Being creative alone

Humans are a creative bunch. We're the ones who invented the airplane, bendable straws, computers, the sports bra, snowboards, light bulbs, the jitterbug, disposable diapers, the safety pin, and *Star Wars*. We invent to save lives: the polio vaccine, air bags, and fat-free cheesecake. We invent just for fun: game shows, roller blades, and professional wrestling. And we invent to express our deepest selves: poetry, painting, filmmaking, dance, and music.

Creativity is at the heart of the new economy, revitalizing every facet of the marketplace in every corner of the globe. Where does this creativity come from? From people very much like you. Really. Now we're not promising to make you into a creative genius overnight, but we do believe that everyone can be a lot more creative than they usually are.

To see what you can accomplish on the creativity front all by yourself, we've whipped up an exercise called the *idea blender.* Work with us here — even if you already have a good business idea in your back pocket. A little creative thinking, after all, can always make a good idea even better.

To use the idea blender, you need a pair of dice, a couple of sheets of paper, and Forms 1-1, 1-2, and 1-3 on the CD-ROM. Before you fire up your own idea blender, however, take a look at Figure 1-1, which shows an example of how the blending process begins. The idea behind the idea blender is to mix and match the entries randomly, based on the throw of the dice. If you're lucky, the pairings will spur some ideas you never thought of before.

Sound a bit off-the-wall? That's exactly the point. Keep in mind that the word *brainstorm* refers equally well to a bright idea or a sudden fit of insanity. That notion is important here, because bright ideas often sound a bit peculiar when they're first expressed. (Think of online chat rooms and skateboards, for example.) Another thing to remember is that most creative ideas often emerge by taking familiar pieces of the world around you and putting them together in new and different ways. In this case, the creativity is in the combination. (Think of TV dinners and car radios, for example.)

MY FAVORITE THINGS		
Three important things about myself:		
1. I love to travel	2. I'm an organizer	3. I shop a lot
Three things I really like to do:		
4. Triathlons	5. Play with computers	6. Collect folk art
Three products or services I enjoy using a lot:		
7. Specialty catalogs	8. Online travel sites	9. Hybrid bicycles
Three products or services I would like to see:		
10. Digital cash	11. Briefcase bikes	12. Instant holograms

Figure 1-1: Identifying personal traits and interests.

Begin by using Forms 1-1 and 1-2, which are on the CD-ROM.

1. **In the first row of Form 1-1, list things about yourself.**

   List things like the following: I love kids, I'm good with computers, I'm a detail person, I work best alone, or I conceptualize well.

2. **In the second row, list things you like to do.**

   Include hobbies like playing video games, listening to classical music, hang-gliding, refinishing antiques, or reading.

3. **In the third row, list great products or services you really enjoy using.**

   Examples include personal organizers, online banking, doggy daycare, or stair machines.

4. **In the fourth row, dream up some products and services you wish really existed.**

   The list may include things like solar-powered cell phones or electric sports cars.

5. **Blend these items together and see what comes up, using Form 1-2.**

   - Roll your pair of dice and enter the number that comes up in the top box marked "a."
   - Roll again and enter that number in the box marked "b."
   - Continue rolling and writing down the numbers that come up in the remainder of the boxes in columns "a" and "b."

   Each of the numbers you've written down corresponds to an item in Form 1-1. Write down the two items together in column "c."

   If you're not sure how to do this, look at the example in Figure 1-2, which shows how rolling the dice results in mixing up the numbered items in Figure 1-1. In this case, the idea blender came up with some pretty weird ideas, such as collecting folk art using a portable bike. But it also came up with some provocative ones. How about a travel site for triathletes? Or an online emporium that uses digital cash?

6. **Try to pull at least two promising business ideas out of Form 1-2 and write them up as short phrases and capture them in Form 1-3.**

   In our example, the idea blender came up with at least two decent business ideas, and we've captured them in Figure 1-3.

THE IDEA BLENDER — MIXING AND MATCHING YOUR INTERESTS GRID

a.	b.	c.
10	3	I like to shop and would like to see digital cash.
6	11	I collect folk art and would like to see portable bikes.
7	5	I enjoy computers and specialty catalogs.
2	9	I'm an organizer and like hybrid bikes.
8	4	I enjoy online travel sites and do triathlons.

Figure 1-2: Mixing and matching your interests in the idea blender.

THE IDEA BLENDER — YOUR BUSINESS IDEA BRAINSTORMS
Brainstorm #1: An Internet emporium of specialty shops from around the world with a centralized ordering and payment system.
Brainstorm #2: A tour company specializing in travel adventures created around sporting competitions and catering to the amateur athlete.

Figure 1-3: Using the idea blender to create new business ideas.

Take a careful look at the combined entries in column "c" to see what kind of weird and — we hope — wonderful ideas have emerged. Bear with us here: Some of these pairings may sound pretty darn strange. Some combine traits you have with products you like. Others combine two traits. Still others bring two products or services together. The point here is to get you thinking *out of the box*. What do we mean by that? Very simply, we want you to look at and focus on the world around you in completely new ways.

Don't dismiss an idea just because it seems a little too far out at first glance. Take our word for it: You don't always recognize a good idea when you first see it. Who would have jumped at the notion of a pet rock, after all? And who would've guessed that those sleek little foldable scooters would become a worldwide runaway success? When you look back at the combinations you come up with, give each one some serious thought. You may just find the seed of an intriguing idea that can grow into the flourishing business you're looking for.

What are the odds that the idea blender will come up with a product or service that revolutionizes the world? Well, we're not in the business of making predictions. And the truth is, revolutionary breakthroughs don't come along every day. But when they do, it's often the result of putting two things together in new and innovative ways.

After you have the hang of it, think about returning to the idea blender from time to time, using different personal traits and new rolls of the dice. You can even think about getting your friends together and using the idea blender as an after-dinner parlor game. It may turn out to be more rewarding than *Trivial Pursuit.* Get in the habit of keeping a pad and pencil (or your personal organizer) handy so that you can take down those bright ideas when and where they hit you.

Where in the world do people get those ideas?

Where do resourceful people get their most creative ideas? When innovative types were asked in an informal survey to name their top idea-generating activity, the following rankings emerged. Take a look at the list. Which activities get your own creative juice flowing? Maybe you want to spend a little more time at them over the next couple of weeks to boost your personal creativity quotient. (Just don't forget that you may find a downside to very long showers, too much napping, or overly-long commutes!)

- Taking a shower (12 percent)
- Commuting (10 percent)
- Going to sleep (10 percent)
- Just waking up (9 percent)
- At quiet moments (8 percent)
- Actively thinking (8 percent)
- Exercising (7 percent)
- Meditating (7 percent)
- Walking (5 percent)
- Talking with friends (5 percent)
- On vacation (4 percent)
- During the night (4 percent)
- In a business meeting (3 percent)
- Reading (2 percent)
- Sitting at the desk (2 percent)
- Under pressure (2 percent)
- Napping (1 percent)
- Dreaming (1 percent)

Being creative together

Often, putting a few heads together can turn a solo brainstorm into a mental hurricane. One person's problem, after all, can be another person's inspiration for an innovative solution. Getting half a dozen dynamic, inspired, and innovative individuals together is a good start, of course. But for a brainstorming session to reach its full potential, you first need to master some important communications skills.

The quickest way to kill an idea right off the bat is to say things like the following:

- It won't work.
- We're not ready for that.
- It's not practical.
- It's already been done.
- That's just plain stupid.

So the first thing you want to do is figure out how to respond to a brand-new idea in a way that doesn't squash it before it's had time to be developed. The best system we know asks you to do three things when you react to a new idea, and it's called LCS:

- L is for *likes,* as in, "What I like about your idea . . . ." Begin by saying some positive things about a new idea. That way, you encourage people to let loose with every creative idea that comes to mind.
- C is for *concerns,* as in, "What concerns me about your idea . . . ." Sharing your concerns about the new idea begins a dialogue that usually opens up and expands the creative process. If you point out a problem, someone else in the group is likely to find a creative solution.
- S is for *suggestions,* as in, "I have a few suggestions . . . ." Offering suggestions moves the brainstorming session along and may lead to the generation of a brand-new set of ideas.

After you've mastered LCS, you're ready to take on a real brainstorming session. Here's how to put one together step by step:

1. **Start with a small group of people you trust and admire.**

   Depending on your situation, you can turn to friends, relatives, professional acquaintances — anyone you think may contribute a new and useful perspective.

2. **Invite a couple of ringers.**

   Consider people you wouldn't necessarily think of asking — people you may even feel a bit uncomfortable with — but people who will definitely stretch your thinking, challenge assumptions, and take the group in new and unexpected directions.

3. **Choose the right time and place.**

   If you want people to be creative, change the scene. Go to a park, a coffee house, or a hotel lobby. The same old places can lead to the same old thinking, so be inventive.

4. **Establish ground rules.**

   Explain what you'd like the group to achieve. Introduce the LCS system so that all participants has a tool that allows them to make positive contributions to the session.

5. **Act as the group's conductor.**

   Keep the process moving forward without turning into a dictator. The following tactics may help:

   - Encourage alternates. ("How else can we do that?")
   - Stimulate visionary thinking. ("What if we had no constraints?")
   - Invite new perspectives. ("How would a child see this?")

   - Ask for specifics. ("What exactly do you mean here?")
   - Clarify the next steps. ("How should we proceed on that?")

6. **Record the results as you go along.**

   Write down as much as you can. Remember, the best ideas are often "beside the point" when they first come up. So try to capture the off-beat comments as well as the mainstream discussions.

7. **Review your notes and thoughts while they're still fresh.**

   Set aside some quality time to distill your brainstorming session into three or four business ideas that you want to continue working on.

Identifying a Business Opportunity

Great ideas aren't that easy to come up with. Creating businesses out of them can be even harder. "Genius is one percent inspiration," Thomas Edison said, "and ninety-nine percent perspiration." The same goes for business. Coming up with the idea is inspiration. When you begin to think about how to turn it into a business, that's when you begin to sweat.

Selecting the finalists

Some of the most inventive businesses can be attributed to particularly fertile brainstorming sessions. But not every good idea is totally new and innovative (and not every totally new idea is good, for that matter.) In fact, a recent survey found that the initial ideas for almost half the 500 fastest growing companies in America grew directly out of the founders' own work environment. In other words, these companies were created by people who looked around at what they were already doing and discovered a better way of doing it. The ideas most worth developing, it turns out, are those that spring up in your own backyard.

Take time out to look at the business you're already in and the work you do every day. Keep in mind that 99 percent of all businesses (both old and new) fall into one of only three broad categories:

- Products for sale
- Services for hire
- Distribution and delivery

Taking a good idea and making it yours

A successful business doesn't necessarily require a unique or original idea. Many thriving ventures are based on adapting existing ideas to particular circumstances. A few years back, a California chef we know went on a vacation to Spain and discovered the joy of *tapas,* traditional finger food that Spaniards eat during their supper hour. On the spot, the chef knew that people in L.A. would go wild for tapas. What's more, they'd love the look and feel of the classy tapas bars that thrive in cities like Barcelona. So he imported traditional Spanish food to southern California and made it his own, opening a series of tapas bars around Los Angeles.

Taking a good business idea and making it yours can mean a number of things. It may be as simple as duplicating a business that's successful in one part of the country — do-it-yourself pottery-painting stores, for example — and introducing it somewhere else. Or it may mean taking a product that's been wildly successful in one market and introducing it to another — alternative medicine for pets, for example. Occasionally, two existing products can be successfully combined into a brand new one — clock radios or WebTV.

So if you're still searching for the idea that's just right for you, put your finger on some existing product or service you really like and think of ways to place your own personal stamp on it.

Use these categories to spur your own creativity. First look at the range of products that your industry produces:

- Can you think of innovative ways to make them better?
- Can you imagine a product that completely replaces them?

Consider the services your industry offers:

- Do you notice problems with consistency?
- What's not being done that should be?
- What do customers complain most about?

Ask yourself similar questions about your distribution and delivery systems:

- What are the most serious bottlenecks?
- Can you think of clever ways to improve distribution?
- Can you envision a radically new delivery system?

Question as much of your industry as you can, and you may find yourself with a whole drawer full of promising business ideas. The real question then becomes: How do you know which promising ideas are really worth pursuing? We're the first to admit that it's not easy to know. Plenty of promising ideas have been shelved without a second thought — only to make someone else a bunch of money later on. The moral: While having good ideas is important, having the sense to recognize a real opportunity may be an even greater gift. Consider the two following suggestions:

- **Focus on ideas you're really excited about.** Often the best ideas for you are the ones that really get your juices flowing. Too many entrepreneurs make the mistake of starting businesses that they're not passionate about.
- **Pursue ideas you can follow through on.** If you feel you don't have the means or the drive to take an idea from the drawing board to the real world, it's probably not the right idea for you.

Consider the armchair inventor we know who, about ten years ago, dreamed up the idea of developing "rain sensors" that would measure the amount of rain falling on a car windshield and then adjust the wiper speed automatically. From time to time, he'd tell friends about his great idea. And everybody he told would nod their heads and say, "Wow, that's a great idea." Trouble is, that's all it ever was. Then a couple of years ago, top-of-the-line cars began featuring our inventor friend's great idea — windshield wipers that adjust their speed to the amount of rainfall. If only he'd been passionate enough about his idea and possessed the means and drive to make it happen.

To help make one of your ideas happen, start by filling out the business opportunity evaluation questionnaire in Form 1-4. Then tally up your scores. Any idea that scores at least 24 or higher — or an average score of 6 on each question — is probably worth pursuing further. Consider one exception to the scoring: If your promising idea scores high on every question but question number 3, you may want to file it away for a friend. It may be a great idea for someone else — but not you. If you're not really all that interested in an idea or excited about the kind of work you'd have to do to turn the idea into a genuine business, you're going to have a real tough time making it succeed.

The business opportunity evaluation questionnaire is just the first test. If an idea passes here, it still has other hurdles ahead. But the questionnaire can at least tell you which of your promising ideas should make the final cut.

Choosing a winner

If you're fortunate and have worked diligently on your choices, you may be sitting on several promising ideas, each representing a real business opportunity. How do you sort them out and choose the one opportunity to run with? Unfortunately, no magic wand can help you.

Here's a suggestion: Take the time at this point to fill in a few important details around what may still be rather sketchy business propositions. Using the general questions in Form 1-5 as a guide, try to flesh out some of the business issues around each of the ideas you're still considering. Give your answers some serious thought. After all, they represent the first step in business planning — evaluating an opportunity to see if it really has what it takes to be turned into a real, live business.

BUSINESS OPPORTUNITY EVALUATION QUESTIONNAIRE
1. Describe your promising idea in two sentences.
2. Being as honest as you can, rate the idea on a scale of 1 to 10: 1 being "the only thing we could come up with in a pinch," 10 being "the best thing since sliced bread." Circle your rating. 1 2 3 4 5 6 7 8 9 10
3. Think seriously about what you would have to do to turn your idea into reality. Is this the kind of idea — and the kind of business — you really want to pursue? Rate your interest on a scale of 1 to 10 by circling the appropriate number: 1 for "so-so" and 10 for "very high." 1 2 3 4 5 6 7 8 9 10
4. Imagine sitting down and persuading an investor to put down hard-earned cash to help turn your idea into a real business. How easy would it be to convince a skeptical outsider that your idea has the potential to make money? Circle your answer from 1 meaning "very difficult" to 10 meaning "a breeze." 1 2 3 4 5 6 7 8 9 10
5. Being as objective as you can, ask yourself what odds your idea has of becoming a real business venture. Rate your chances from 1, meaning "it's a long shot," to 10, meaning "it's a guaranteed overnight success." 1 2 3 4 5 6 7 8 9 10

Form 1-4: Business opportunity evaluation questionnaire.

BUSINESS OPPORTUNITY FRAMEWORK
1. Describe your business opportunity in two sentences.
2. List the three most important features of the product or service you propose.
3. What basic customer needs does your product or service fill?
4. Briefly describe who is likely to buy your product or service.
5. List two or three existing products or services that already meet a similar need.
6. Why would customers choose your product or service over others?
7. How will you reach your customers?
8. How do you plan to make money?

Form 1-5: Business opportunity framework.

If you find yourself struggling to come up with the answers to questions in Form 1-5, your idea may still be a little threadbare. If you charge ahead now, you could find the whole notion of your business unraveling before it has even begun. We're not suggesting that you abandon any idea at this point. But we are suggesting that you make sure you clearly understand each business opportunity before you take any one of them to the next stage and start planning in a serious way. If you can't easily describe the customer need you're fulfilling, for example, or how you plan to make money, you still have some homework to do.

Doing Your First Reality Check

Every entrepreneur thinking of going into business for him- or herself feels a stomach-wrenching moment of doubt at some point when he or she asks: "Is this really such a good idea? Who am I kidding, anyway?"

In fact, moments like these aren't unusual at all. And they don't mean you lack confidence. What they do mean is that you're smart enough to know that from time to time, you need a timeout. You need to stop, step back, and make sure that the road you're on is leading you where you want to go. In short, you need a *reality check.*

In many ways, writing a business plan is an ongoing series of reality checks. By forcing you to stop and carefully think through every aspect of your business — from the product or service you offer to the competitors you face and the customers you serve — writing a business plan brings you face-to-face with all the realities of doing business. This section guides you through your first reality check to make sure that your preliminary planning is on track.

Getting a little help from a friend

One way to determine whether you're on solid ground is to discuss your business idea and preliminary plans with a trusted friend or confidante. Now we don't mean just anybody: Make sure the person has some experience in the business you're talking about — or at least in a similar business. And make sure it's someone who has the courage to tell you the absolute honest truth — whether it's, "You bet that's a great idea. Go for it!" or, "If I were you I'd take a little more time to think this over . . . ." At the same time, make sure the person is someone you respect and admire — someone from whom you can take candid criticism without feeling defensive.

We're really describing a *mentor* here, and the person who fills the bill will prove to be invaluable to you at many steps along the way. So take time to elect a few candidates. Consider colleagues you've worked with in the past, teachers or professors, friends from college, and other contacts you've made along the way. Look through your address book or personal organizer for ideas. Try to come up with at least three people you can turn to when you really need to bounce around ideas and get a frank and serious response.

You may be tempted to turn to personal friends or family in these situations, and sometimes they can offer the advice and perspective you need. Often, however, emotional ties get in the way of absolute honesty and objective advice. You may say you're open to all suggestions and comments, but you may find yourself resenting what you hear. So set some ground rules first. Ask for constructive criticism and prepare to hear both the good and the bad without taking what you hear too personally.

While you're thinking about possible candidates for the role of mentor, also consider designating someone as your official devil's advocate. That person's task is to be as critical as possible of each idea that's put on the table — not in a negative or destructive way, of course, but in a skeptical, show-me-the-money, I'll-believe-it-when-I-see-it kind of way. If you find someone willing to play that role, you're guaranteed to understand the flip side of every argument you make.

Relying on yourself

Okay, you've proven to yourself that you have a real business opportunity in hand. But that still leaves a personal question unanswered: Do you have what it takes to make the opportunity succeed? This is an extremely important question to consider. After all, you're not the only person out there who wants to go into business for him- or herself. We hear stories about young CEOs who become multi-millionaires before they're 25. And we have mental images of entrepreneurs cruising around in Porsches and issuing orders over their cell phones, blissfully watching the value of their stock options soar. Who wouldn't want the same thing?

Well, speaking of reality checks, keep one central idea in mind here: Entrepreneurs who succeed are always talented and hard working. Their kind of success just doesn't drop from the sky. And not everyone has what it takes to be a high-flyer. For that matter, not everyone has what it takes to be self-employed — to have the discipline, the confidence, and the capacity to live with the uncertainty that's part and parcel of being out on your own.

In fact, everyone has strong suits and weak suits: In our experience, the people who are most likely to succeed in a business venture are the ones who can honestly appraise themselves, and then compensate for their weaknesses and make the most out of their strengths. Before you can do that, however, you have to be aware of what those strengths and weaknesses are.

The survey in Form 1-6 is meant to help you identify your own personal strengths and weaknesses, so try to be as candid as you can when you fill it out. You're not trying to impress anyone, and you're not going to win any points for getting a perfect score.

Take some time to review your responses to the 20 statements presented in Form 1-6. Those items receiving a "poor" rating represent your weakest areas, and you may eventually need to figure out how to compensate for them. Areas receiving an "excellent" rating represent your real strengths. These strengths are the personal resources you can call upon when you start your business venture.

Not all personal strengths or weaknesses are equal when creating a successful business. How important any one of them is depends in part on the kind of business you're thinking about. If you plan to be a sole proprietor, for example — and someone who works mostly alone — the ability to manage a staff doesn't matter all that much. But being self-motivated is absolutely essential. If you're involved in a business that depends on face-to-face customer service, on the other hand, your interpersonal skills are indispensable.

Using Form 1-6, place a star next to the top six traits that you think are most important to the kind of business you're planning. (Ignore, for the moment, how you rated yourself.) When you're done, organize these key traits — based on whether they represent potential strengths or weaknesses — in Form 1-7 (on the CD-ROM). Figure 1-4 shows how one of the authors — we won't say which one — ranked himself on the traits key to his own business. The grid shows that tending to the details of a project is an ongoing challenge for one of us. Knowing that, of course, allows him to compensate by, say, hiring a personal assistant (or cajoling a colleague) to take care of all those loose ends. Taking risks is another weakness. But again, awareness is always the first step in dealing with a limitation.

PERSONAL STRENGTHS AND WEAKNESSES GRID

Poor	*Fair*	*Good*	*Excellent*
Tending to the details of a project			Organizing a schedule and getting things done
		Setting goals and achieving them	Juggling several tasks at once
	Taking risks	Adapting to changing circumstances	

Figure 1-4: Using a personal strengths and weaknesses grid.

PERSONAL STRENGTHS AND WEAKNESSES SURVEY			
Being as honest as you can, rate your abilities in the following areas:			
1. Setting goals and pushing yourself to achieve them on time:			
Poor	*Fair*	*Good*	*Excellent*
2. Making decisions and completing tasks:			
Poor	*Fair*	*Good*	*Excellent*
3. Organizing a complex schedule and getting things done efficiently:			
Poor	*Fair*	*Good*	*Excellent*
4. Staying focused on the specific task at hand:			
Poor	*Fair*	*Good*	*Excellent*
5. Juggling several tasks at one time:			
Poor	*Fair*	*Good*	*Excellent*
6. Judging a person's character:			
Poor	*Fair*	*Good*	*Excellent*
7. Getting along with other people and bringing out the best in them:			
Poor	*Fair*	*Good*	*Excellent*
8. Listening to several sides of an issue and then making a decision:			
Poor	*Fair*	*Good*	*Excellent*
9. Leading a team, even when there is disagreement among the members:			
Poor	*Fair*	*Good*	*Excellent*
10. Understanding what motivates other people:			
Poor	*Fair*	*Good*	*Excellent*
11. Resolving disputes among people:			
Poor	*Fair*	*Good*	*Excellent*
12. Saying what you mean and meaning what you say:			
Poor	*Fair*	*Good*	*Excellent*

Form 1-6: Personal strengths and weaknesses survey — page 1 of 2.

13. Keeping your cool even when everyone else is losing theirs:			
Poor	*Fair*	*Good*	*Excellent*
14. Telling someone no:			
Poor	*Fair*	*Good*	*Excellent*
15. Tending to the details of a project:			
Poor	*Fair*	*Good*	*Excellent*
16. Looking at the big picture:			
Poor	*Fair*	*Good*	*Excellent*
17. Acting decisively under pressure:			
Poor	*Fair*	*Good*	*Excellent*
18. Adapting to changing circumstances:			
Poor	*Fair*	*Good*	*Excellent*
19. Taking risks:			
Poor	*Fair*	*Good*	*Excellent*
20. Taking responsibility, even when things go wrong:			
Poor	*Fair*	*Good*	*Excellent*

Form 1-6: Personal strengths and weaknesses survey — page 2 of 2.

Everyone has personal strengths and weaknesses. In fact, we know plenty of entrepreneurs who aren't good at taking risks, who agonize over decisions, or who have a tough time saying no to employees. And yet they've still created successful companies. Identifying a personal weakness doesn't mean that you don't have what it takes to turn your idea into a business. But it does mean you may to have to work extra hard in that area to compensate.

Put a copy of your personal strengths and weakness grid into your personal organizer or post it near your computer. By having it close by, you'll constantly remind yourself of who you are and what you can draw on as you begin the challenge of planning a business.

Forms on the CD-ROM

Check out the following business idea-generating forms on the CD-ROM:

Form 1-1	**The Idea Blender — Your Personal Traits and Interests**	The first step in an exercise that helps you think creatively about new business possibilities
Form 1-2	**The Idea Blender — Mixing and Matching your Interests**	The second step in an exercise that helps you think creatively about new business possibilities
Form 1-3	**The Idea Blender — Your Business Ideas**	The final step in an exercise that helps you think creatively about new business possibilities
Form 1-4	**Business Opportunity Evaluation Questionnaire**	Questionnaire that helps you decide which business ideas are worth pursuing further
Form 1-5	**Business Opportunity Framework**	Questions designed to fill in some important details around your business proposition
Form 1-6	**Personal Strengths and Weaknesses Survey**	A survey designed to provide you with an honest profile of your business abilities and traits
Form 1-7	**Personal Strengths and Weaknesses Grid**	A tool that allows you to compare your abilities and traits with qualities important to the kind of business you're considering

Chapter 2

Starting Your Planning Engine

In This Chapter

- Understanding the importance of a business plan
- Identifying the people who will read your plan
- Putting the proper information into your plan
- Planning your business timeline
- Asking for help and advice

The fact that you're holding this book in your hands is a very good sign (and we're not saying that just because we wrote it). It means you're seriously considering creating a business plan.

In this chapter, we tell you why planning is so important — not just when you're starting a business, but at many stages along the way — and why setting aside valuable time upfront to create a written business plan is well worth the effort. We help you think clearly about who your business plan is for and introduce you to the key parts of a business plan. In planning, of course, timing is crucial, so we also help you choose a time frame that will make your goals and objectives challenging but not unreasonable. Finally, we point you toward some resources you may find useful as you prepare for the planning challenges ahead.

Convincing Yourself that a Plan Is Important

If you're starting a new company, you have a thousand and one things to think about. So why take precious time to create a business plan? For the same reason that an explorer takes the time to gather up maps, an architect draws up blueprints, and a sailor consults charts. You'd never dream of setting off in a sailboat for a trip across the ocean without a clear plan and the charts to guide you, right? And you'd never try to build a house without detailed blueprints. For the same reason, you need a plan in place before you start a business venture.

Think of your business as if it's a ship you're about to sail. Your business plan pinpoints your destination, of course, but it also describes how you intend to get there. What's more, a business plan takes account of the supplies you have on board, your crew, the anticipated cost of the voyage, and what the weather and sea conditions are likely to be. Your plan tries to anticipate the potential dangers that may lurk over the horizon and identify other sailing ships that may be attempting to beat you to your destination.

Back on dry land, the simple fact is that a good business plan gives you all kinds of important advantages, not just in the early stages of your business venture but well down the road, too. Take a few minutes to read through the business planning situations listed in Form 2-1 and check off the ones that apply to your own particular circumstances.

As you may be able to tell from the situations described in Form 2-1, business planning is an ongoing process. That's because the only constant in every business we can think of is change. Markets evolve. Innovative technologies emerge. New competitors appear. So the business plan you create will need to be revised and updated along the way to adapt to the changing business conditions you'll face.

The good news in all of this is that as your business evolves, a strong and carefully-considered business plan pays off in ways that you may never have anticipated. Check out some of the benefits of a business plan we've put together in the following list. They're meant to motivate you as you begin to think seriously about business planning.

- A clear statement of your business mission and vision
- A set of values that can help steer you in times of trouble
- A blueprint you can use to focus your energy, making sure that your company stays on track
- A clear-eyed analysis of your industry, including both opportunities and threats
- A detailed portrait of your potential customers and their buying behavior
- A rundown of your biggest competitors and your strategies for facing them
- An honest assessment of your own company's strengths and weaknesses
- A roadmap and timetable for the future made up of targeted goals and specific objectives
- A description of the products and services you offer
- An explanation of your marketing and pricing strategies

TYPICAL BUSINESS-PLANNING SITUATIONS
☐ *We think we have a good idea, but we're not sure if we're being overly optimistic.* The process of putting together a business plan can be a powerful reality check. While crafting your plan, you'll put your good idea to the test. Does your business proposition make sense? Are the assumptions you're making, in fact, true? Does your strategy fit in with prevailing business conditions? Do you have the resources you need? Will you really be able to attract customers? Can you actually make a profit? Do you have contingency plans in place if things go wrong?
☐ *We know we have a great idea. We're just not sure how to turn it into a real business.* Turning a great idea into a successful business is exactly what a business plan is all about. One key part of your plan is likely to be a business model, for example, which describes exactly how your business intends to take in and make money. (Planning a not-for-profit? Your business model will describe where the money's coming from and how you plan to allocate it.) Most business plans also include detailed goals and objectives, which together create a road map for exactly how to turn that great idea of yours into a going — and growing — concern.
☐ *We need to convince investors that our great idea can make them lots of money.* The only way to convince investors is with a solid business plan. Sure, you can point to a time in the heady days of the Internet boom when investors may have written a check simply because an idea sounded good or the entrepreneurs were energetic and talked the talk. But booms never last very long. Most of the time, investors want to see a strong and convincing business plan — one that makes a persuasive case that your company can turn a profit. They will take an especially close look at your business model and your financials. And the same goes for lenders. A complete and convincing business plan can help you get the loans you need to get your business up and running.
☐ *We're having a tough time attracting talented people in a highly competitive labor market.* A strong business plan will help. Prospective employees need to feel confident that they're signing on with a company that knows what it needs to do to succeed. They also need to share in your vision and excitement. If your business plan points clearly toward an attractive destination, you'll have a very good chance of enlisting the kind of skilled and enthusiastic people you're looking for. If the plan also helps inspire new hires with a strong vision and mission, all the better.

Form 2-1: Typical business-planning situations — page 1 of 3.

☐ *I'm thinking of going into business for myself, but I'm not sure where to start.*

Sole proprietors going into business on their own are often less likely than bigger companies to take the time to write a detailed business plan. But they really have as much or more to gain. Writing a business plan — particularly creating a detailed set of goals and objectives — gives you a simple framework to think about where to begin and how to follow through. If you're going into business on your own for the first time, a plan can help you side step problems and focus clearly on what you do best. Most important of all, a detailed and well-thought-out business plan gives you the confidence you need to go out and start your own business in the first place.

☐ *Our company has hit a few big bumps in the road, and we're struggling to get back on track.*

Part of the business-planning process involves an analysis of your own strengths and weaknesses as well as a recognition of the opportunities and threats in your business environment. Establishing specific goals and objectives as part of a coherent, overall plan is especially important when your company is in trouble. An effective business plan ensures that all your employees are focused on the same goals when you most need them to be

☐ *We've had a few financial and personnel problems lately, and staff morale is low.*

A strong and inspiring business plan can bring your employees back together and boost morale. Two key parts of a good business plan — the mission statement and the vision statement — help make clear to employees not only what the company does, but why it's in business. The two statements express both your purpose and what the company wants to become in the future. Many businesses use their mission and vision statements to inspire their people, boost productivity, and sharpen their competitive edge.

☐ *We want to sell off part of the company so we can focus on what we're good at.*

You have two good reasons to write a business plan. One of the purposes of your plan will be to get the part of the company you're spinning off in shape and ready to sell — at the best price. The other purpose of your plan will be to help you set out goals and objectives for the remaining part of the company, allowing you to focus your efforts on what you do best. Whenever a company undergoes the kind of sweeping change you describe; after all, it really becomes a new company. That's why writing a new business plan in this situation is so important.

Form 2-1: Typical business-planning situations — page 2 of 3.

☐ *We have the opportunity to grow our business, but we're worried about growing too fast.* Success can be a double-edged sword. It's great while the money keeps rolling in, but the pressure to grow has also derailed many a company. Effective planning can help you chart the best way for your own business to grow. A solid business plan will also help ensure that you have the necessary resources in place to support and power your growth.
☐ *We're thinking about introducing a new product or service, but we need some guidance.* Introducing a new product or service — or entering a brand new market with a product or service you already have — is very much like starting a business. You need to think through all the same issues, from whom your customers and competitors are likely to be to avoiding threats and seizing market opportunities. The process of creating a business plan helps you develop a strategy for introducing your new product or service, and then ensures that it becomes a successful part of the larger business.

Form 2-1: Typical business-planning situations — page 3 of 3.

- An analysis of your revenues, costs and projected profits
- An action plan that anticipates potential detours or hurdles you may encounter
- Benchmarks you can use to track your performance and make mid-course corrections
- A "handbook" for new employees describing who you are and what your company's about
- A "résumé" you can use to introduce your business to suppliers, vendors, lenders, and others

Identifying Who Your Plan Is for

A comprehensive business plan covers a lot of territory and addresses all sorts of issues. That means it's going to be an invaluable resource to many people around you.

Your audience

All the people who have an interest in your business venture — from investors and lenders to your employees, customers, and suppliers — represent different *audiences* for your business plan. You may find that certain audiences are more important to you than others, depending on your situation. If you're starting a company that's looking for investment capital, for example, your all-important target audience is likely to be filled with future investors. And you may have to include prospective employees in this group if you plan to offer stock options in lieu of high salaries.

But suppose you're going into business for yourself, and you don't need cash to get up and running. Instead of investors or lenders, your plan may be primarily targeted toward your potential clients. If you're like a freelance writer we know, your plan may be for you and you alone — to focus your efforts, chart a course ahead, and help you anticipate problems before they arise.

Form 2-2 presents a list of the most common audiences for a business plan. Take a few minutes to consider each audience and check off those groups that you think will be most important to your business, given your current situation. (In case we've left somebody out, we've put a blank space at the end of the list.)

Your message

With a clear idea of whom your plan is aimed at, you'll have an easier time coming up with the key messages you need to get across. And you ensure that the messages address the people who matter most. Identifying your target audience helps you set the tone of important sections in the written plan and tells you where to put the bulk of your planning efforts.

Consider the actions of a small city magazine that had seen its circulation fall and its revenues slump. The publisher and senior editors got together and decided to develop a revised business plan designed to keep their entire enterprise from going belly up. They were smart enough to turn their attentions first to the target audiences they absolutely needed to address:

- **Investors:** One thing the management team knew it needed was a serious infusion of cash to remake the look and feel of the magazine and expand the content. That meant the team needed a business plan that would speak directly to potential investors.
- **Customers:** The team also knew that the biggest problem facing the magazine was a loss of readership. So the team members wanted to concentrate their attention on customer analysis and on specific action plans designed to win back readers. Their readers weren't likely to read the business plan itself, but the team wanted to keep its customers front and center as it developed a revised plan.

- **Contributors:** The magazine's senior editors knew they needed to draw in local talent, from writers and editors to photographers and artists. So they wanted the business plan to create a strong sense of the magazine's new direction in an effort to reach out to this creative audience. In addition, they decided the plan should include specific steps to attract and keep top-notch talent.

CHECKLIST OF COMMON BUSINESS PLAN AUDIENCES
☐ Yourself
☐ Your Board of Directors
☐ Investors and lenders
☐ Senior management team
☐ Current employees
☐ New hires
☐ Independent contractors
☐ Vendors and suppliers
☐ Customers or clients
☐ Donors (for not-for-profits)
☐ Distributors
☐ Regulators
☐ Advocacy groups
☐ Others ______________________

Form 2-2: A checklist of common business plan audiences.

Table 2-1 shows how the management team at the magazine ended up outlining the key messages they wanted to get across to each of their target audiences.

Table 2-1 Business Plan Target Audiences and Key Messages

Target Audience	*Key Message*
Investors	Show how changing demographics favor a new role for the magazine
	Describe new editorial approach and its break with the past
	Highlight new editorial sections and their appeal to potential advertisers
	Run financial numbers with detailed revenue projections and profit targets
Customers (subscribers and newsstand buyers)	Explain how the magazine will attract new readers who were turned off in the past
	List new features: local celebrity profiles, expanded restaurant reviews, new columnists
Contributors	Detail new relationship with writers and photographers based on agreements designed to create a stronger sense of loyalty
	Include a strategy to bring more media attention to the magazine itself
	Highlight plans for a contributors' page

Now take some time to complete Form 2-3 (on the CD-ROM) around your own business planning, by following these steps:

1. **Identify the three most important audiences you intend to address with your plan.**

   Refer to Form 2-2 for additional help.

2. **Jot down two or three key points you need to make to each target audience.**

   This doesn't require fancy prose. Just get your ideas down on paper so you can refer back to them later when you begin writing the business plan itself.

Understanding What's in a Business Plan

Written business plans are as varied as the companies that put them together. We've seen business plans that run to almost 100 pages and others that barely fill three. We've seen plans that start with executive summaries and plans that plunge right into a detailed description of products and services. Some plans are printed; others are entirely Web-based documents. Some plans include page after page of financial projections; others list anticipated costs, expected revenues, and projected profits — and that's all.

Are some business plans better that others? You bet. Are all plans written for the same reasons? No way.

Reviewing plans from top to bottom

Business plans may come in all shapes, sizes, formats — even colors! — but they all share a general framework. So before you become overwhelmed by the details and differences between business plans you may have seen, take time to look at what they all have in common.

Look over each of the components in the following list to get a flavor of the issues and areas that are addressed in a typical business plan.

- **Table of contents:** The table of contents (TOC) provides a simple way for readers to find key sections in your business plan. It's especially useful if your plan exceeds ten pages.
- **Executive summary:** An executive summary is a short write-up that summarizes the key points in your business plan. An executive summary is especially useful if your plan runs more than ten pages and you want to convey important information right upfront. Many people in your audience will go no further than your executive summary, so keep it short, sweet, and as captivating as it can be — in fact, try to keep it down to two pages or less.
- **Company overview:** This section makes important observations about your company and the nature of your business. In the company overview, you may want to include parts of your company's mission and vision statements, as well as your values, key products and/or services, ways your company is unique, and what business opportunities you're capitalizing on. Of course, you can leave a lot of the details for later. (Check out Chapter 3 for more information.)
- **Business environment:** This section takes a look at everything beyond your control. This section includes a careful analysis of your industry and the forces at work in your market, an in-depth description of both

your direct and potential competitors, and a close look at your customers, including who they are, what they want, and how they buy products or services. (Check out Chapter 4 for details.)

- **Company description:** This section describes in detail what makes your company special. Include information about your management team, your organization, any new technology you have, your products and services, your company operations, and your marketing potential. In particular, try to point out in which areas you have real advantages over your competition. (Check out Chapter 6 for details.)
- **Company strategy:** The company strategy is your roadmap to the future. This section brings together the information you know about your business environment and your company's resources, and then lays out a strategy for going forward. Describe why you think the strategy is the right one, but recognize the uncertainties involved by including possible alternatives as well as ways you plan to avoid unforeseen pitfalls and take advantage of new opportunities. (Check out Chapter 5 for details.)
- **Financial review:** This section includes a detailed review of dollars and cents, including the state of your finances today and what you expect your financial picture to look like in the future. This section typically contains a number of financial statements, including an income statement, your balance sheet, and a cash flow statement. Some of your audience will doze off here. Others will find it fascinating. (Check out Chapter 7 for details.)
- **Action plan:** The action plan includes the specific steps needed to carry out your business plan. Typically, this section focuses on your assessment of the important steps you need to take in the near term in order to put your plan into effect, including any immediate goals and objectives you've set for yourself. (Flip to Chapters 3 and 13 for more information.)
- **Appendixes:** This section includes documents and other information that supports your business plan. This section may include articles, reports, surveys, legal documents, and spreadsheets. In short, you can put anything here that you think is important but not important enough to clutter up the main sections of your plan.

The major components of a typical business plan are also listed in Form 2-4 (on the CD-ROM), along with the kinds of information they usually contain. This framework is general, but captures the full range of issues and areas that you probably want to address in your business planning, now or in the future. When you get down to the business of actually writing your plan, refer to the list in Form 2-4, checking off the major components as you complete them.

After you get beyond the common framework we've described, business plans go off in all directions. The fact is, we can't give you just one single textbook example of a written business plan from beginning to end. Why? Because there is no one right way to organize a plan. What matters is that the material in your plan is arranged and presented to meet your needs, addresses your target audiences, and ultimately moves your business ahead. So instead of relying on one master business plan model throughout this book, we look at several different kinds of businesses and several ways to organize and present materials in a written plan.

One step at a time

If you're like most people we know who are starting to write a business plan, you have questions — usually questions that come with a lot of hand wringing — like the following:

- Do I really have to include all these sections?
- Do I really need to write it all down?
- Just how long does my plan have to be?

To put your mind at rest, we have some answers.

Do I really have to include all these sections?

Nope. Your business plan should include only what's important to you and your business. If your plan is short — or written mostly for your own purposes — you can dispense with the executive summary, for example. And if you're a company of one, you probably don't need a section on the organization of your business (unless you want to give yourself tips on how to get organized yourself!)

That said, the more complete your business plan is, the better. If you're a sole proprietor, for example, you may figure you can do without a mission statement. You already know what your business is all about, right? But you may find that the writing of a mission statement forces you to focus on what you really plan to do with your business. And that can be an extremely valuable exercise for any company, large or small.

Do I really need to write it all down?

We hear this all the time, especially from small business owners and individuals in business for themselves. Is it really worth taking the time to write down a formal business plan? You bet it is. Creating a written plan forces you to face tough issues you may otherwise ignore. Questions you find yourself asking include: How big is my market? Why will customers come to me and not my competition? How much money do I honestly need to get the business off the ground? When can I realistically expect to make a profit? What other opportunities can I take advantage of? What threatens my business? As you can see, putting your thoughts down on paper forces you to give your business-planning efforts some extra attention.

Write a plan, make more money

If you need any more convincing that a business plan is important, consider this. When the Kauffman Center for Entrepreneurial Leadership surveyed the winners of its Entrepreneur of the Year award, it found that companies with written business plans had 50 percent greater sales growth and 12 percent higher gross profit margins than companies without plans.

Now there's a real incentive. As the saying goes, a dollar earned is worth a thousand words — or something like that.

The following is just one example of why the process of writing a plan can be so important. A lawyer friend we know decided to hang up his own shingle after ten years of working for a big corporate law firm. It's not quite fair to say he made the decision on an impulse. But he never really got down to thinking seriously about what actually goes into setting up a practice. Oh sure, he'd made a few back-of-the-envelope calculations about how much money he had tucked away to tide him over. But that was about the only real planning he did.

His first surprise: discovering how much it would actually cost to set up a small law office — computers, faxes, a telephone system, furniture, and all the rest of it. He also realized rather quickly that clients weren't going to simply beat a path to his door on their own. He was going to have to do some marketing, something he had very little experience with. In the rush of excitement about going out on his own, he had never really thought about the competition, either. Needless to say, he wasn't the only lawyer in town. And he quickly understood that he was going to have to compete with several existing firms for the same group of clients.

We're happy to say that he eventually made his one-man practice work. But only after many very rocky months — and a lot of frustration that he could have avoided. In fact, three months after starting the business, he finally sat down and wrote a formal business plan. It wasn't all that long, and it wasn't complicated. But it did spell out exactly what he needed to do to get the business on track — and how much that would cost.

His plan also described the kinds of clients he hoped to attract and a strategy for reaching out to them. He took the time to analyze the competition — who the other lawyers were, where they practiced, and what sort of clients they were going after. By doing this analysis, in fact, he was able to identify an area of family law that wasn't being practiced by any of the lawyers in town. He also created a set of goals and objectives — a road map for what he needed to do when, and where he wanted to be at the end of the year.

Just how long does my plan really have to be?

The simple answer: Only as long as it needs to be and not a single word longer. A business plan as thick as a Stephen King novel isn't going to impress anyone. In fact, it's likely to scare them to death. (A 100-page business plan may be 75 pages too long.) What really impresses investors, clients, employees, and anyone else who may read your plan is simple, straightforward, to-the-point thinking. Don't get us wrong. We don't want you to leave anything important out of your plan for the sake of keeping it brief. But we would like you to state your plan as concisely as possible. In our experience, even the most comprehensive plan shouldn't be more than 20 to 30 pages (not including the appendixes.)

Writing down your plan is one of the last steps you take in the process of business planning. Before putting pen to paper (or finger to keyboard), you'll do a lot of brainstorming, researching, and decision-making. So you don't have to start polishing your prose until you've organized your thoughts, finished your homework, and carefully considered all the questions that are the major part of your business-planning effort. We devote Chapter 12 to the nuts and bolts of actually creating a written plan — after all the background work of research and analysis is complete.

Planning Your Time Frame

Your *time frame* represents how far out into the future you plan to plan. The answer isn't "forever," although we couldn't be happier if the business you start keeps right on growing. To make that happen, however, you need a current business plan that includes a realistic start and finish, with a number of measurable checkpoints in between.

Start to finish

Timing is essential in almost anything you do, from making dinner to playing a game of tennis. And its absolutely critical in business. For example, your business proposition is probably designed to take advantage of some opportunity you see out there in the world. Well, opportunities don't last forever. No doubt someone else is having a similarly bright idea — maybe even as you read this chapter. And if your new business is designed to exploit a new technology, you have to be quicker still. The clock is always ticking.

How far out should your planning horizon be? The answer depends on the kind of business you're in and the pace at which your industry is moving. Some Internet ventures have only six months to prove themselves. So their time frames are incredibly short. On the other hand, not-for-profit organizations with substantial endowments are in for the very long haul. Their business plans may look at five- or ten-year horizons. Many of the business plans we're familiar with use one-year, three-year, or five-year benchmarks — odd numbers are popular, for some reason.

Business planning is an ongoing process. From year to year — and sometimes more often than that — companies review and revise their plans. So don't worry that the time frame you choose today is somehow set in stone. You'll have the chance to revise it along the way if circumstances change. At the same time, you can't expect to succeed unless you commit yourself to a planning process within a realistic time frame.

Milestones in between

Your planning efforts involve the crucial task of setting business goals and establishing measurable objectives. (Take a look at Chapter 3 to find out more.) And when you set goals and objectives for your business, you can't just say you'll get around to doing them . . . whenever. (At least not if you plan to make money.) In order to give yourself the best odds of being successful at your business venture, you not only need to establish a clear time frame, you also have to set specific milestones along the way.

Figure 2-1 shows how Digital Fun, a retail store specializing in digital equipment (cameras, recorders, and other devices) answered five basic questions in order to determine a reasonable time frame for its expansion plans. Based on its answers, the most reasonable business-planning time frame for Digital Fun is probably one year. A year gives the company plenty of important milestones along the way. It also provides a clear goal for the end of year one: profitability.

Set aside some time to answer the same time frame planning questions for your own business venture, using Form 2-5 on the CD-ROM. You don't have to answer all the questions, of course — answer only those that are relevant to your business. When you're done, review your answers and choose a sensible business plan time frame, making sure your planning horizon is far enough ahead to include key milestones and to take into account major business trends and cycles.

To get a jump-start on the process of developing business goals and objectives, take a few minutes to come up with a preliminary timeline for what you need to accomplish, given the planning horizon you've set for yourself. Include the major milestones you've identified. Nobody's going to hold you to this timeline, but it will almost certainly prove useful later on in your planning process.

BUSINESS PLAN TIME FRAME QUESTIONNAIRE		
1. Identify three milestones that represent essential steps you need to take to get your business up and running. Estimate a time frame for each.		
• **Milestone 1:**	Secure business loans.	(2 months)
• **Milestone 2:**	Lease and develop four locations.	(5 months)
• **Milestone 3:**	Get all shops up and running.	(8 months)
2. Is the success of your business tied to a major business trend? If so, what is the time frame?		
The emerging market for digital devices — already underway, with new products scheduled for release every quarter		(5 months)
3. Is your business seasonal in nature? When do you need to have your product or service available to take advantage of the peak season?		
Holiday sales represent 50 percent of our revenue.		(8 months)
4. How soon do you need to make your product or service available to stay ahead of your competition?		
Consumer electronics is extremely competitive.		(ASAP)
5. When do you absolutely need to start making a profit?		
Moderate financial pressure on the company.		(Within 1 year)

Figure 2-1: Answering questions helps determine an appropriate planning time frame.

For example, the following timeline shows the target months in which the digital equipment retailer, Digital Fun, plans to complete the major milestones it has identified.

- **Month 1:** Complete business plan
- **Month 2:** Secure business loans
- **Month 3:** Begin search for retail space
- **Month 4:**
- **Month 5:** Lease and develop retail space; begin hiring
- **Month 6:**
- **Month 7:** Open all shops; run holiday ads
- **Month 8:** Holiday shopping season begins
- **Month 9:**
- **Month 10:**
- **Month 11:**
- **Month 12:** New stores become profitable

Preparing for the Real World

We're going to assume that you've convinced yourself that a business plan is important, and you've given some thought to who'll use the darned thing and why. You may even have come up with a time frame and perhaps a first stab at a planning timeline. (If not, look back at the preceding sections in this chapter.)

So you're ready to begin your plan (see Chapter 3), but first, consider the tips and tools discussed in the following sections.

Locating information resources

You're going to have a lot of questions as you get underway. Trends? Customers? Competitors? Strategy? Goals? Finances? Chances are, you'll need to do a little digging to come up with the answers. Luckily you can find plenty of places to turn to. Here's a quick checklist:

- **The Internet:** You may be surprised how much you can dig up if just look for it, including information on markets, your customers, competition — you name it.
- **Your local college or university library:** While a college library is best, even your local public library probably has a good collection of business journals and other useful periodicals.
- **A nearby business school:** Many schools offer seminars or night classes that are open to the public, and professors are usually quite happy to answer your questions.
- **Industry trade journals:** Yes, the subscriptions are sometimes pricey, but they're often well worth the money.
- **Newspapers:** No matter what your business, *The New York Times* and *The Wall Street Journal,* along with a local paper, will keep you on top of issues you should probably know about.
- **Trade shows or industry symposiums:** These get-togethers are usually a great way to get up to speed, because you find out about products, services, customers, and your competitors — all under one roof.
- **U.S. Small Business Administration (SBA):** A rich resource for all kinds of information about starting and running a small business. They're online at `www.sba.gov`.
- **Search and research companies:** Search and research firms are always expensive, but sometimes a NEXUS/LEXUS search or a market-research study is the only place to find must-have data.

- **Professional groups:** Almost every profession has a professional group, from the American Medical Writers Association to the Society of Wetlands Scientists.
- **Local business networking groups:** These groups are full of people in the same position you are, often with experience and insights to share.
- **Your local Chamber of Commerce:** While this group may sound old-fashioned, your local Chamber of Commerce can usually supply you will all sorts of relevant information.
- **Anyone else you run across with background in the kind of business you're planning:** A quick call to someone with some experience can provide a treasure trove of information.

Expert advice

When you can't find the answers to specific questions, don't be afraid to ask for advice. We've found in our own work that people are remarkably willing to help. Are you thinking of starting a retail business in town? Ask other retailers to fill you in on what you need to know. Are you planning to break away from the corporate grind and go into business for yourself? Invite someone who has made the same career move out to lunch to talk about what it takes. For the price of a decent meal, you'll discover that you can gather a lot of really useful information.

We recently met with a Chicago dress designer who had been dreaming about starting her own private clothing label for years. But she had absolutely no idea where to go for information about what was involved. Sure, she knew plenty of insiders in the business, but she was afraid to talk to people who could be potential competitors. And given her lack of experience, she was also afraid she'd seem just plain naive.

After months of stewing, she finally screwed up her courage and sent off an e-mail to a friend she'd gone to design school with — someone who worked at one of the big New York fashion firms. Her friend was more than willing to help. And along the way, he recommended three other people she should contact. All of them were happy to talk about the ins and outs — and ups and downs — of starting a designer label. By the time she had made the rounds, the Chicago dress designer had received a complete tutorial on the business side of fashion design — precisely the kind of advice she needed to point her in the right direction.

If you plan to interview people in your own industry — or people who have had experience starting similar businesses — use the following simple (but, we hope, useful) advice:

- **Prepare your questions in advance.** By jotting down ahead of time what you want to ask, you make sure you don't forget to discuss something really important.
- **Explain exactly why you're asking for help.** You can't expect people to be open and honest with you if you aren't honest with them.
- **Be prepared to really listen.** Even if someone is telling you something you don't want to know, listen to what he or she says. Believe us, anybody who warns you about obstacles ahead is doing you a big favor.
- **Keep the conversation open-ended.** Always ask whether you should be thinking about other issues or addressing other topics.
- **Build your network of contacts.** Ask for introductions to anyone else that your contact suggests you talk with or any other sources of useful information.
- **Be grateful.** Offer to take them out for lunch or dinner. Write a quick thank-you note. Remember: You may need to turn to the same people later for additional advice or help.

Helping hands

If you're going into business on your own, chances are you're going to have to shoulder most of the business-planning effort yourself. But that doesn't mean you can't enlist the help of friends or colleagues to read over what you've written and tell you whether it makes any sense. In fact, we think it's a great idea to involve other people. Outsiders bring a new perspective to your plan. Just remember one thing: You need honest opinions, so make sure the people you choose feel free to praise and criticize. The last thing you want is a yes person giving you guidance.

If you're going to be part of a business team, don't work on your plan all by yourself. (And we're not saying that just to make your life easier.) Enlisting the help of people in the company has all sorts of important benefits. For one thing, different people with different backgrounds will have different perspectives. And those perspectives add breadth and depth to your business plan. What's more, by involving key people in the planning process, you ensure that they have a strong stake in getting results after the written plan is finished.

If you're in a fairly big company, you may be forced to delegate a lot of the work involved in creating and writing a business plan. Some companies even end up hiring outside people to handle parts of the process. But assigning a dedicated planning staff of any sort presents its own pitfalls. The plan you end up with, for example, may not reflect what's really happening in the company. Worse yet, you may fail to win the commitment of the managers who are ultimately responsible for putting the plan into action. Instead, you want to make very sure that the senior management team has a central role to play in putting the business plan together in the first place.

Take some time now to identify the key people who should be involved in your business-planning process. Depending on the size of your company, you may end up delegating sections of the plan to different groups, based on their expertise. The folks in marketing, for example, may be charged with writing the company-strategy section. The CFO and staff are obvious choices for completing the financial review. You may want to identify someone in corporate communications to write the executive summary, because it needs to be crisp, clear, and to the point. (We don't recommend starting the summary until all the other parts of the plan are completed, of course; otherwise, you won't know what to summarize.)

We've listed the major components of a typical business plan in Form 2-6, along with spaces for names and dates. If you intend to delegate, you can use this form to keep track of who's in charge of which business plan component — and when it's due. If you're planning all by yourself, you can still use the form to keep track of your progress.

BUSINESS PLAN TRACKER		
Plan Component:	*Who's In Charge:*	*When It's Due:*
Executive summary		
Company overview		
Business environment		
Company description		
Company strategy		
Financial review		
Action plan		
Appendixes		

Form 2-6: Business plan tracker.

When you enlist help in putting together a plan, you're probably asking the people around you to take on more than their usual workload. That's fine, of course. But be careful not to overwhelm them. Create a reasonable schedule for getting the work done. And to keep your team motivated, sell them upfront on the importance of the planning process. (Look at the "Convincing Yourself that a Plan Is Important" section, earlier in this chapter, if you need ammunition.) The more enthusiastic people are, the more creative they're likely to be. And if you're asking people to put in overtime, don't forget to reward them for their efforts. A dinner out to celebrate important milestones in the planning process can go a long way toward keeping smiles on everyone's faces.

The business-planning process involves a lot of brainstorming, discussion, vision, and revision, so don't be surprised if you generate a lot of paperwork. To keep track of it all, we recommend that you name one person to be in charge of keeping a loose-leaf notebook with all the forms you fill in as well as any other documents related to your plan. If you're on your own, that person is you. If you're heading up a planning team, make sure to assign a person who's a natural-born organizer.

Finally, consider using computer software to help you through the business-planning process. All sorts of tools are available — everything from freeware and shareware programs to full-service commercial software. We've included a number of software tools, trial versions, and demos on the CD-ROM — take a look at the Appendix for details.

Forms on the CD-ROM

Check out the following forms on the CD-ROM designed to help you get ready to start your business plan:

Form 2-1	**Typical Business-Planning Situations**	A selection of business situations in which business planning can be extremely important
Form 2-2	**Checklist of Common Business Plan Audiences**	A checklist of groups and individuals who may have a stake in your business plan
Form 2-3	**Business Plan Target Audiences and Key Messages**	Your three most important audiences and the key messages you want to get across
Form 2-4	**Major Components in a Typical Business Plan**	A checklist of the most common sections found in a typical business plan

Form 2-5	**Business Plan Time frame Questionnaire**	A questionnaire to help you determine the best time frame to use in your business planning
Form 2-6	**Business Plan Tracker**	A form you can use to keep track of who's in charge of each business plan component and when it's due

Chapter 3

Laying Down the Ground Rules

In This Chapter

- Crafting your company's mission
- Establishing goals and objectives for your company
- Discovering your company's values and vision

In any kind of work, you can easily get buried in day-to-day demands. It happens to everyone: You get so caught up in details that you miss the bigger picture.

That's where planning comes in. Writing a business plan gives you a chance to step back, think about where you've come from and where you're headed, and ask fundamental questions about your business and your company:

- Why are you in business?
- What does your business do?
- What do you want your company to become?
- How do you get there?

Sure, these are basic questions, which is exactly why they are so important. We know lots of scary stories about companies with great promise — and sometimes tons of money to boot — that suddenly saw their fortunes falter and their promise fade. We're not saying that all these companies would have been successful if they'd taken time to ask themselves basic questions, but many of them could have steered a surer course, avoiding trouble along the way.

In this chapter, we help you set your own course by coming up with a clear and compelling mission statement. We also show you how to write achievable goals and specific objectives to turn that mission into a reality. Finally, we show you why thinking about your company's values and creating a vision for the future is crucially important. Even better, we help you do it.

Giving Your Company its Mission

One of the foundations of a successful business plan — and a fundamental part of business planning — is a mission statement. By all rights, putting one together should be straightforward. The mission statement, after all, answers a simple question: What business are you in? Well, it may sound simple, but answering this question means thinking carefully about the products and services you offer, who your customers are, what sets you apart from the competition — and what you hope to achieve. In short, it means taking a long, hard look at all the key parts of your business.

Not convinced it's really worth the trouble? Consider this:

- If you're starting a business, a compelling mission statement can convince potential investors that you know who you are and where you want to go. A great mission statement won't make up for a poor business plan, but an ill-defined or uninspired mission statement can make investors think twice about putting their own money on the table.
- If you're a company of one, a clear mission statement keeps you focused on what you do best — and it can help keep you on track if you run into problems along the way.
- If you run a small business, a strong mission statement can help turn employees into team players and keep your entire team pointed in the same direction.

No matter what kind of business you're in, a solid mission statement communicates the purpose of your business to people inside and outside the organization. It tells them who you are and what you do.

Asking basic questions

Where should you begin? If you're part of a small organization — and that includes a business of one — you can always write a mission statement totally on your own. But getting someone else's perspective never hurts, even if the people you turn to aren't directly involved in your company. Of course, if you're part of a medium-sized or larger company, enlisting help is essential. You'll get new ideas and insights, plus you'll encourage a sense of ownership in the mission statement, which, in turn, will help forge a stronger business team.

Before you put a group together, however, you may want to get a head start. Using Form 3-1 as a handy guide, take a few minutes to think through the eight fundamental questions that your mission statement will try to address. Don't worry about polished phrases right now. Just jot down the first honest answers that come to mind.

YOUR MISSION STATEMENT QUESTIONNAIRE
1. What exactly do we do?
2. What products and services do we offer?
3. Who is our ideal customer?
4. What customer needs do we meet, and what benefits do we provide?
5. What markets and geographic areas do we serve?
6. What sets us apart from our competition?
7. What's the best thing a satisfied customer can say about us?
8. What gets us most excited about the company's future?

Form 3-1: Your mission statement questionnaire.

Choose a group of creative and energetic people to help you with your mission statement. If your company is big enough, make sure all the major areas of you business are represented. Then schedule several brainstorming sessions, each with a clear agenda. (For more information on brainstorming, see Chapter 1.) Here's what we suggest:

- **Session 1:** Discuss the reasons why a mission statement is important. Explain briefly what a mission statement should include. Ask your team to fill out answers to the questions in Form 3-1.
- **Session 2:** Get the group together to discuss their answers. Try to make the discussion free and open, so that every idea is given its fair hearing. Begin to build a consensus on the best answers for each question.
- **Session 3:** Using the framework described in the following section, begin to outline your company's mission. If your initial brainstorming group is too large, select a smaller group of people to work on the mission statement itself.
- **Session 4:** Meet again to review, revise, and polish the mission statement draft.

Framing your mission

Mission statements come in all shapes and sizes, reflecting the nature of the companies they describe. (See the "Thumbs up, thumbs down" section, later in this chapter, for examples.) Some begin with who the company is; others begin with what the company does; still others begin with the customers the company plans to serve.

Although we can't put our finger on the perfect way to frame a mission statement, we suggest that you start by using a simple framework to link your ideas together. Consider the example in Figure 3-1 showing how a company that offers information and referrals for alternative medical treatments might complete the framework.

Now it's your turn. Using the framework in Form 3-2 on the CD-ROM, describe your own company: what you do, who your customers are, and how you plan to distinguish yourself from your competitors.

Crafting your statement

After answering some basic questions about your business and seeing how your answers relate to one another, you're ready to transform your ideas into a real mission statement.

YOUR MISSION STATEMENT FRAMEWORK
OUR PRODUCT OR SERVICE IS holistic health services.
WE PROVIDE reliable advice about alternative therapies
FOR people with chronic illnesses like cancer or diabetes
WHO ARE DISSATISFIED WITH standard medical care.
UNLIKE other referral networks in our area,
WE OFFER both information and referrals to local providers.

Figure 3-1: An example using the mission statement framework.

A few do's and don'ts

While we can't give you the one perfect way to organize or present a mission statement, we can share a few simple rules:

- **Include everything that helps describe who you are, what you do, and what sets you apart.** At the same time, try to keep your mission statement as short and sweet as it can possibly be.
- **Use plain language.** A mission statement serves as a guide for people who know the business and for people who don't. So make sure that everyone who reads your statement will understand it. If you can't explain your idea clearly, either you don't know what you're talking about — what is a "multi-platformed B-to-B integration database solution," anyway? — or you haven't gotten down to the basics yet.
- **Be specific.** "We will be a leading provider of software" doesn't say much. However, consider the mission of Praevius, Inc: "Our goal is to provide the finest business and productivity applications for the Macintosh platform." Now that gets down to the nitty-gritty.
- **Be enthusiastic.** A mission statement is meant to sell your message and inspire your troops, so don't be afraid to give it a strong sense of conviction and commitment.
- **Avoid hype and hyperbole.** The latest buzzwords — from "quantum leap forward" to "a mega-paradigm shift" — may sound great. But they don't mean much to most people. Stick to simple, straightforward explanations.

Elevator talk

If you find yourself breaking into a cold sweat at the sight of a blank piece of paper, relax. One way to get those words flowing into your mission statement is to think about how you would describe your company to a stranger you happen to meet in an elevator. Here's some elevator talk, using the medical services company described in Figure 3-1.

I'm involved in a holistic health services firm that helps patients with chronic disease get the best alternative treatment when standard medicine hasn't worked. We have a large network of local providers who are carefully screened. We offer our clients objective information about alternative medicine, and we direct them to the most appropriate resources.

Take a minute to look at the framework that you filled in on Form 3-2. Then put it away, take a deep breath, and tell that imaginary someone on the elevator exactly who you are and what you do. When you're finished, grab a pen and write down the gist of what you just said. Chances are, you'll end up with a pretty good first draft of your mission statement.

Thumbs up, thumbs down

Before you start revising your first draft, take a look at a few mission statements from real companies, both large and small, in Form 3-3. Chances are you'll be impressed with some and not others. That's the point. Give these dozen examples thumbs up or thumbs down, and then take a moment or two to jot down what you like about the winners and what you don't like about the losers. Your answers will give you a stronger sense of what you want your mission statement to look like.

Take your favorite mission statements from Form 3-3 as models to shape your own polished version, using Form 3-4 on the CD-ROM to get it down on paper. (Form 3-4 is basically a blank box, but using it helps you keep your documents organized.) Your own mission statement should be prominently featured in your written business plan. After all, it tells the world what your business is all about.

Putting your mission statement to work

A strong, inspiring mission statement is only as good as your ability to put it to work. So if you're on your own, make sure your mission statement is something you can commit to. And if you have a staff, give everyone a chance to review and comment on your company's mission. That way, they'll also have more of a stake in making it a reality.

Proclaim your mission loud and clear. Your mission statement should be something that everybody in the company knows by heart. If you're a company of one, make a spiffy-looking copy and frame it on the wall. If your company is bigger, make sure your mission is included in your employee handbook. Be creative. Print your mission statement on the back of business cards, for example, so that it will be everywhere you want it to be.

EXAMPLES OF REAL-WORLD MISSION STATEMENTS
To be the leading global provider of handheld computing products and to provide developers with the industry-standard platform for creating world-class mobile solutions. (Palm, Inc.) ☐ Thumbs up ☐ Thumbs down Why?
The mission of the Metropolitan Police Department is to prevent crime and the fear of crime, as we work with others to build safe and healthy communities throughout the District of Columbia. (Washington D.C. Police Department) ☐ Thumbs up ☐ Thumbs down Why?
Get it there. (FedEx) ☐ Thumbs up ☐ Thumbs down Why?
To explore, enjoy, and protect the wild places of the earth; To practice and promote the responsible use of the earth's ecosystems and resources; To educate and enlist humanity to protect and restore the quality of the natural and human environment; and to use all lawful means to carry out these objectives. (Sierra Club) ☐ Thumbs up ☐ Thumbs down Why?
To provide our customers with safe, low-cost, good value, point-to-point air services. To offer a consistent and reliable product at fares appealing to leisure and business markets from our bases to a range of domestic and European destinations. (easyJet.com) ☐ Thumbs up ☐ Thumbs down Why?
The NBA's mission is to be the most respected and successful sports league and sports marketing organization in the world. (National Basketball Association) ☐ Thumbs up ☐ Thumbs down Why?
To manufacture world class quality molds to fill our customer's needs, provide satisfying careers for all our employees, and to earn a fair return in order to allow continuous improvement, and thereby enable our customers, and ourselves, to succeed in the future together. (Stellar Mold & Tool, Inc.) ☐ Thumbs up ☐ Thumbs down Why?

Form 3-3: Examples of real-world mission statements — page 1 of 2.

United Community Center is a human service agency providing emergency assistance, daycare, social services and recreational activities for low-income children and families at risk in inner city Atlanta, Georgia. (United Community Center)

☐ Thumbs up ☐ Thumbs down

Why?

To make guests happy. (Disney World)

☐ Thumbs up ☐ Thumbs down

Why?

To create an online community, like no other, encompassing every facet of every municipality in the United States; to aid in online economic revitalization in partnership with local businesses and local, state and national government agencies; to publish, maintain and connect a network of community websites designed to entertain, educate and enlighten the residents of our great nation, while maintaining the highest standards of personal morals, business ethics and web etiquette. (A2Z Computing Services)

☐ Thumbs up ☐ Thumbs down

Why?

Dell's mission is to be the most successful computer company in the world at delivering the best customer experience in markets we serve. In doing so, Dell will meet customer expectations of:

- *Highest quality*
- *Competitive pricing*
- *Best-in-class service and support*
- *Superior corporate citizenship*
- *Leading technology*
- *Individual and company accountability*
- *Flexible customization capability*
- *Financial stability*

(Dell Computer)

☐ Thumbs up ☐ Thumbs down

Why?

The YMCA of San Francisco, based in Judeo-Christian heritage, seeks to enhance the lives of all people through programs designed to develop spirit, mind, and body. (YMCA of San Francisco)

☐ Thumbs up ☐ Thumbs down

Why?

Form 3-3: Examples of real-world mission statements — page 2 of 2.

One last piece of advice: Sit down with your colleagues to talk about how to put the company's mission statement into action. (Check out the "Setting Goals and Objectives" section that follows.) After all, words on paper are just that. And your mission statement is ultimately worth only what you and everyone around you make of it.

Setting Goals and Objectives

We probably don't need to convince you that setting goals is important. Just think about what football would be without goal posts. Or the Indianapolis 500 without a finish line. *Goals* establish where you intend to go, and they tell you when you've gotten there. Well-chosen goals point a new business in the right direction and can keep almost any company on the right track. Goals inspire and motivate your business team and push everyone to go that extra mile.

While goals tell you where you want to go, objectives tell you exactly how to get there. *Objectives* are the specific steps you and your company need to take in order to reach each of your goals. They specify precisely what must be done — and when. While goals are typically described in words, objectives often have numbers and specific dates attached to them.

Suppose, for example, that your goal is to double the number of people using your Web-conferencing service. Your objectives may be as follows:

- Get final approval for a weekly online giveaway of $1,000 (by June 1)
- Place print ads in four regional markets (by June 10)
- Sign contracts for daily radio spots in two major markets (by June 15)
- Send out 2,500 targeted e-mails weekly (by July 10)
- Send follow-up e-mail reminders (by July 25)

The whole point of most business goals is to improve your overall effectiveness as a company — whether you're trying to increase your share of the market, for example, or improve your customer service. The more carefully you define your goals, the more likely you are to do the right thing and actually achieve what you really wanted to accomplish in the first place.

Whereas goals are meant to increase your effectiveness, carefully chosen objectives to back them up make you more efficient. After all, if you think carefully through all of the steps you need to take to reach each goal, chances are you'll end up doing things right. In other words, you make sure your efforts are as efficient as they can possibly be.

Ultimately, your business success hinges on how effective and efficient your company is. And that depends on how well you define your goals and set objectives. Together, goals and objectives form the road map for your company's future. Without them, you risk making wrong turns and wasting precious energy.

In this section, we offer you three ways to think about the goals and objectives that are essential to your business's success. We encourage you to try all three approaches. Don't worry if you come up with more goals than you can handle. We'll help you sort through your list to choose the most important ones.

Who should be involved in the goal-setting process ahead? That depends a lot on how big your enterprise is. The best rule we know is to involve everyone who will have the responsibility for achieving the goals and objectives you're about to set.

Revisiting your mission

In this approach to goals and objectives, you begin by dusting off your company's mission statement. (Don't have one yet? See the "Giving Your Company its Mission" section, earlier in this chapter.) Because if your business plan is to be right on target, your major goals must be closely tied to your company's mission. And your objectives, in turn, should be tied directly to each goal. The connections are easy to visualize if you use a flowchart similar to the one shown in Figure 3-2. In this example, key phrases in the mission statement are highlighted and used to define the company's major goals, which then lead into a series of specific business objectives.

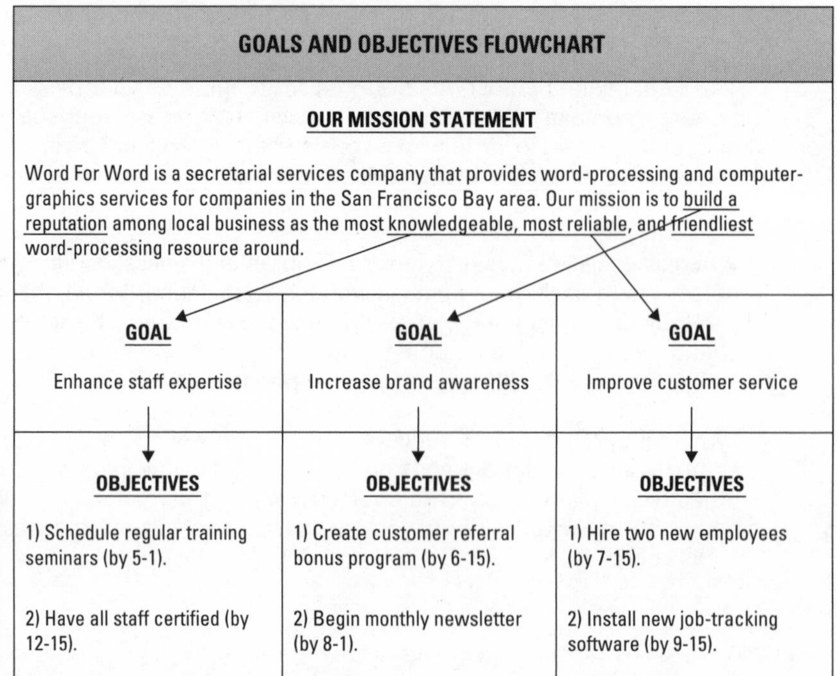

GOALS AND OBJECTIVES FLOWCHART

OUR MISSION STATEMENT

Word For Word is a secretarial services company that provides word-processing and computer-graphics services for companies in the San Francisco Bay area. Our mission is to build a reputation among local business as the most knowledgeable, most reliable, and friendliest word-processing resource around.

GOAL	GOAL	GOAL
Enhance staff expertise	Increase brand awareness	Improve customer service
OBJECTIVES	**OBJECTIVES**	**OBJECTIVES**
1) Schedule regular training seminars (by 5-1).	1) Create customer referral bonus program (by 6-15).	1) Hire two new employees (by 7-15).
2) Have all staff certified (by 12-15).	2) Begin monthly newsletter (by 8-1).	2) Install new job-tracking software (by 9-15).

Figure 3-2: Using the goals and objectives flowchart.

Use Form 3-5 on the CD-ROM to create a flow-chart of goals and objectives based on your own company's mission statement. Don't worry about actually committing to the goals just yet. And don't think you have to come up with a complete list of objectives right away. Simply jot down what comes to mind as you consider your mission statement. If your mission statement doesn't suggest a list of goals, you may want to take another look at it to see whether it really captures what your business is all about.

Goal-setting ACES

Most of your goals will describe positive aspects of your business you plan to promote and achieve. We don't want to spoil the party here, but odds are that in the future, you'd also like to avoid some pitfalls and eliminate a few weaknesses. This leads us to ACES — an inspired acronym for another nifty way of thinking about goals and objectives. ACES poses four key questions that cover all bases involved in most business planning:

- **Achieve:** What do you want to attain in the future?
- **Conserve:** What do you want to hang on to?
- **Eliminate:** What do you want to get rid of?
- **Steer clear:** What do you want to avoid?

Establishing mileposts

Daunted by the list of goals you've created? Good. (If you don't feel a little overwhelmed, you may need to raise the bar a little higher.) Goals are supposed to challenge and inspire.

At the same time, make sure that your goals don't discourage you or your team because they seem impossibly big. The simplest way to make even the most ambitious goal seem do-able is to break it down into parts or specific objectives. Objectives act as **mileposts** along the way, showing you how far you've come in reaching your goal and how much farther you need to travel.

Review all the goals you've committed yourself to reaching and break down each goal into the steps that are necessary to achieve it. Use the goals and objectives flowchart (Form 3-5 on the CD-ROM — see the example in Figure 3-2) to capture your full business picture, starting with your mission statement, including your major business goals, and listing the specific objectives you need to accomplish those goals.

Consider the following guidelines when putting together your objectives:

- Make sure your objectives are in line with your goals.
- Make sure your objectives are focused and measurable.
- Set a time frame for achieving each objective.

Figure 3-3 shows how a brand-new online shopping emporium, a small start-up company with big dreams, decided to answer the four ACES questions and then use them to create a set of business goals.

Take some time to answer the four ACES questions for your own business in Form 3-6, which is on the CD-ROM. Feel free to put down the first things that come to mind — you always have the option to revisit and revise your answers. After you fill in the grid in Form 3-6, take a fresh look at each box and see if you can identify a clear set of business goals.

Covering all bases

To make absolutely sure you haven't left out something important, we suggest one more way to think about business goals. We've found that goals typically fall into one of four following categories.

- **Day-to-day work goals** are directed at making you and your company more effective in doing what you do all the time. These goals may involve things like order tracking, office management, or customer follow-up. As a start, think about at least one change in your day-to-day operations that could make a difference in your overall effectiveness. Write it down in the form of a business goal.
- **Problem-solving goals** address specific challenges or problems that may confront your business, whether it's low employee morale, for example, or quality-service issues. Take a few minutes to think about the two biggest problems facing your company. Try to come up with goals that would help solve them.
- **Development goals** are usually established to help encourage employees to acquire new skills and expertise. But you don't need to have employees to think about development. Enhancing your own skills or expertise makes you more effective even if you're a freelancer or an independent contractor. So how about formulating at least one development goal for yourself or your company?
- **Innovation goals** are directed at finding new ways to improve the products or the services you offer, how you market yourself, or how you distribute and deliver what you sell. As you look ahead, can you identify any innovative approaches that could make your business more effective in the future? If so, formulate an appropriate goal.

Finally, glance through Form 3-7, a checklist of common business goals. Check off any that ring true for your own company and add them to your list.

GOALS AND OBJECTIVES BASED ON "ACES"	
ACHIEVE Web site up and running with at least 25 different "storefronts" Successful second round of venture capital	**CONSERVE** Strong sense of employee morale and enthusiasm Staff expertise
ELIMINATE Unnecessary duplication of efforts The competition (ha, ha)	**STEER CLEAR OF** A financial crunch Losing valued staff to other dot-com companies
SET OF BUSINESS GOALS: • Revise business plan and financial projections. • Review storefront vendor acquisition strategy. • Streamline management decision-making process. • Redesign employee benefits packages. • Develop a new-hire training curriculum.	

Figure 3-3: Using the four ACES to come up with business goals.

Making final choices

After you have a fairly respectable working list of goals — maybe more than you really want. Select the five goals that you think are absolutely essential to your business. (If you come up with only four, don't worry. If you can't get away with fewer than six or seven, no problem.) The point is to identify the goals that are absolutely, positively critical to your future success. After you decide on your list, fine-tune these remaining goals, using the following guidelines:

- Keep each goal clear and simple.
- Be as specific as you can.
- Be realistic.
- Don't be afraid to push yourself.
- Make sure your goals are in sync with your mission.

CHECKLIST OF COMMON BUSINESS GOALS
☐ Improve customer satisfaction
☐ Establish or increase brand awareness
☐ Find new markets for products or services
☐ Expand product or service lines
☐ Decrease time to market
☐ Improve employee satisfaction
☐ Increase management communication
☐ Reduce operational costs
☐ Generate new sources of revenue
☐ Become more entrepreneurial
☐ Increase networking with partners

Form 3-7: Checklist of common business goals.

Capture your final set of business goals using either the goals and objectives flowchart in Form 3-5 or the simpler Form 3-8, both of which are on the CD-ROM.

The major business goals you finally settle on are certainly going to be a part of your written business plan. Your longer-range goals will be wrapped into your business strategy, while your more immediate goals will find their way into your action plans.

Exploring Values and Vision

Your mission statement, along with your business goals and objectives, provide a road map that helps you steer your company as you move ahead into an always uncertain future. They help challenge you and inspire you to reach a little further than you thought you could. But they aren't enough all by themselves. You also need a good, reliable compass — something you can count on to point in the right direction, particularly during rocky times. That's where a clear set of values and a strong vision come in.

A *values statement* is a set of beliefs and principles that are always there, behind the scenes, to guide your business activities and the way you operate. A *vision statement* is a precise, well-crafted set of words that announces to the world what your company eventually hopes to make of itself. For detailed information about the central role of values and vision for many businesses across industries, check out *Business Plans For Dummies* by Paul Tiffany and Steven Peterson (Hungry Minds, Inc.). In this section, we give you some basics to help you think about your own values and vision.

Understanding why values matter

Plenty of real-life examples illustrate just how important a strong sense of values can be when a company faces a crisis. Consider a few recent cases:

- When Coca-Cola products were rumored to have made several hundred people sick in Europe not long ago, the company was slow to respond. The governments of France, Belgium, Luxembourg, and the Netherlands finally had to order Coke products off the shelves — and the company was left scrambling to repair its tarnished image. Coke's top executive was forced to apologize to European customers. His apology amounts to a values statement:

  "The Coca-Cola Company's highest priority is the quality of our products. One hundred thirteen years of our success has been based on the trust consumers have in that quality. That trust is sacred to us."

  Had his company acted on those values faster, Coke could have saved itself a tremendous amount of damage to its reputation and image.

- Most oil producers have taken a wait-and-see attitude toward concerns over global climate change. Not British Petroleum (BP). The company recently announced a "firm overall target" to cut greenhouse gas emissions by ten percent of their 1990 levels by 2010. This pledge made BP the first oil producer to weigh in with a measurable commitment in this area. The move, guided by the company's environmental values, also had a public relations payoff. The executive director of the Environmental Defense Fund called the announcement "a really magnificent example of a corporation acting responsibly."

- When customers discovered that Amazon.com required publishers to pay for the benefit of having their books featured on the company's Web site, they were furious. Many readers made their anger known in a barrage of e-mails. The company responded quickly, announcing a more lenient policy for book returns. Amazon also pledged to disclose whenever a company paid to have a book featured on its site. "We're always listening to our customers, and it was clear that our customers had a higher expectation for us than for the physical bookselling world," said a company spokesman in Seattle.

The fact is, a strong sense of values can bolster any company's image and guide it through troubled times. It can also improve the bottom line. A recent management study found that "honesty, transparency, and effective communication has a clear and fundamental financial value." The study looked at man-made catastrophes and their consequences for the various companies involved. Some firms were *recoverers* — they emerged with their reputations intact. Others — the *nonrecoverers* — didn't. The hallmark of recoverers was their ability to recognize their responsibilities to customers, shareholders, employees, and the public at large.

The examples we've mentioned all involve big companies. That's hardly surprising; after all, how often does a little business like Mary & Pete's Dry-Cleaning Service make the pages of *The Wall Street Journal?* But values remain important even when you're self-employed or part of a very small company. The following is just one example:

A chiropractor who worked for a large medical group in San Francisco quit to begin a small practice of his own in northern California. One of the major reasons for his decision was dissatisfaction with the way patients were treated by the large HMO. His new practice was so successful that he soon had more patients than he could treat. So he began to make plans to enlarge his practice, move to a larger facility, and hire two more chiropractors.

Then he stopped and took stock. The original reason he had begun a private practice — and one of his guiding values — was his belief that patients deserved individualized, personal care. By growing his business, he realized, he would spend more time managing staff and less time treating patients. The one thing he valued above all would be diminished. So he decided not to enlarge the practice. Instead, he formed a networking relationship with other private practice chiropractors to whom he could refer patients.

Uncovering values you already hold

So what are the values you hold for your company and your business? Don't be too surprised if you can't come up with a list of them off the top of your head. Values tend to be things we all take for granted — beliefs and principles that serve as a hidden foundation for what we choose to do and how we choose to get things accomplished.

One way to uncover some of your core values is to consider what you would do in a series of hypothetical situations — situations that call on you to make difficult decisions. Read through the scenarios presented in Form 3-9 and check the boxes that best describe what you would do. Remember, these questions don't really have right or wrong answers. The whole idea of this survey is for you to get a better handle on the set of values you already hold.

Writing a values statement

Look at your responses to the hypothetical situations in Form 3-9 and use them as a guide in drafting a formal statement of the values you think are most important to your company and your business. The statement doesn't have to be long and fancy. In fact, we think the best form for a values statement is a simple checklist, with values written down as plainly and clearly as possible.

The example in Figure 3-4 is one we particularly like. It was created by a young entrepreneur who is planning to combine his love of art and his commitment to folk artists into an Web-based folk art emporium.

OUR VALUES STATEMENT

Folk Art Bazaar is dedicated to the following values:

- Using the Internet to form a community of artists and collectors
- Encouraging the preservation of folk art tools and methods
- Offering struggling folk artists a means to make a decent living
- Educating collectors about the value and importance of folk art

Figure 3-4: Writing down a values statement in the form of a checklist.

VALUES QUESTIONNAIRE		
You discover that a product you offer poses a risk if used incorrectly. You've already dropped it from your online catalog, and the manufacturer has promised to send out warnings to everyone who's filled out a warranty card. What other steps would you take?		
☐ Let the matter drop, assuming the manufacturer has taken care of things.	☐ E-mail customers who have bought the product, alerting them to the problem as well.	☐ E-mail customers with a warning and an offer of a full refund, no questions asked.
An unhappy customer asks to return an item they purchased from you, even though it's beyond the thirty-day-return and there's absolutely nothing wrong with it. If you take it back, it can't be resold. What would you most likely do?		
☐ Tell them you're sorry, there's nothing you can do after 30 days.	☐ Bend the rules and refund them the money, betting on repeat business.	
You have meetings with two different clients, both on the opposite side of the country. They've each offered to pay your expenses as well as your fees. You plan to make only one trip to the coast. When it comes time to bill out your travel expenses, what would you do?		
☐ Split the airfare evenly between the two clients, giving each a small financial break.	☐ Bill the airfare out to the client you're least interested in working with long term.	☐ Bill each client for the full airfare, assuming this is what they each agreed to.
You learn that by changing suppliers, you could substitute sustainable materials into your product, substantially improving its environmental friendliness. Unfortunately, your costs would rise by about 25 percent. What alternative would you choose?		
☐ Continue producing the product in the most cost-effective way.	☐ Switch suppliers and absorb as much of the additional costs as you can.	☐ Pass the costs along after educating customers about the environmental benefits.
You discover that a long-term supplier has been consistently under-billing you for the last five years. What action would you take?		
☐ Wait for the supplier to discover the error, assuming it's not your problem.	☐ Correct the current bill.	☐ Alert the supplier and offer to repay all the past under-charges.
You are faced with filling a key position in your company. Where would you most likely turn?		
☐ Hire an outside person with the right job skills but no industry experience	☐ Promote someone inside with talent and drive, and agree to train them in the needed skills.	

Form 3-9: Values questionnaire — page 1 of 2.

Your are forced to let one of your team members go. Who would you tend to dismiss first?

☐ The young, inexperienced but energetic college grad who was just recently hired.

☐ The 20-year veteran, loyal and hardworking, but somewhat set in his ways.

An employee suggests that the company institute a strict recycling program. Your offices are already cramped and you worry about cutting into productivity. What's more, not all your employees want to be bothered with recycling. How would you proceed?

☐ Explain that the benefits aren't worth the costs to the company at this point.

☐ Agree to a three-month trial and then evaluate how well it's working.

☐ Ask your employees to vote on the new program and let the majority rule.

You have a smart, creative, and productive person working for you. Unfortunately, the individual is also disruptive, often flouts the rules, and is the source of many complaints in the office. What would you do?

☐ Tolerate the behavior, assuming a bit of tension is good and worth the results.

☐ Try to work with the person to get her to understand what absolutely needs changing.

☐ Terminate the employee to keep the office peace.

You are faced with a dilemma: Either work overtime and miss your child's championship soccer game, or risk letting an important business deadline slip. What would you do?

☐ Work until the project was complete, and then try to make it up to the family.

☐ Work around the soccer game, assuming things will somehow work out at your company.

An employee asks if you are is willing to help defer the costs of night school courses. What would your response be?

☐ You agree, but only to reimburse courses directly related to your business needs.

☐ You agree, but only if the employee agrees to work at least a year after course work is complete.

☐ You agree to pay without any preconditions, assuming you'll have a better employee.

You're putting together a compensation package for your top managers. What sort of incentives would you most likely include?

☐ Incentives based primarily on rewarding individual effort and performance.

☐ Incentives that promote team effort and company-wide performance.

Select the top three in terms of their importance in running your business.

☐ Maximize company profits

☐ Satisfy customers

☐ Be as ethical as possible

☐ Create fulfilling jobs

☐ Promote new technologies

☐ Develop employees

☐ Win product-quality awards

☐ Maintain long-term growth

☐ Promote worker safety

☐ Dominate markets

☐ Protect the environment

☐ Beat the competition

Form 3-9: Values questionnaire — page 2 of 2.

Using the checklist model shown in Figure 3-4, jot down the four to six phrases that best capture the core values you plan to run your own business by. Use Form 3-10 on the CD-ROM to get your values statement down on paper. Your values will make their way into your written business plan as part of your company overview.

Writing a vision statement

Remember, a mission statement describes who you are and what you hope to achieve. Goals and objectives set the mileposts that help you get there. And a values statement reminds you of why you're in business in the first place.

But many companies, large and small, have found that they can also use a plain *statement of their vision:* a short phrase or sentence that describes their enduring purpose. Based on your set of values, the vision statement cuts through all the details in a way that expresses, in the simplest possible language, what you intend to accomplish. A vision statement helps you decide what to preserve and what to change over the long haul. It captures the essential reasons you're in business: the intentions that will remain constant even while strategies and practices — and even your products and services — change in response to a changing world.

The best way to get a sense of what a vision statement can accomplish and how it is different from a mission statement is to look at a specific example. Folk Art Bazaar is a brand-new business venture started by an entrepreneurial friend of ours and has a set of business values listed in Figure 3-4. His company's mission statement reads as follows:

> To create an online marketplace that brings together unique and creative folk artists from around the world with serious collectors from beginner to expert.

His business vision:

> To promote the continuing production of folk art and the livelihood of folk artists around the world through internet technology.

We've collected additional vision statements in Form 3-11 that take a range of approaches, but all of them get to the core of what each company is all about. Check off the ones that really grab you. You can refer to them as you write up your own vision.

EXAMPLES OF REAL-WORLD VISION STATEMENTS
☐ *To be a role model and tool for social change.* (Lost Arrow Corporation)
☐ *To make technical contributions for the advancement and welfare of humanity.* (Hewlett-Packard)
☐ *To be a world-class system integration and technology management business that provides best value solutions to our customers, an exceptional career experience to our people and excellent returns to our shareholders.* (Lockheed Martin)
☐ *To solve unsolved problems innovatively.* (3M)
☐ *To give unlimited opportunity to women.* (Mary Kay)
☐ *To make alternative and complementary health care available to cancer patients in the community.* (Holistic Health Services)
☐ *To preserve and improve human life.* (Merck)
☐ *To strengthen the social fabric by continually democratizing home ownership.* (Fannie Mae)
☐ *To be a leading provider of injection molds to industry, well respected for technical expertise, quality, timely delivery, and adherence to highest ethical standards, by our customers and competitors.* (Stellar Mold & Tool, Inc.)
☐ *To help people with mental impairments realize their full potential.* (Telecare)
☐ *To give ordinary folk the chance to buy the same things as rich people.* (Wal-Mart)
☐ *To experience the joy of advancing and applying technology for the benefit of the public.* (Sony)
☐ *To provide a place for people to flourish and to enhance the community.* (Pacific Theaters)

Form 3-11: Examples of real-world vision statements.

Looking back over your values statement, try to capture in 25 words or less the core vision you have for your company. Use the examples you like in Form 3-11 as a starting point, and use Form 3-12 (on the CD-ROM) to get it down on paper. Your vision statement will make its way into your written business plan as part of your company overview.

The vision you have for your company is something you should be very proud of. So show it off to the world. Make handsome, framed copies of your vision statement and distribute them to everyone you work with. If you work for yourself, print out an attractive version of your vision and attach it to your computer monitor or the inside cover of your daily calendar. Consider making your vision statement a part of your company brochure. Some companies even put their vision statements right up on their letterhead to remind everyone of the essential reasons they're in business.

Forms on the CD-ROM

Check out the following forms on the CD-ROM if you need help setting up the ground rules for your business:

Form 3-1	**Your Mission Statement Questionnaire**	A questionnaire designed to generate ideas about your company's mission
Form 3-2	**Your Mission Statement Framework**	A form created to help you bring your ideas together into a statement of your mission
Form 3-3	**Examples of Real-World Mission Statements**	A selection of actual company mission statements, along with space to record your own impressions
Form 3-4	**Our Mission Statement**	A form on which you can record the final version of your company's mission statement
Form 3-5	**Goals and Objectives Flowchart**	A form to capture your company's major goals and objectives as they relate to your mission statement
Form 3-6	**Goals and Objectives Based on ACES**	A form to capture goals and objectives based on things you want to achieve, conserve, eliminate, and steer clear of

Form 3-7	**Checklist of Common Business Goals**	A checklist of common business goals that many companies say they'd like to accomplish
Form 3-8	**Our Major Business Goals**	A form to record the major business goals you've set for yourself
Form 3-9	**Values Questionnaire**	Situations designed to help you identify the values you already hold
Form 3-10	**Our Values Statement**	A form on which you can record the final version of your values statement
Form 3-11	**Examples of Real-World Vision Statements**	A selection of actual company vision statements, along with space to check off which ones you like
Form 3-12	**Our Vision Statement**	A form on which you can record the final version of your vision statement

Part II
Building Your Plan's Components

"You can become a 'corporation' or a 'sole proprietor,' Mr. Holk. But there's simply no legal way of filing yourself as a 'formidable presence'."

In this part . . .

No two business plans are the same, but almost all of them share certain features: They describe the company and what it proposes to do, they take a close look at the business environment, and they lay out a business strategy. A good business plan also crunches the numbers to make sure the company has enough money in the beginning to get off the ground, as well as enough money down the road in the form of profits.

In the four chapters in this part, we walk you through all of the essential business-planning elements. We take a look at your marketplace — sizing up your customers and checking out your competition. We also look at your strengths and weaknesses to see how they match up with the opportunities and threats you face. Then, by examining your key business capabilities, we make sure your business plan focuses on what you do best. Finally, we help you tackle the numbers, walking you through the details of creating an income statement, a balance sheet, and a cash flow statement, along with the financial projections and the budget you need.

Chapter 4

Assessing the Business Environment

In This Chapter

- Examining the industry your business is in
- Getting to know your customers
- Keeping track of your competition

So you're ready to run with your very own business venture. Maybe you've already crafted a mission statement and have a clear vision of what you want your company to become (see Chapter 3). Perhaps you've even settled on specific goals and objectives you want to achieve, along with targets and time frames (also discussed in Chapter 3). In any case, you've no doubt whipped up plenty of excitement and anticipation about your new enterprise.

We couldn't be happier for you. We'd like, however, to suggest a reality check here. Remember that a great business idea isn't enough — even if you're convinced that your brainchild is the biggest thing since Post-it notes. For one thing, you'll need to have customers who also think it's a great idea. You'll also have to establish a very good reason (or two) for those customers to come to you and not to your competitor around the corner or across the Internet. In short, before you plunge ahead, you have to take a long, hard look at your business environment.

In this chapter, we guide you through a straightforward analysis of your industry with a special look at some of the forces that can have an impact on your business success. We also help you take a closer look at customers, including customers that may themselves be other businesses. Finally, we walk you through the process of scoping out your competition, helping you identify who your competitors are and what their next moves may be.

Taking a Close Look at Your Industry

You may think that your business is one-of-a-kind, with products and services in a class by themselves. But chances are, you're part of a larger industry: retail, telecommunications, entertainment, travel, publishing — or any of a hundred others. Even if you're part of a not-for-profit organization (discussed in Chapter 11), you're probably in competition with many other worthy causes. This section helps you describe your industry and how you fit into it.

Understanding the business you're really in

What business are you really in? You may think that you already have a pretty good idea, but business history is littered with the corpses of companies that thought they knew — only to discover that the industry wasn't quite what it seemed.

- Take the railroad industry, for example. During its heyday in the 30s, 40s, and 50s, the big railroad companies assumed they were in the railroad business. Then along came powerful competitors that had nothing to do with railroads — automobile manufacturers, the interstate highway system, jet aircraft, and regional airports. Railroads weren't really in the railroad business — they were in the transportation business. Perhaps if they had realized it a little sooner, they may have had a rosier future.
- Eastman Kodak is over 120 years old. And over the years, the firm has made most of its money processing film. So much money, in fact, that the company came to believe it was in the chemical-imaging business. That all changed with the digital revolution. Today, Kodak competes with Sony and Philips and a host of other companies. The business? Well, it sure isn't chemicals. As it turns out, people are interested in capturing their memories — on film, video, or computer. And Kodak has been in the memories business all along.
- Here's an example from Main Street, U.S.A: In a bustling resort town on the Gulf Coast of Florida, Mom and Pop's Toys had been thriving for years. Then one day someone else set up shop right across the street. Mom and Pop's Toys prepared for the competition by reducing prices on their best-selling merchandise, assuming that customers would respond favorably to lower costs. Across the street, Toy Mania had another idea: They realized that in this Florida resort town, they were really in the entertainment business. So they created a fantasy land right inside their store, with puppets, animated cartoon characters, giant wind-up toys, and store clerks dressed up in outrageous costumes. They even held their own variety shows three times a day. Within a year, Mom and Pop's Toys had to close its doors. They couldn't compete because they didn't understand the business.

As you can see, you must ask yourself this not-so simple question: What business are you really in?

To make answering this basic question a bit easier, we've drawn up three related questions to guide you. In Figure 4-1, you can see how one company we've worked with answered them. This particular firm provides text-editing services over the Internet, mainly to the marketing and communications departments of large companies.

BASIC BUSINESS DEFINITION FRAMEWORK
1. What basic needs do you fulfill in the marketplace? For each of our corporate clients, we make sure that all printed and Internet text materials are grammatically correct and conform to the company's style requirements.
2. Beyond specific products and services, why do customers come to you? The reliability and quality of our service. Peace of mind. Not having to worry that the company will look bad in print. Confidence that what's published is correct and understandable.
3. What are the three nicest things your customers could say about you? That we're thorough and reliable. That we have excellent turnaround. That we're friendly and easy to work with.

Figure 4-1: Answering questions to determine the business you're really in.

Looking back over these answers, the execs at the company were struck by the phrase "peace of mind." Sure they were in the text-editing business, but in a way they were also in the insurance business — making sure that marketing and communications managers weren't tripped up by an embarrassing typo or inconsistency. They were also in the hand-holding business. They realized that many of their clients were so pressed for time that they had trouble finding people simply to look over text for clarity and readability.

In response, the company decided to change a few of its procedures. They put a managing editor in place to oversee the largest projects — someone who could hold clients' hands and give them feedback as they went through the editorial process. Someone, in other words, to reinforce that sense of peace of mind. Within six months, they were getting more work than they could handle.

Now it's your turn. Invest some time and effort in thinking about the three questions we pose in Form 4-1 (on the CD-ROM). Jot down whatever comes to mind, and then polish your ideas. While your answers may not go directly into your written business plan, they will influence almost everything around your business planning efforts.

Looking at your industry's big picture

Understanding the larger forces at work in your industry is a crucial part of business planning. What are the long-term trends around you? Is the industry growing fast or treading water? Is entering the market difficult? How important is technological change? Answers to questions like these are key to creating a robust business plan. By taking the long view, you get a better sense of how and where your own venture fits in. Chances are, you'll find out a few things you didn't know — insights that help you sidestep trouble and chart a better course.

Industry forces out there are bigger than you or any of your competitors. We've seen too many companies go belly up because they based their business plans on faulty or naïve assumptions about their industry. And we've watched too many promising ventures miss out on real opportunities because they didn't see the big picture.

As a first step toward analyzing your industry, fill out the questionnaire in Form 4-2. Completing this questionnaire gives you a good idea of what you already know about your industry — and, more importantly, what you still need to find out.

When you don't know the answer to a particular question, circle the number beside it. If you circle a few numbers because you don't know the answers, take time out now to do a little additional digging. Anything you don't know about your industry — the fact that a few suppliers control all your material costs, for example — can come back to haunt you sooner than you may think.

Look over your answers and choose the most important aspects of the big picture you've created. How serious is the competitive threat? Who really drives your industry — customers, distributors, or suppliers? Are you going to be able to ride the rising tide of an expanding industry, or are you going to have to find ways to succeed in spite of a general industry slowdown?

Analyzing your industry can be a daunting task, no doubt about it. And any one of the forces, trends, or issues you've identified can be the one that's absolutely critical. Using what you've learned from the industry analysis questionnaire and the legwork you put into it, create a written summary describing the big picture view of your industry as you see it. Your written plan should include this industry overview as part of the business environment section.

INDUSTRY ANALYSIS QUESTIONNAIRE			
1. How may competitors do you have?			
☐ Many	☐ Some	☐ Few	
2. Has a new competitor entered the market recently?			
☐ Yes	☐ No		
3. Have any companies in your area gone out of business recently?			
☐ Yes	☐ No		
4. How difficult is it for new companies to come into the business?			
☐ Very difficult	☐ Difficult	☐ Easy	
5. How important is technological change to your business?			
☐ Very important	☐ Somewhat important	☐ Not important	
6. What's the current market demand in your industry?			
☐ Growing	☐ Stable	☐ Declining	
7. Is there an untapped market that your industry can take advantage of?			
☐ Yes	☐ Maybe	☐ No	
8. What do customers care about most in your business?			
☐ Price	☐ Features	☐ Service	☐ All of the above
9. How easily can customers find alternatives outside your industry?			
☐ Very easily	☐ With difficulty	☐ Not at all	

Form 4-2: Industry analysis questionnaire — page 1 of 2.

10. How much bargaining power do big customers have in your industry?		
☐A lot	☐ Some	☐None
11. How much influence do large suppliers have in setting terms?		
☐A lot	☐ Some	☐None
12. How much power do distributors wield in your industry?		
☐A lot	☐ Some	☐None
13. What are typical profit margins like in your business?		
☐Strong	☐ Average	☐Weak
14. What is the trend for overall costs in your industry?		
☐Declining	☐ Stable	☐Rising
15. How would you describe the general health of you industry?		
☐Very healthy	☐ Somewhat healthy	☐Ailing

Form 4-2: Industry analysis questionnaire — page 2 of 2.

Paying the price of admission

Business-planning efforts are often centered around new business opportunities — either you're just starting up or you're branching out into new markets. In either case, your business plan has to tackle the hurdles you're going to face as a newcomer.

No matter what industry you're in, specific obstacles are bound get in the way, increasing the difficulty for new competitors to join the party. Business gurus call these obstacles *entry barriers.* If the entry barriers are low, almost anyone can join. Setting up an online Web site is a fairly straightforward task, so barriers to entry on the Internet are relatively low — hence the mad rush of dot-com companies into cyberspace.

Diamonds are forever, but what about De Beers?

For most of the 20th century, De Beers wasn't just part of the diamond industry, it *was* the diamond industry. With both aboveboard and underhanded practices — including the use of West African mercenaries — De Beers managed to control the world's entire supply of diamonds. The result: It managed to keep diamonds scarce and diamond prices high.

But by the mid 1980s, the company had detected the beginnings of change in the industry that threatened its monopoly. Rich new diamond mines were opening in Canada and Australia. Conflicts in Africa were creating widespread smuggling of diamonds, over which De Beers had little control. The collapse of the Soviet Union was eroding its influence over diamond producers in that area. In response, the company was forced to stockpile billions of dollars worth of diamonds to keep supply down and prices up.

But it just wasn't enough. When De Beers saw that its profits were going nowhere fast, the company decided to fundamentally change the way it did business. It announced that it would not only begin to sell off its stockpiled diamonds, but it would also increase production from mines around the world. Instead of trying to control the world market, the company would now focus its efforts on increasing demand for diamonds worldwide.

We'll have to wait and see how these changes will affect the company's fortunes — or the price of a diamond ring. But we're encouraged to see this venerable old company still analyzing its industry and making changes to its business plan as it adapts to changing conditions. If it's successful, De Beers, like diamonds, could be forever.

When barriers are high, you have fewer competitors. But there's a downside: As a newcomer, you also face plenty of hurdles to get into the market in the first place. Consider the following examples:

- Suppose you're thinking about starting a printing business. Right off the bat, one barrier to entry is the high capital cost associated with acquiring the production equipment you'll need. To overcome the barrier, you may come up with creative ways to lease the equipment or figure out how to outsource a portion of your production operations until you get up to full speed.
- If you're planning a clothing shop that will eventually have to compete with chain stores, you face an entry barrier: the built-in advantage of economies of scale. Simply put, larger retailers can buy their merchandise at much lower cost than you ever can, because they buy so much of it at a time. To overcome the barrier, you may want to think about competing on something other than price: the quality of your fabrics, for example, or the uniqueness of the fashions you carry.

- Perhaps you've decided to open a new hair salon in a town that already has a handful of successful beauty shops. Chances are, the biggest barrier to entry you face is customer loyalty. After people find a hair stylist they like, they're usually reluctant to change — who knows what kind of a 'do they may end up with! To overcome this strong sense of loyalty, you have to come up with good reasons for customers to change: a "bring-a-friend for free" campaign, for example, or an onsite daycare service.

We've created a short list of the typical barriers to entry that new competitors often face in a variety of industries. Review Form 4-3 and check off those barriers that may apply to your own industry and marketplace. If we've forgotten something, fill it in at the end.

BARRIERS TO ENTRY CHECKLIST
☐ Capital costs (lots of money required up front)
☐ Distribution systems (difficult to reach your customers)
☐ Organization (complex operations are needed)
☐ Raw materials (hard to get supplies)
☐ New technology (sophisticated skills required)
☐ Scale economies (the bigger you are, the lower your costs)
☐ Regulations (legal obstacles)
☐ Patents (competitive hurdles)
☐ Customer loyalty (market advantage)
☐ Customer switching costs (it costs the customer to change)
☐

Form 4-3: Barriers to entry checklist.

Take a moment to look over the items you checked and rank them on a scale of 1 to 10, 1 being the most important. Look closely at the top three on your priority list. These represent the biggest hurdles you face in getting your business up and running. When you write your business plan, you need to acknowledge these barriers and discuss precisely how you intend to get over, under, or around them.

Sizing Up Your Customers

When you get right down to it, the key to success for any business is having customers. Without enough of them, in fact, you don't have a business at all. So successful planning depends on understanding precisely who your customers are and exactly what they want from you. We don't expect you to find out everything about what makes them tick, but if you're going to succeed, you need to figure out what makes your customers buy the first time and what makes them come back to buy again.

Describing the ideal customer

If customers are important to a business, the ideal customer represents the pot of gold at the end of the rainbow. But how do you know who your ideal customer is? The ideal customer is likely to be different for every business and every company. And building up a description of your own perfect customer takes a little time and effort on your part.

Weighing the good and the bad

Begin by separating good customers from bad ones. "Bad customers?" you say. "How can a customer be a bad customer?" Easy. Some, in fact, are downright awful — and may threaten the best business. You can typically identify bad customers because they

- Don't end up buying very much from you
- Ask you to do things you're not particularly good at
- Require too much service and attention
- Are always dissatisfied, no matter what you do for them

On the other hand, good customers

- Ask you to do things you do well
- Appreciate what you do and are willing to pay for it
- Challenge you to improve and expand your skills
- Take you in new and profitable directions

Take a few moments to compare the qualities of a good customer with those of a bad customer in your own business. Come up with a list of four or five traits that really capture the difference between these two groups. Jot them down in Form 4-4, which you'll find on the CD-ROM.

Considering perfection

After you have a better idea of what a good customer is — at least in comparison to a bad one — you can focus on the qualities that turn a good customer into the perfect customer.

Indulge in a little fantasy here. Sit back and imagine your absolute ideal. (We're still talking customers here.) Imagine the sort of person who will eagerly buy your products and services, rave about you to friends and colleagues, and keep coming back time and again to buy on a regular basis. We're making an assumption that your customers are individuals, not other businesses. But don't skip this section even if you do business mainly with other companies. You're sure to find out something about your business customers here that you can apply when you turn to the "Doing business with business customers" section, later in this chapter.

To get your imaginative juices flowing, use Form 4-5, a questionnaire designed to cover all the important aspects of the ideal customer you're trying to describe.

To see just how important a good description of your ideal customer can be in clarifying your business plan and directing your company's activities, consider the case of a rather unusual e-business: a Web site startup specializing in selling underwear with sex appeal. The first time the company's young entrepreneurs sat down to write a paragraph describing their ideal customers, they came up with this:

> We're going after Internet shoppers with a sense of humor, adventure, and playfulness — but who are a bit reluctant to purchase intimate apparel at a bricks-and-mortar store. Our customers are likely to be women buying our products for themselves or for their significant others.

IDEAL CUSTOMER QUESTIONNAIRE		
1. What does your ideal customer want or need?		
2. What special features or benefits are they looking for?		
3. What do they place the most value on?		
4. What motivates your ideal customer to buy a product or service?		
5. How will you best reach your ideal customer?		
6. What is it about your ideal customer that will motivate them to buy from you rather than someone else?		
7. Why will they keep coming back to you?		
8. Where is your ideal customer most likely to live?		
9. Describe your ideal customer:		
• Age range	**• Gender**	**• Family size**
• Education	**• Occupation**	**• Income**

Form 4-5: Ideal customer questionnaire — page 1 of 2.

• **Ethnicity**	• **Nationality**	• **Religion**
Any other important or unique attribute		
10. How does your ideal customer spend his or her time:		
• **Hobbies**	• **Social functions**	• **Vacation time**
• **Any other special activities**		

Form 4-5: Ideal customer questionnaire — page 2 of 2.

No doubt a fine beginning. But this snapshot leaves out some crucial aspects. How is the ideal customer likely to find the sensual underwear site in the first place? Why would she choose to buy underwear here rather than somewhere else? What motivates her to buy — price, quality, special features? Is she likely to be a repeat buyer? What will convince her to come back and shop again? Encouraged to flesh out (sorry) their snapshot of the ideal customer, this is what they added:

> Most of our customers will hear about us by way of advertising on other selected Web sites and through ads placed in national women's magazines. Our ideal customer is between the ages of 18 and 35. Most are single or recently married and live in urban areas, especially on the east and west coasts. Because they are Internet savvy, they also tend to be somewhat upscale and have a certain sense of sophistication. Quality matters more than price to these customers. And quality is determined both by the materials used and our designs. The bottom line: We create products that make our customers feel sexier. We hope that if we deliver on this promise, our customers will keep coming back to us.

Now the young entrepreneurs were getting somewhere. The expanded description includes a few key demographic characteristics — where the ideal customer lives, her age, her marital status. And it begins to zero in on what drives her buying decisions.

When the senior management team looked over the snapshot they'd drawn, they began to understand a few new things about their customers and themselves — insights that helped them hone their marketing strategy. First, they realized that what their customers really wanted was to feel sexy and desirable. The intimate apparel was just the path to that end. Sure, the company was selling underwear, but it was really marketing sex appeal. Suddenly the entrepreneurs realized how important the images and models used on the site would be in generating traffic and sales.

When they went back to review their ideal customer snapshot they also found one weak link — that bit about "if we deliver on this promise, our customers will keep coming back to us." Repeat buyers would be crucial to their strategy, but with very little money available for marketing and advertising, this company would succeed only if customers kept coming back on their own — and told all their friends, as well. True, good service and high quality were a big draw, but the managers began to realize that they would need something else to create loyal customers.

So the simple exercise of writing a descriptive snapshot of an ideal customer sparked a series of creative meetings devoted to the issue of encouraging repeat buyers. Beyond offering a line of sensual underwear, the new Web site would also create an online mini-magazine including weekly health and beauty tips, a monthly make-over column written by a leading cosmetologist, and even a racy Q & A written by a famous sex counselor.

Would their revised strategy work? Only time and their customers will tell. But thinking about the business from their best customers' point of view make this company's odds of success much greater.

To create your own descriptive snapshot of your ideal customer, review your answers to the ten questions in Form 4-5, circling those characteristics that seem most important to your business relationship with the perfect customer. After you have a clear picture of you ideal customer in mind, create your ideal customer snapshot using the template in Form 4-6, which is on the CD-ROM.

If the underwear e-business entrepreneurs we just described were to fill out the template, it would probably look something like Figure 4-2.

Take your completed template and write up a short sketch — two or three paragraphs in plain English — describing your ideal customer. This description will become a part of your written business plan. It also keeps you focused on exactly the kind of customer you'd like to have. After all, the better you come to know your best customers, the more effective you'll be in creating a business that caters to their needs and keeps them loyal.

Doing business with business customers

Many companies do business with other businesses rather than individual consumers. *B2B* (short for *business to business*) has already become a well-known buzzword in the Internet world. And, of course, many bricks-and-mortar industries — the steel industry, for example — have always sold their goods to other companies (not many individuals are in the market for steel girders, after all).

IDEAL CUSTOMER SNAPSHOT
OUR TARGET CUSTOMERS CAN BEST BE DESCRIBED AS 18- to 35-year-old women, single or recently divorced, living in coastal urban areas.
THESE CUSTOMERS ARE LOOKING FOR adventure, playfulness, and sex appeal through the purchase of intimate apparel.
WE WILL REACH MANY OF OUR TARGET CUSTOMERS THROUGH online advertising, ads in women's magazines, and word-of-mouth.
THESE CUSTOMERS WILL BUY FROM US RATHER THAN OUR COMPETITORS BECAUSE THEY appreciate our styling and quality and enjoy the privacy, ambience, and convenience of our online store.

Figure 4-2: Creating a descriptive snapshot of the ideal customer.

In some ways, business customers are a lot like individual consumers. They're concerned about price, quality, service, reliability — those aspects of buying and selling that you're already familiar with. But you can also find important distinctions. If you sell to other businesses, for example, your customers aren't as likely to be swayed by holiday sales or promotional blitzes, and they're not usually impulse buyers. In fact, your business customers' buying behavior is most often determined by their own customers and what's happening in their own industries.

If you've ever had to deal with other businesses as customers, you'll probably recognize two additional differences that really set business customers apart: the people who are involved in purchasing a product or service and the way they go about buying it. If you think you need to find out more about the decision makers and the decision-making process that goes on in companies before they make a purchase decision, we suggest you check out *Business Plans For Dummies* by Paul Tiffany and Steven Peterson (Hungry Minds, Inc.).

In many cases, you already have access to a lot of information about your potential business customers. All you really need to do is organize it by creating a business customer profile on each of them. Give yourself some time to think about the companies you hope to do business with. For each company, fill out the questionnaire provided in Form 4-7.

BUSINESS CUSTOMER PROFILE ON COMPANY: ________________		
1. Company description:		
• **Company name**	• **Industry**	• **Yearly revenue**
• **Number of employees**	• **Years in business**	• **Location**
• **Principal contact**		
• **Other relevant information**		
2. What are the major benefits you offer this company?		
3. What are the essential qualities the company is looking for in a supplier?		
4. Do the key decision-makers in the company tend to be engineers or marketing people?		
5. Does this company use both small and larger suppliers?		
6. Does the company have a policy of requiring more than one supplier?		
7. Does the company purchase centrally, or are buyers scattered around?		

Form 4-7: Business customer profile — page 1 of 2.

8. Does this company require several levels of approval for purchases?
9. Is the company's business booming, steady, or facing increased competition?
10. Are there major changes inside this company that might result in opportunities for new business?

Form 4-7: Business customer profile — page 2 of 2.

After you complete these profiles for your key business customers, go through and circle the important characteristics that the companies have in common. Use these common traits to put together an ideal business customer snapshot — two or three paragraphs describing the business customers you want to target. If you need help, use Form 4-6, which is on the CD-ROM.

A snapshot description of the business customers you intend to serve will find its way into your written business plan. The snapshot spells out who these customers are and, as a result, who you need to be in order to get and keep their business over the long haul.

Discovering more about all your customers

You may think you already know a lot about the customers you're trying to attract. But you may not always have an easy time figuring out what makes your customers tick — what they really need and want, where they shop, and exactly how they buy. How can you get more information?

Large companies often hire consulting firms for big bucks. These consultants send out long and detailed customer surveys or conduct elaborate focus group sessions to discover subtle customer traits and motives. Take a look at "The minivan versus the SUV" sidebar, for example, to read about some of the latest market research in the automobile world.

The minivan versus the SUV

Sport utility vehicles (SUVs) and minivans look pretty much the same on the surface — ideal for picking up groceries, taking long trips, or playing the soccer parent. And in many ways, the owners of SUVs and minivans seem to have a lot in common as well. They're usually affluent, most in their 40s, and married with children. The drivers are more likely to be men than women.

Automakers routinely spend lots of money trying to figure out what consumers really look for in a vehicle. And in the last few years, they've wanted to know why certain people in the above category always buy a minivan and others wouldn't have anything but an SUV.

Now they have an answer. Recent market research has revealed that the buyers of minivans and SUVs are really very different, if you know where to look. Minivan buyers, for example, tend to be self-confident and "other-oriented" — likely to spend time with family, friends, and community organizations. SUV drivers, on the other hand, tend to be restless, self-oriented, and, well, almost always on their own. SUV drivers are more concerned with what the vehicle looks like on the outside. Minivan drivers want to know how it feels on the inside, and whether the interior space is comfortable and practical.

There are even bigger differences when you look at what these different buyers do to have a good time. The list of favorite activities for minivan owners includes conversations with friends, family gatherings, reading, church functions, and volunteer work. SUV owners, on the other hand, would rather dine out, go to sporting events, work out, hunt, or go mountain biking.

Who cares? The car makers, of course. Armed with new information, they've tailored their marketing campaigns and even re-designed their vehicles to make the most of these critical differences. Minivan ads now feature mothers and children. SUV ads feature mountains and beautiful women. The newest minivans are designed from the inside out, with an eye on comfort and practical use. The latest SUVs are designed for outside looks and sex appeal.

If you can't afford to spend money on customized market research, you can sometimes find simpler and cheaper ways to get a clearer picture of what your customers are really like. Consider the following ideas:

- **Stop, look, and listen.** You can discover a lot by observing customers. If you're in the retail business, for example, watch where customers go while inside your store and what products they linger over longest. When you go to an industry trade show, watch which booths and exhibits people visit most often. You can even do your own informal surveys by chatting with people, asking them informal questions about various products and services. Whatever business you're in, be creative in finding simple ways to observe your customers and their behavior.

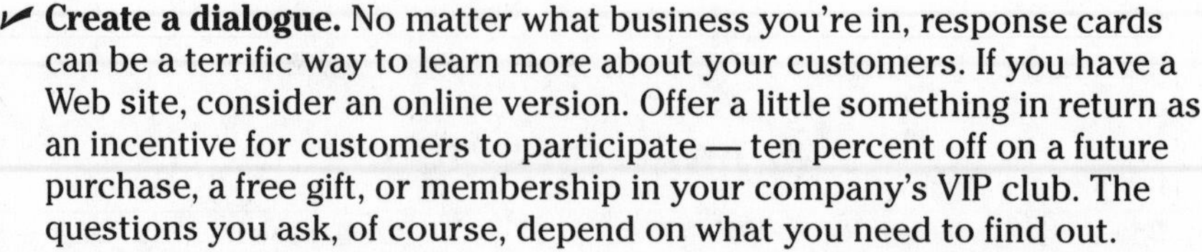

- **Create a dialogue.** No matter what business you're in, response cards can be a terrific way to learn more about your customers. If you have a Web site, consider an online version. Offer a little something in return as an incentive for customers to participate — ten percent off on a future purchase, a free gift, or membership in your company's VIP club. The questions you ask, of course, depend on what you need to find out.

  If you're thinking of improving a product or developing a new service, consider asking your best customers to become part of the creative process. Ask them what they like and don't like about existing offerings. What would they change? What new features would they like to see?

  The closer you can get to your customers, the more successful you're going to be in your marketplace.

- **Cast a wider net.** The Internet has become a vast database of customer responses to everything from the latest bestseller to the most sophisticated digital camera on the market. Publishers (and authors) can discover which books are selling well hour by hour. Winemakers can find out which vintages are being snapped up. Consultants can explore business topics that are hot this month. Digital gadget makers can survey customer reaction to cutting-edge technology as they design the next generation of electronic toys.

  As you start to follow your customers through cyberspace, take time to discover which Web sites are worth tracking in your own industry and market. Check out any site that allows customers to weigh in on what they think, and you're bound to get an earful.

- **Go virtual.** If you want specific customer feedback, and you can't afford a full-fledged focus group, consider going *virtual* — especially if you already have an Internet presence. The idea is simple: You arrange for a group of customers to get together in an online chat room to talk about a particular aspect of your product or service. If you do business online, contact a number of your customers by e-mail to ask if they'll participate in an online focus group: Offer them a little something in return for the favor.

If you want to find out more about your customers on an ongoing basis — and we think that's a very good idea — take our suggestions and begin to create your own agenda for times, places, and ways to get closer to your customers. Consider it your personal customer intelligence plan. To get you started, we've created the customer intelligence checklist in Form 4-8.

Grouping your customers together

Every company wants each of its customers to feel special. "Have it your way," one fast food chain promises. "We do business one customer at a time," boasts a major investment firm.

CUSTOMER INTELLIGENCE CHECKLIST
1. Places and times to observe real customers in your marketplace: • • • •
2. Ways to interact with customers around your products and services: • • • •
3. Web sites relevant to your customer feedback, behavior, and analysis: • • • •

Form 4-8: Customer intelligence checklist.

Sounds good. But the fact is, most companies — particularly large ones — can't really think about every customer as an individual. Instead, they do the next best thing. They try to separate their markets into groups of customers who seem to have something in common. In other words, they try to create *market segments* (sorry for the marketing jargon.)

By lumping similar customers together, companies can design specific products and services and target their advertising efforts to reach not just one person, but a whole group of people who all respond in similar ways. The fast food company, for example, may develop a promotional program using clowns and stuffed animals to attract its youngest customers. At the same time, it may advertise during televised sporting events to tempt its young adult clientele and place discount coupons in local papers to attract senior citizens.

For more details about the ins and outs of market segmentation, turn to *Business Plans For Dummies* by Paul Tiffany and Steven Peterson (Hungry Minds, Inc.). In this section, we give you a basic market segmentation framework to use as you think about ways to divide your own customers into categories based on their similarities. The framework involves three simple questions:

- Who is buying?
- What do they buy?
- Why do they buy?

Consider the example of a new online retailer specializing in selling underwear with sex appeal. After gathering some data and thinking carefully about their market segments, this startup company found that it could marshal scarce marketing dollars and use them to the greatest effect. Figure 4-3 shows how the company answered the three questions in our market segmentation framework.

BASIC MARKET SEGMENTATION FRAMEWORK
1. Who is buying?
80% of customers are women who are single or recently married and are under 30 years old.
75% of customers are from urban areas.
2. What do they buy?
85% of customers ranked style and sexiness as important.
60% mentioned privacy and convenience as important.
35% of customers ranked materials and quality near the top.
3. Why do they buy?
75% of customers mentioned a desire to be attractive and playful.
60% said they were embarrassed to go into intimate apparel stores.

Figure 4-3: Answering three questions to divide customers into segments.

Looking over their answers to the segmentation questions, the company's managers realized that not all of their female customers actually lived in urban areas. By offering gift certificates to visitors who filled in short online questionnaires, they found that 25 percent of their customers lived outside big cities. One of the major reasons these customers shopped online was that they had no other place to go. To help this broader audience identify more closely with the Web site, the e-tailer slightly changed the range of models used in its images.

The fledgling company was also struck by the fact that they could segment their customers by gender — 80 percent were women; 20 percent, men. The managers had always assumed that they would be marketing solely to women. Now they decided that they shouldn't just ignore their male market segment. In fact, they agreed that it would be worth addressing this customer base with some highly targeted advertising. By placing several ads in leading men's magazines, the company hopes to increase its sales among men by 25 percent.

The moral of this story: Know your customer.

Complete the market segmentation framework for your own business by answering the three questions about your customers in Form 4-9, which you can find on the CD-ROM. Don't worry if you have to be a bit tentative at this point. If you don't have all the customer information you need, add the task to your company's goals and objectives (see Chapter 3) or make sure it's on your customer intelligence checklist, discussed in the preceding section.

Include the market segmentation you come up with in your written business plan as part of the business environment section.

Checking Out the Competition

Unless you're very clever — and extremely lucky — chances are you're not the only one out there with a great idea and a serious plan to win over eager customers in a particular market. Even in brand-new industries, a throng of new competitors quickly appears, each fighting tooth and nail to grab their own piece of the market pie. If you need any evidence, just glance online and see how intense the competition for cyberspace customers has become.

What's that? You say your idea is so new and so creative that you really won't have any competition? Think again. Unless you're a government agency or a communist state, you have competition. Someone else out there is always ready and willing to offer a similar product or service to similar customers. One classic mistake that companies often make is forgetting that they're not alone with their customers. In a very real sense, the success of your business depends largely on how well you understand your competitors and how successful you are at distinguishing yourself from them in the eyes of your potential customers.

In the business world, competition is often compared to the battlefield and warfare. And because business books are forever quoting dead people, we can't resist doing it just one time. The great military strategist Sun Tzu wrote (a *very* long time ago), "If you know yourself, but not your enemy, for every battle won, you will lose another."

He's got a point. And while equating business competition with warfare may be going a bit far — especially if you're planning to open a yoga studio or a environmental consulting firm — they can both be equally brutal. The lesson: If you want to win more battles than you lose on the business front, be prepared to really know your competition.

Competition isn't necessarily a bad thing. Having competitors to challenge you makes you stronger. Competitors encourage you to run your own business better by first forcing you to clarify what you do and then asking you to distinguish yourself from the crowd.

Take some time to identify your five biggest competitors — those other players who are most likely to take business away from you, if you're not careful. Can't come up with five? Then list as many as you can, using Form 4-10 (on the CD-ROM) to track them. And because the competitive landscape can change rapidly, make sure you keep an eye on your list of competitors all the time.

Identifying your stealth competitors

You can usually spot direct competitors pretty easily. They're the ones that look a lot like you. They offer similar products or services and go after the same markets. But watch out for the other competition — the *stealth competitors*, who often catch you off guard, winning competitive battles before you even realize they're around. Your stealth competitors go after the same customers you do, but in different, sometimes unexpected ways.

Suppose you're thinking of starting a yoga studio, for example. Your biggest competitors are likely to be other yoga centers within, say, a 20-mile radius. But chances are, you have other, less obvious competitive threats. Yoga classes may be offered at local fitness centers or at the YMCA. Parks and recreation departments may offer yoga instruction. And you can find a slew of yoga videotapes that are available to rent or to buy. Why do people sign up for yoga classes in the first place? To relax, to become more fit and flexible, and to help ease joint pains. Any place that may cater to these needs — gyms that offer water aerobics classes, for example, or meditation centers — are all stealth competitors, as well.

When you think about your competition in the broadest sense, think about your potential customers and the choices they have to make. For local businesses used to catering to local customers, competition has traditionally centered around other local businesses. But the concept of a local business is quickly fading away, thanks to the Internet, which has opened up new choices to customers everywhere. The corner bookstore used to compete against other bookstores around the corner. Now it must compete against nationwide online booksellers, as well.

In today's rapidly changing business environment, new technologies such as the Internet can create the most dangerous kind of competitive threat: a competitor who comes along and makes you irrelevant, completely eliminating the need for the product or service you once provided. The following are two quick examples:

- The local travel agent used to be an indispensable resource when planning any kind of a trip for business or pleasure. Now, of course, the Internet allows individual travelers to explore various travel destinations and to book hotels, flights, car rentals — even ski equipment — on their own. Suddenly, travel agencies are lonely places. They're discovering rather painfully that many of their traditional customers don't really need them any more — at least not in traditional ways. The agencies that remain are focusing their efforts on particular market segments and services, such as group sales and high-end, customized tour packages.
- The makers of flea collars and flea shampoos were for a long time the unsung heroes of pets and pet owners alike. But they've recently been bitten by stealth competitors disguised as a group of new wonder drugs that can be applied to the family pet once a month, totally eliminating fleas and ticks. Unfortunately for the collar and shampoo makers, the drugs threaten to eliminate them, too.

Do we have your attention yet? You bet these stories are scary. That's why you need to take the extra time here to come up with a list of as many potential stealth competitors as you can. Use the questionnaire in Form 4-11 to help you identify competitors you may not recognize right off the bat.

Based on the answers you come up with, select your top candidates for potential stealth competition. Keep track of them in Form 4-12, which is on the CD-ROM. While you may not have the luxury of giving these companies all the attention you lavish on your biggest competitors, don't let them languish for too long. Remember, one of them can easily become your worst nightmare.

Using cloak-and-dagger methods

If your plan is to open a new gift shop on Main Street, scoping out your direct competition isn't all that difficult. All you have to do is browse through shops in the neighborhood that cater to the same kinds of customers you hope to attract. You may also want to check in with City Hall to see what other businesses are planning to open in the near future. And you'll want to identify potential stealth competitors, including any Internet competition you may have to face.

POTENTIAL STEALTH COMPETITORS QUESTIONNAIRE
1. What technologies could change your business overnight, and what companies might make them happen?
2. What businesses can you think of that may consider expanding into your markets in the future?
3. What companies may develop products and services to compete directly with you in the future?
4. Which of your customers could potentially become your competitors?
5. Which of your suppliers or vendors could turn around and compete with you?

Form 4-11: Potential stealth competitors questionnaire.

For many businesses, however, finding out all you need to know about the competition isn't always that easy. You may have to work hard to get answers to key questions, such as:

- What products or services do they offer?
- Who are their customers?
- What are their strengths?
- Where are their weaknesses?

Corporate strategists call this information *competitive intelligence* or CI. (We've always thought that somebody ought to start a consulting firm called Competitive Intelligence Associates, or the CIA). We're not suggesting that you resort to hidden microphones or picking through waste baskets to conduct a little CI of your own, but you need to be clever and persistent to get your hands on the information you need.

Fortunately, a number of good resources can help you in your research. One obvious tool is the Internet, which has become a terrific source for information of all kinds, no matter what business you're in. If you're planning to start an e-business, you can uncover a great deal by prowling around the Web to see what potential competitors are up to. But even if your business has nothing to do with the Internet, the Web can be a great source of information about your competition. As a corporate intelligence type recently observed, "Information on rivals has long been a key to success. Now it looks like the cloak-and-dagger may be giving way to the mouse-and-keyboard as an avalanche of information becomes available online."

So what are you waiting for? Go to your competitors' Web sites and homepages. They may prove to be a treasure trove of information — from product specifications to client lists. Many company sites include press-release archives, which often contain useful information about future strategies and plans.

Another resource is right down the street: the good-old library. The reference section usually contains a wealth of reference books about business in general as well as specific companies. Consult the *Readers' Guide to Periodical Literature* to find magazine articles about a given industry or company. Or ask for a Nexus/Lexus search (this may cost you a few bucks) to find articles in business sections from newspapers large and small around the country.

To guide you in your sleuthing, we've created a competitive intelligence checklist in Form 4-13. It provides a road map to the kinds of information worth uncovering about your competition. Don't worry if you can't fill in every detail. Any information at all will help you as you try to understand exactly who you're up against.

Keep your competitive intelligence checklist up-to-date by checking off the information you've managed to uncover about each of your biggest competitors.

COMPETITIVE INTELLIGENCE CHECKLIST ON COMPANY: ________________
☐ Mission and vision statements
☐ Years in business
☐ Organization charts
☐ Executive biographies
☐ Job postings
☐ Customer base
☐ Information on products and services
☐ Pricing data
☐ Research and development plans
☐ Distribution and delivery channels

Form 4-13: Competitive intelligence checklist.

Staying a step ahead

One way to stay a step ahead of the competition is to anticipate what their next moves are likely to be and be ready to counter them. Predicting the future isn't easy, of course, but by thinking through your competitors' options, you'll be better prepared. Keep in mind that in chess competition, a chess master routinely thinks five or six moves ahead.

The next moves your competitors make are likely to depend, in part, on where they think their relative capabilities lie — in other words, where they feel they may have advantages over their competition. Perhaps a competitor feels its strength is in R&D: A potential move may be a new product introduction. Or maybe a competitor is strong in marketing and sales: A potential move may be a market expansion. Perhaps customer loyalty is its strong suit: A potential move may be a further market penetration.

Unfortunately, we can't give you a simple, straightforward list of guaranteed competitive strategies that companies use to fight for and gain market share. Strategic planning is more complicated than that. But we can point out a few tried and true generic strategies. More often than not, in fact, companies end up competing on the basis of the following:

- **Lower prices:** Offering similar products or services at consistently lower prices than their competitors
- **Better service:** Pampering customers with personal attention and the little extras, and doing it better than their competition
- **Customer focus:** Going after well-defined markets by serving small groups of customers with very specific wants and needs
- **Something different:** Delivering unique products or services that stand out and call attention to themselves

Using Form 4-14, list your five top competitors (refer to Form 4-10), and then jot down what you see as their strongest suit or key capability and the strategic move you think they're most likely to make in the next year or so. Don't worry: We're not going to hold you to your predictions. But we can guarantee that taking the time to think through the possibilities will enable you to fine-tune your own business plans and be better prepared for the competitive battles ahead.

OUR BIGGEST COMPETITORS AND THEIR LIKELY MOVES		
Competitor	**Key Capability**	**Likely Strategic Move**
1.		
2.		
3.		
4.		
5.		

Form 4-14: Your biggest competitors and their likely moves.

A general description of your competition, including their strengths, capabilities, and likely moves, will find its way into your written business plan as part of the business environment section. Beyond that, the competitive landscape you face influences every other piece of planning you do.

Forms on the CD-ROM

Check out the following forms on the CD-ROM to help you assess the business environment you're likely to face:

Form 4-1	**Basic Business Definition Framework**	A set of questions designed to help you determine which business you're really in
Form 4-2	**Industry Analysis Questionnaire**	A questionnaire designed to tell you what you know and what you don't know about your industry
Form 4-3	**Barriers to Entry Checklist**	A checklist of the typical hurdles new competitors often face in a variety of industries
Form 4-4	**Good Customer / Bad Customer Comparison**	A form allowing you to make a side-by-side comparison of good customer and bad customer traits
Form 4-5	**Ideal Customer Questionnaire**	A questionnaire to help you gather information about your ideal customer
Form 4-6	**Ideal Customer Snapshot**	A framework to help you create a descriptive snapshot of your ideal customer
Form 4-7	**Business Customer Profile**	A questionnaire to help you create a profile of your business customers
Form 4-8	**Customer Intelligence Checklist**	A form to jot down times, places and ways to get closer to your customers on an ongoing basis
Form 4-9	**Basic Market Segmentation Framework**	A set of questions designed to help you think about ways to group customers into market segments
Form 4-10	**Our Biggest Competitors**	A form to record the list of your top five competitors

Form 4-11	**Potential Stealth Competitors Questionnaire**	A questionnaire to help you identify potential competitors before they become a threat
Form 4-12	**Potential Competitors We Need to Watch**	A form to record the list of your top five potential competitors
Form 4-13	**Competitive Intelligence Checklist**	A form to keep track of information you've gathered on each of your biggest competitors
Form 4-14	**Your Biggest Competitors and Their Likely Moves**	A form to keep track of your biggest competitors and what their next strategic moves may be

Chapter 5

Explaining Your Strategy

In This Chapter

- Analyzing your strengths, weaknesses, opportunities, and threats
- Figuring out how to make money
- Deciding whether you want to grow bigger

When you're right in the middle of creating a business plan, you may feel like a juggler. On the one hand, you're trying to evaluate the industry you're in. On the other, you're trying to get to know your customers better. All the while, you're attempting to keep both eyes on the competition. With so much going on, you may have a hard time focusing your attention on anything else.

You also need to keep your eye on what's happening *inside* your business. Knowing where your company strengths lie and where you're a little weak, looking out for opportunities and watching out for threats, defining how you'll do business, and having a sensible long-term strategy are all essential elements of business planning.

You may think you already know everything about your business. After all, if you don't, who does, right? But the truth is, being objective about yourself is difficult. People tend to accentuate the positive — and play down the negative. And anything but an honest assessment of your company's resources and capabilities can mean big trouble down the road.

In this chapter, we give you an opportunity to size up the strengths and the weaknesses of your company and look at the opportunities and the threats you may have to face. We also show you how to put all these things together into a SWOT (strengths, weaknesses, opportunities, and threats) analysis. And because how you plan to make money is an important part of your strategy, we help you define your business model. In addition, we show you different ways to think about growing your company. Finally, we help you outline an exit strategy — how you want your company to wind up if all goes according to your plans.

Putting Together Your SWOT Team

SWOT teams usually conjure up images of police cars, sharpshooters, and bad guys. But we're taking about another kind of life-and-death activity here. In the business world, *SWOT* is an easy acronym for bringing your strengths and weaknesses together with the opportunities and threats you face. SWOT analysis is an extremely important part of business planning for one simple reason: It works.

Before you can actually carry out a SWOT analysis, however, you need to look at each of the pieces separately. In this section, we start by sizing up your business strengths and weaknesses. After that, we take a look at your opportunities and threats.

Sizing up strengths and weaknesses

A company's strengths and weaknesses come in all shapes and sizes. The best approach we've found for getting a handle on what you do well — and where you fall short — is to look at eight key *capabilities,* which together make up the essential elements of any business:

- **Research and development (R&D):** Your ability to design and develop new products, services, or technologies.
- **Operations:** Having what it takes to produce the highest quality products or services in the most efficient ways possible.
- **Sales and marketing:** How well you get your products or services into the marketplace and onto customers' radar screens.
- **Distribution and delivery:** The ability to get your products reliably into customers' hands.
- **Customer service:** Everything you do to satisfy customers in order to create a loyal clientele, supporting you with their purchases and their praise.
- **Management:** The ability to provide leadership, direction, and a vision for the company.
- **Organization:** The procedures and company structures that enable you to make the most of your staff and resources.
- **Financial condition:** Both the long- and short-term financial health of your company.

Not all of these capabilities are equally important to every business. (For a more complete description of each, take a look at Chapter 6.) A state-of-the-art distribution and delivery system may be essential to the success of one firm but not be particularly important to another. Research and development may be crucial for A2Z Computers, for example, and not important at all to Relax-a-Way Massage Centers. And if you're on your own, management abilities may seem totally irrelevant.

Don't jump to conclusions too fast, however. Chances are, your company is engaged, in some way, shape or form, in all of the eight areas on the list. Sure, you may need to be a bit flexible in the way you think about each category, but look at each business element and relate it to your own company and its situation.

Consider a small gourmet catering service we know called Soup's On. The company's management team was interested in expanding the business to form a local chain of stores in four nearby cities. They needed to act quickly, but they weren't quite sure that they were up to the task. So the managers went on a retreat to seriously consider the resources and assets the company could bring to the expansion plan. To help them in their analysis, they completed a company strengths and weaknesses survey like the one in Figure 5-1. The figure shows how the management team ranked the importance of the eight key capabilities to their business and then graded themselves on how well the company was doing — poor, fair, good, or excellent — in each area.

COMPANY STRENGTHS AND WEAKNESSES SURVEY

Capability	Importance to Business			How Does the Company Rate?			
Research and development	Low	**Medium**	High	**Poor**	Fair	Good	Excellent
Operations	Low	Medium	**High**	Poor	Fair	Good	**Excellent**
Sales and marketing	Low	Medium	**High**	**Poor**	Fair	Good	Excellent
Distribution and delivery	Low	Medium	**High**	Poor	Fair	Good	**Excellent**
Customer service	Low	Medium	**High**	Poor	Fair	**Good**	Excellent
Management	Low	Medium	**High**	Poor	**Fair**	Good	Excellent
Organization	Low	**Medium**	High	Poor	Fair	**Good**	Excellent
Financial condition	Low	Medium	**High**	Poor	**Fair**	Good	Excellent

Figure 5-1: Filling out a survey of company strengths and weaknesses.

Here's a little background on what went into their thinking. Typically, R&D wouldn't be of much importance to a gourmet catering company. However, part of their strategic plan was to establish a snazzy Web site where customers could go to view the current selection of dishes available, create personalized menus, and schedule their own catered events. Getting up to speed on the Internet would require R&D of sorts, so they gave research and development a ranking of medium importance. They used the category of operations to describe how accurately the orders were filled and how well the meals were prepared. And they defined distribution and delivery as how efficiently they got the food to their customers' events and supervised set-up, serving, and clean-up. All these capabilities, of course, are very important to the catering business.

Using the questionnaire, the Soup's On management team began to collect valuable information on the important success factors in their business, as well as their own relative strengths and weaknesses. Next, they turned to another way of organizing the same information, which offered additional insights. Figure 5-2 shows how the company's capabilities lined up in a strengths and weaknesses grid.

COMPANY STRENGTHS AND WEAKNESSES GRID

How Does the Company Rate?	Importance to Business		
	High	*Medium*	*Low*
Excellent	• Operations • Distribution and delivery		
Good	STRENGTHS • Customer service	• Organization	
Fair	• Management • Financial condition		
Poor	WEAKNESSES • Sales and marketing	• Research and development	

Figure 5-2: Using a grid of company strengths and weaknesses.

A completed grid allowed the management team of Soup's On to see at a glance where the most important strengths and weaknesses fell. The news was both good and bad. On the plus side, operations and distribution and delivery both ranked high in importance to the catering business — and the company received "excellent" grades in each area. That was great. Customer service also ranked high in importance, and it scored a "good" rating for the company. That was still okay.

But then the red flags began to flutter. While the management team and the company's financial condition were rated as "highly important," the company received only "fair" grades in these areas. And they found an even more troubling note in the area of sales and marketing. The plan called for an expansion into new geographic areas, yet in its current location, the company depended on repeat business and word of mouth for new customers. So in all honesty, the management team had to grade themselves as "poor" in sales and marketing. They also saw problems with research and development and, therefore, their Internet strategy. Because no one on staff had any experience with Web site development, another "poor" grade showed up.

After carefully reviewing the company strengths and weaknesses grid, the managers agreed to take a time-out from their expansion plans. The goal: to work on improving several of the key business capabilities where Soup's On had scored badly.

Set some time aside to complete the company strengths and weaknesses survey in Form 5-1, which is on the CD-ROM. First rank the eight key capabilities based on their importance to your business. Then grade yourself in each area. Be honest! (We're not going to give out gold stars at the end of the chapter in any case.) The more honest you can be about your company's strengths and weaknesses right now, the more useful this exercise will be in helping you develop a business plan that will be of real use to you in the future.

If your company is already in business, assessing these eight capabilities can be a fairly straightforward task. If you're creating a brand new business plan, however, you may have to think harder about how well equipped you are — right here, right now — to succeed in each of these areas.

To see at a glance where your most important strengths and weaknesses fall, use your rankings from the survey in Form 5-1 to fill in the company strengths and weaknesses grid in Form 5-2 (you can find it on the CD-ROM). Reading the grid is quite simple:

- Capabilities at the top left represent important company strengths — and very good news.
- Those at the top right of the grid represent strengths, too, but they're not quite as important to your business.

- Capabilities at the bottom left are potentially serious company weaknesses. You need to focus on these, because this is where you're most vulnerable.
- Those at the bottom right are weaknesses, as well, but because they're less important to your business, you don't need to worry quite as much about them — at least for now.

When you're the one and only

If you're completely on your own — the boss and the entire staff of your little company — you may feel a bit overwhelmed with all this talk about strengths, weaknesses, and business capabilities. After all, what could research and development or operations possibly have to do with being a freelance designer, a personal trainer, or an interior decorator?

Plenty. Many of the same issues that confront big companies are just as important to a business of one. All you have to do is think small. For example, we know a computer-networking specialist who decided to go out on her own after getting tired of the corporate rat-race and her long commute. Here's how she filled in the blanks to make sense out of those eight key business capabilities in her own world:

- **Research and development:** This includes staying current with new software and hardware technologies using online training courses and certification programs.
- **Operations:** This is stuff like billing, accounting, and scheduling. I also need to set up an answering service to field calls when I'm out and make sure I'm always reachable in an emergency.
- **Sales and marketing:** This includes business cards, stationary, and maybe a Web site in the future. This also includes my ability to make cold calls to prospective clients.
- **Distribution and delivery:** This includes reliable transportation to and from clients' locations. Also, I have to make sure I have the right equipment and software in the right place at the right time.
- **Customer service:** This is my close working relationship with local clients who have information technology needs.
- **Management:** This includes my sense of direction and vision, plus the goals and objectives I set for myself. I also define this as my ability to be my own boss.
- **Organization:** This includes the support services I'll need, such as accounting, secretarial, and so on.
- **Financial condition:** This means having enough cash to stay afloat until invoices start getting paid, plus having a financial cushion so that I can buy testing equipment along with the other hardware and software I need.

So no matter what the size of your company, we encourage you to define these key business capabilities in whatever way makes the most sense to you. All we ask is that you give each one careful consideration.

Don't be afraid to toot your own horn in your written business plan, especially when you can identify important company strengths. Give those strengths the full 76 trombones, if you like. After all, these strengths provide the evidence that you have what it takes to be successful in your chosen business. At the same time, however, you can't afford to ignore the weaknesses you've discovered. So acknowledge the fact that you need to seriously address certain business capabilities and make sure your plan includes a detailed strategy for turning those company weaknesses around.

One more word of advice: Because your company's strengths and weaknesses are likely to change over time, return to the grid in Form 5-2 on a regular basis to take a fresh look at where you stand.

Looking for opportunities and threats

After you take a hard look at your company's strengths and weaknesses, take a look around you at the outside business forces that will ultimately shape your company's destiny. Whether those forces represent opportunities or threats depends in large part on the strengths and weaknesses you possess as a company. Opportunities and threats can come in any form and all directions, from the sudden appearance of a new competitor to the emergence of a totally unique technology. Shifts in population and popular taste, politics and changing regulations, economic ups or downs — even an unforeseen fad or fashion craze — can represent big opportunities or major threats.

When the small gourmet catering service called Soup's On began planning to expand from one store to a small chain, the management team put together a list of the opportunities and threats that they thought they should take seriously. Figure 5-3 shows what the managers came up with.

Looking over the list, the Soup's On management team was encouraged. After all, at least their opportunities outnumbered all the threats they could think of! And given this plus-and-minus list, the managers were convinced that they could capitalize on the opportunities they saw and counter any threats they identified.

You can create your own list of opportunities and threats you see out there on the business horizon. Use Form 5-3 on the CD-ROM to jot down what you come up with. Don't forget to think about the less obvious shapes that an opportunity or threat can take and the numerous directions they can come from. For a complete rundown of the kinds of business opportunities and threats you may encounter along the way, take a look at *Business Plans For Dummies* by Paul Tiffany and Steven Peterson (Hungry Minds, Inc.).

COMPANY OPPORTUNITIES AND THREATS	
Possible Opportunities	**Potential Threats**
• Increasing number of couples who work and have money but don't have the time to cook • Growing interest in healthy, organic, high quality ingredients • Growing sophistication of consumers and a demand for "true" gourmet take-out food • Business boom in the area, creating a strong market for catering of business events • Promise of the Internet to improve marketing and customer service	• Difficulty in finding reliable staff in a very tight regional labor market • Indirect competition from "do-it-yourself" catering and take-out at local grocery stores • Direct competitors, especially the "waiters-on-wheels" who will deliver from a number of local restaurants

Figure 5-3: Listing possible opportunities and potential threats to the business.

If you're having a tough time coming up with specifics, fill out the strengths and weaknesses survey again (Form 5-1). Only this time, use it to describe the strengths and weaknesses of your leading competitor. You won't know as much about them as you know about yourself, but chances are, you know enough to know what areas they're strong in and where they have weaknesses. Their strengths represent potential threats to you. Their weaknesses represent possible opportunities.

Conducting a SWOT analysis

How well will you be able to exploit business opportunities and sidestep potential threats? We don't own a crystal ball, but we do know that part of the answer depends on how well your strengths and weaknesses line up against the opportunities and threats you face. And that's where a SWOT analysis comes in. It's an easy-to-use tool that helps you do the lining up.

SWOT stands for strengths, weaknesses, opportunities and threats. Small businesses and large corporations, freelancers and schools, not-for-profits and small towns have used SWOT to evaluate their own situations. A SWOT analysis allows you to bring together all the internal factors you've identified and weight them against the external forces you see. Exactly how they line up tells you something about the next steps you need to take in planning your business.

The management team of the gourmet catering business Soup's On made a number of significant decisions around their business plan as a result of a SWOT analysis. Figure 5-4 shows how they filled in the SWOT grid.

COMPANY SWOT ANALYSIS GRID		
	Opportunities	**Threats**
Strengths	Use superior operations and delivery to go after increasingly sophisticated high-end take-out and catering markets CAPITALIZE ON THESE	We depend on our high quality and service, but it's harder to attract and keep good people MONITOR THESE
Weaknesses	Big growth in catered events market, but we're weak in marketing Promise of the Internet, but we have no R&D IMPROVE THESE	Our poor marketing and precarious financial condition are dangerous, given the increased competition we face ELIMINATE THESE

Figure 5-4: Completing a company's SWOT analysis.

Based on their SWOT analysis, Soup's On brought a consultant on board who had marketing expertise and a background in developing restaurant chains. They researched Web site development to get a sense of the resources they would need to commit if they wanted to achieve a true Internet presence. They also tightened up their management structure so that they would be prepared for the growth they were expecting. Finally, with the help of two big investors, they improved their financial condition to the point where the entire team felt comfortable signing on to the expansion effort.

So Soup's On is about to grow bigger. While it's certainly true that they'll have increased competition for catering and take-out services, demand is growing, which leaves room for several companies to prosper. What's more, Soup's On is confident that by focusing their new resources on quality, consistency, and sophisticated menus, the company can compete successfully against both grocery stores and restaurants. And Soup's On has increased its chances of success, because the company spent extra time upfront understanding their own strengths and weaknesses and dealing with the opportunities and threats they faced — before inviting all those new guests to dinner.

Use Form 5-4 (on the CD-ROM) to conduct your own SWOT analysis. The rules are simple: Divide all your strengths into two groups — those that will help you take advantage of opportunities and those that will help you head off potential threats. Do the same with your weaknesses. As a guide, look over your company strengths and weaknesses grid (Form 5-2) and your list of opportunities and threats (Form 5-3).

The strengths, weaknesses, opportunities, and threats you feature in your SWOT grid have to be more than broad generalizations if you want your resulting analysis to be at all useful in your business plan: Each item should be detailed, specific, and supported by the facts you have at hand.

Using your SWOT analysis as a guide, make sure your written plan addresses each of the following:

- How you intend to capitalize on your company's strengths where they match up with major business opportunities
- How you plan to eliminate the weaknesses you've identified in areas where you face serious outside threats
- How you plan to improve on weak areas where you may be able to take advantage of future business opportunities
- How you intend to monitor and maintain your other strengths, so that you'll be ready for threats before they appear

Don't forget that your company's capabilities and the external forces you face are constantly changing. That's just the nature of business. So plan on revisiting your SWOT analysis on a regular basis to see how the balance of strengths, weaknesses, opportunities, and threats may have shifted or changed. That way, your business plans will be based on the way the world around you *is,* not the way it *was.*

Defining Your Business Model

Your business model isn't something you have to build from the ground up — you're not going to need any balsa wood or glue. And we're not talking about elaborate diagrams on flipcharts, either, with circles and squares and arrows pointing every which way. In fact, when management types talk about a business model — as in, "So what's your business model?" — they're really just being polite. What they're actually asking is a much more direct and basic question: How do you plan to make money?

With all the early excitement over the Internet and dot-com companies and all the talk about new business rules and the new economy, people — entrepreneurs, investors, managers, and yes, even business gurus — seemed to have forgotten the part about making money, and business models weren't all that popular for awhile. That all changed when some of the initial enthusiasm wore off. Suddenly, everybody's asking about business models again.

Considering where the money comes from

Whether you like it or not, at some point you have to devote a chunk of time getting into the nitty-gritty details of your company's finances — income statements, balance sheets, cash flow, budgeting, and all that scary stuff. We try to make it as painless as possible in Chapter 7. For now, though, we want you to do something much more basic: Show us the money. Not literally, of course. But tell us how you expect to make money in your business.

The answer may seem simple, at first. Your customers will give you money in exchange for the products or services you provide, right? But in fact, business models aren't always as straightforward as that.

- You may think that your local movie theater gets most of its revenue from the cash you plunk down at the ticket booth. In reality, most theaters make their real money from the concession stands, where they turn a tidy profit selling Milk Duds and buckets of buttery popcorn. They also make money off the game arcades that have recently been added to expand the theater experience.
- The largest fitness center chains make money on enrollment fees and monthly dues, but the chains have also discovered that they can rake in cash by selling fitness-related supplements, exercise clothes, gym bags — and the services of personal trainers.
- Magazines like *Time, Newsweek,* and *Health* get a portion of their revenues from subscriptions and the newsstand price you pay. But the lion's share of their money comes from advertising revenues. There's always an exception to every business model, of course. *Consumer Reports* is different because it depends entirely on subscription revenues. Why? The magazine doesn't what to be seen as endorsing the products they advertise.
- Some companies are happy to sell their products at a loss — and then make their real money on the so-called *consumables.* Gillette, for example, doesn't mind selling razors at cost, knowing that the company makes its profit on razor cartridge refills. As long as Gillette can keep customers satisfied with the total shaving experience, the money will flow in month after month, year after year.

Staying in the black

You don't need an in-depth financial analysis to know that, if you want to stay in business over the long haul, your revenues have to be bigger than your costs. No rocket science here! If your revenues exceed your costs, you're *in the black.* Otherwise, you could find yourself drowning in *red ink,* which means you're losing money.

As any new business owner knows, you have plenty of costs — from renting an office and buying equipment to paying out salaries and buying supplies. Some of these costs — office rental or salaries, for example — are called *fixed costs.* They don't change much, and they have to be paid on a regular basis no matter how good (or bad) your business is. Another category of costs, called *variable costs*, do change, depending on how much business you have. They include the materials that go into producing your product or service.

Why do these distinctions matter? Because they place different demands on your budget. You have to make sure you have enough cash coming in to meet your fixed costs, for example, or you may find yourself out of funds — and out of business — very quickly. And if you want to make a profit, you had better make sure that the price you charge for your goods or services is high enough to cover both your variable costs and your fixed costs. Otherwise you'll never be able to turn red ink to black.

Consider Windy City Bistro, a restaurant planning to open in the Chicago area. The owners are looking for investors, so they need to present a convincing business model as a part of their business plan. And that means they must convince potential investors that the amount of money they plan to take in will exceed their costs, leaving room for them to make a persuasive profit. On the revenue side, they must calculate how much they will make on each meal and how many meals they plan to serve. On the cost side, they need to calculate both the fixed costs (rent, loans, utilities, insurance, wages) and their variable costs (food, supplies, part-time help, and so on).

The owners did a quick financial projection, the back-of-the-envelope calculation shown in Figure 5-5, as they began to create a convincing business model for local investors. For a more in-depth look at finances, flip to Chapter 7.

Based on these rough estimates, Windy City Bistro should turn a profit of about $1,950 a week, or almost $8,000 a month. It won't happen right away, of course — that's part of the reason the owners are looking for investors in the first place. Given their previous experience in the restaurant business, they estimate that the bistro needs nine months to a year to gear up. The owners expect to operate at a loss for the first six months. They plan to break even during months seven and eight, and then begin to make a profit starting in month nine. For a brush-up on planning time frames, check out Chapter 2.

QUICK FINANCIAL PROJECTION WORKSHEET		
Projected Revenues		
Anticipated number of meals served:	250 / week	
Average gross revenue per meal:	$ 37.50	
Total weekly gross revenue:		*$ 9,375.*
Projected Fixed Costs		
Restaurant space rental:	$ 1,000. / week	
Loan payments on equipment:	$ 350. / week	
Utilities, insurance, and other costs:	$ 225. / week	
Full-time personnel costs:	$ 2,350. / week	
Total weekly fixed costs:		*$ 3,925.*
Projected Variable Costs		
Food / wine wholesale costs:	$ 3,000. / week	
Temporary service staff:	$ 500. / week	
Total weekly variable costs:		*$ 3,500.*
Expected Profits		
Total weekly profits:		*$ 1,950.*

Figure 5-5: Projecting revenues and costs as part of a business model.

Understanding that timing is everything

How you expect to make your money is only one part of your business model. Another important part of the model has to do with *when* that money will come in. Your company may begin incurring costs and spending cash months (or maybe even years) before a revenue stream begins to flow. And if that's the case, your business model must include a timeline that takes the following into account:

- The upfront costs you expect to incur when setting up your business
- The source of funds to pay for your upfront costs
- A schedule showing when your expect revenues to pour in

The question of timing isn't just for very big companies with factories to build and products to design. It can have a real impact on businesses of any size.

A business model with a timeline is especially important to companies that depend on seasonal customers. Take the example of Bide-a-Wee, a bed and breakfast (B&B) on Cape Cod. The tourist season there begins on June 1st and ends with the big Labor Day weekend in September. Except for a few holiday weekends in between — Thanksgiving, Christmas, and New Year's — virtually all of the B&B's revenue comes in during those three summer months. Their business model must ensure that the money coming in during that short period is enough to pay Bide-a-Wee's fixed costs — mortgage, utilities, taxes, salaries, upkeep — all year 'round.

Many retail businesses that operate all year actually take in most of their revenue during one season — the Christmas holiday rush. In some cases, retailers rake in half of their annual revenues during late November and December. Timing for these establishments is quite literally a make-or-break affair.

Knowing how customers pay

An effective business model takes into account how your customers pay. When customers buy a product or service, they typically have a number of payment options. The most common choice is paying in one lump sum or spreading out the purchase price over easy monthly installments. But customers may also be given the choice either to pay as they go or to pre-pay for unlimited uses of a product or service. They may decide to buy or rent. Or they may choose to finance a purchase or lease it. All of these options have financial consequences that affect the business model.

Blockbuster Video, along with your local video store, has a straightforward business model: They buy videotapes in large quantities and at steep discounts, and then turn around and rent them over and over again. Customers pay for the privilege of viewing a particular video over a one-, three-, or five-day period. Recently, however, the business has been shaken up by the introduction of a new technology: DVDs. And a new company, called Netflix.com, has come along with a brand-new business model.

Netflix.com stocks only DVDs and offers them only through a subscription program over the Internet. For a monthly fee (similar to a premium cable channel), customers can rent as many movies as they like. The only limitation: They can keep only four titles at any one time. When customers are through viewing a DVD, they just pop it in the mail using a handy prepaid envelope. After it's received, Netflix.com automatically sends out the next title in the customer's online rental queue. Obviously, this business model offers customers new benefits, but it also creates a challenge for the company. Netflix.com must continuously analyze the rates at which customers rent DVDs so that they can set an appropriate subscription fee and make sure that their model is working.

Creating a business model of your own

You can probably find examples of many more business models than you may have thought. Some are as old as the marketplace itself; others as new as the Internet. Some have been proven to work time and time again; others are almost experimental. Your own business model needs to take into account the unique aspects of your industry and your company. What's more, your business model may need to change over time as your company and the business environment change.

Form 5-5, a business model questionnaire, helps you get started as you begin to think seriously about your own business and how you intend to make money. After completing it, ask yourself the following questions:

- Can you spot additional potential sources of revenue that you may be able to develop in the future?
- Can you come up with alternative payment plans — such as membership or subscription fees — that would entice new customers and increase your revenue stream down the road?

After you list your revenue sources and the costs you anticipate, take the time to make a quick financial projection using Form 5-6 on the CD-ROM. It doesn't have to be fancy (see Chapter 7 to do some serious financial footwork), but it should give you a good idea whether your business model makes sense. For more guidance, refer to Figure 5-5.

A description of your business model will make its appearance very early in your written plan, most likely in your Executive Summary and in the Company Overview (see Chapter 2 for details on these sections). After all, the model lies at the very heart of your prescription for creating a successful business over the long term.

Charting Ways to Grow

If your business strategy and business planning pay off, your company is likely to grow bigger. But simply assuming that growth will take care of itself isn't enough. You must also plan *how* your business will grow — and how big you want it to get.

Understanding your options

After you strip away all the big words and tall business theories floating around, you find that companies grow in three basic ways:

- The first way to get bigger is to go on doing what you do, finding ways to get more and more customers to buy your current products or services:
  - Advertise to bring in additional customers
  - Encourage good customers to use you more often
  - Find new uses (and customers) for what you already do
- Another way to grow is to provide your existing customers with new and different products or services:
  - Make changes in your product line based on customer feedback
  - Package service options together in useful and unique combinations
  - Use your knowledge of the marketplace to develop related products and services
- Perhaps the most difficult way to expand your business is to go after brand-new markets with completely new products or services:
  - Use your current capabilities to develop brand-new products or services
  - Leverage the assets your company already has to woo brand-new customers
  - Stay patient and be prepared for the long haul

You can find hundreds of variations on these three basic themes, but three examples may be useful:

- Your company may find a new market for a product you already have. This often happens in the pharmaceutical industry. After marketing the drug Paxil as a treatment for depression, for example, SmithKline Beecham discovered that the same pills also help people with a condition called social anxiety disorder. Voilà! The company was able to tap a brand-new market for an existing product.
- You may decide to better serve your existing clients by expanding the services you offer. A not-for-profit organization in California has been serving "meals on wheels" to people with AIDS for many years. Recently, the volunteers realized that many of their clients also needed help around the house — not to mention some social interaction. So the organization created a separate service area, enlisting volunteers willing to go out and offer informal counseling and household help to their clients.
- You can deliberately set out to conquer brand new markets with totally new products and services. Amazon.com, for example, began as an online bookseller. But the Internet giant really wants to go head-to-head with the likes of K-Mart and Wal-Mart. Over the past few years, the company has added all sorts of new departments to its online storefront, everything from cameras to kitchen wares, from health and beauty supplies to lawn and patio furniture.

BUSINESS MODEL QUESTIONNAIRE
1. List all your principle sources of revenue. (Don't forget to include things like product accessories, service agreements, upgrades, and so on.) • • • • • •
2. List where you expect your fixed costs to come from. (Remember the obvious, such as utilities, a bookkeeping service, city taxes, insurance, and so on.) • • • • • •
3. List the sources of your variable costs. • • • • • •
4. Jot down the key timing issues your business faces. (Make sure to include the start-up interval, seasonal variations in sales, and any cost or price cycles.) • • • • • •
5. Describe how customers will pay for your products or services (single or multiple payments, weekly or monthly fees, subscriptions, and so on.)

Form 5-5: Business model questionnaire.

Planning for growth

How do you plan to grow your own company bigger? Before you answer this question, you may want to look over the goals and objectives you've already laid out for yourself (flip to Chapter 3). Chances are, a number of your goals involve growing your business in some way or another — either reaching more customers, expanding your product line or services, or entering new markets. And more than likely, these goals require certain critical resources.

Form 5-7 provides a handy checklist of the things you may need to plan for as you begin to grow bigger. Check off those that are most important to your strategy. (If we've forgotten something, fill it in at the bottom.)

After you complete the critical resources checklist in Form 5-7, you'll have a better idea of how you need to prepare for your company's getting bigger. To help you plan for that growth, we've put together some basic questions in Form 5-8. If you're having trouble answering any of them, you may want to look over your SWOT analysis (refer to Form 5-4).

Deciding how big you want to become as a company is just as important as knowing how you want to grow. And not every entrepreneur has the same goal. One independent contractor we know wanted to grow her business just enough to keep her busy and her bank account healthy. She wasn't interested in growing so big that she would have to hire employees and change the way she liked to work. In contrast, a young entrepreneur came to us recently with a very different plan in mind: He wanted to grow his company fast so that he could move away from doing the work himself and concentrate on expanding his business.

A discussion of your plans to grow your company will find its way into several sections of your written business plan, including the Executive Summary, the Company Strategy section, the Financial Review, and your Action Plans (check out Chapter 2 for the lowdown on these sections). For some companies, after all, the plan to grow bigger *is* the business plan.

Outlining an Exit Strategy

An exit strategy — what's that again? You're right in the middle of starting, growing, or re-energizing your company, so why in the world should you think about exiting the business? It turns out that most business planners are so gung-ho about getting started that they don't spend much time upfront thinking about getting out. But knowing where your business is headed — and how you may someday exit, stage right — is a crucial part of an effective long-term plan.

An *exit strategy* describes the very last stage of your business planning — how you want things to end if all goes well. As such, an exit strategy should be the final step in any smart, long-term business plan.

RESOURCES FOR GROWTH CHECKLIST
☐ Raising additional capital
☐ Developing management expertise
☐ Acquiring new office space
☐ Purchasing or leasing office equipment
☐ Hiring new employees
☐ Training and developing staff
☐ Establishing human resources guidelines
☐ Installing accounting and information systems
☐ Investing in research and product development
☐ Spending on advertising and promotions
☐ Outsourcing certain functions
☐ Forming strategic alliances with other companies
☐ Acquiring other companies
☐

Form 5-7: Resources for growth checklist.

PLANNING FOR GROWTH QUESTIONNAIRE
1. What are your goals for company growth over the next year? (Use revenues, profits, number of clients, market share, or any other measure that makes the most sense to you.) • •
2. What are your three- and/or five-year goals for growth? • •
3. What will it take to get your company where you want it to be? (List three or four key requirements.) • • • •
4. Which of your key strengths will be most important in helping you meet your goals for growth?
5. What company weakness could be most significant in limiting your company's growth?
6. What are the major milestones you intend to reach along the way? • • •

Form 5-8: Planning for growth questionnaire.

For certain kinds of companies, describing an exit strategy is an all-important part of business planning. We're talking here about businesses that require investors and deep pockets of cash upfront. Anyone on the outside who's willing to put money into a company wants to know how they'll get it back — along with a handsome return on their investment. Entrepreneurs dream of making companies and then taking them public, turning everyone, from the receptionist to the CEO, into millionaires. More power to them, we say. But unless you have a convincing exit strategy describing exactly how you'll make that happen, attracting serious investors will be an uphill battle.

Not every company wants or needs a detailed exit strategy. Some people start their businesses with the idea of selling: They have their sights set on how much money they'll make at the end. But other people go into business simply to be in business: They like the idea of what they'll be doing. If that sounds like you, terrific. Still, take some time to think about what you're creating as you put together your company.

When you start a business, you create something that may have lasting value, long after you're ready to call it quits. Maybe you've created a brand name that people recognize. Perhaps you've won over a group of loyal customers. Maybe your network of contacts or your relationships with suppliers are of real value to someone else. When it comes time to close up shop, you should be aware of the intrinsic value of what you own. Don't simply throw it away.

Whatever kind of business you're in, ask yourself three basic questions:

- What are my reasons for going into business in the first place?
- How long do I plan to stay in business?
- What do I hope to end up with in the end?

If you need any guidance here, look at the mission and vision statements you put together in Chapter 3. Taken together, your answers to these questions will begin to shed some light on what your own exit strategy may be.

Take a look at the some of the most common exit strategies described in Form 5-9. Put a check beside the ones that make sense for you. Of course, we're just talking possibilities at this point. No one can guarantee that a big company will come along and acquire your little company, after all. But if being acquired is one possibility you're thinking about down the line, it's important to know that now, so you can plan for it along the way.

For each of the options you check off in Form 5-9, make a short list of the business capabilities and resources that absolutely need to be in place if you want the exit strategy to eventually become a reality.

CHECKLIST OF COMMON EXIT STRATEGIES
☐ **Going public** Your private company goes public by selling shares to be traded on a stock exchange through an initial public offering, or IPO
☐ **Being acquired** Your company is bought by another company outright, and you may or may not have a role to play in the larger business
☐ **Being sold** Your company is bought by an individual or group of individuals who may or may not want to keep you as part of the management team
☐ **Merging** Your company joins forces with another existing company on an equal footing, and a joint management structure is put in place
☐ **Being bought out** One or more of the owners of your company buys out the other owners to assume control of the business
☐ **Franchising** You sell your business concept to others who replicate it, paying you fees for the use of the name, business model, and other assets
☐ **Going out of business** Your company's assets are sold, the doors are shut, and the books are closed for good

Form 5-9: Checklist of common exit strategies.

In most cases, your written business plan will at least give a nod to your exit strategy. A description of the final stages you see for your business is particularly important if you expect to use your business plan to make sure that the final chapter unfolds the way you want it to.

Forms on the CD-ROM

Check out the following forms on the CD-ROM to help you explain your company's strategy in your business plan.

Form 5-1	**Company Strengths and Weaknesses Survey**	A survey that helps you collect information on the important success factors in your business and your relative abilities in each key area
Form 5-2	**Company Strengths and Weaknesses Grid**	A grid designed to highlight your company's strengths and weaknesses
Form 5-3	**Company Opportunities and Threats**	A form on which you can jot down the possible opportunities and potential threats you face in your business
Form 5-4	**Company SWOT analysis grid**	A grid designed to line up your company's strengths and weaknesses against the business opportunities and threats you face
Form 5-5	**Business Model Questionnaire**	A questionnaire to help you create a business model that describes how you plan to make money
Form 5-6	**Quick Financial Projection Worksheet**	A worksheet that's designed to help you make a quick financial projection as you develop your business model
Form 5-7	**Resources for Growth Checklist**	A checklist of critical resources you may need as your company begins to grow bigger
Form 5-8	**Planning for Growth Questionnaire**	A questionnaire designed to help you plan your company's growth
Form 5-9	**Checklist of Common Exit Strategies**	A checklist presenting the most common exit strategies for businesses

Chapter 6

Describing Your Company

In This Chapter

- Letting others know what your company does
- Describing your business capabilities
- Focusing in on the value you deliver

After reading the title of this chapter, you may be tempted to skim these pages — or skip them altogether. After all, how hard can it be to sit down and describe who you are and what you do? Well, we can tell you from experience that it's not as simple as it sounds.

We know you're the expert and are probably very familiar with your business, but the people reading your business plan may not have the faintest idea what you do. Your job is to describe what you do as clearly as you can, without getting lost in the details — and without resorting to all kinds of industry jargon.

For your business plan to be really effective, you have to paint a compelling picture of who you are. You need to focus in on the most important aspects of your company and include all the pertinent details precisely where and when they're needed. What's more, you must do all of this as briefly and concisely as possible. Remember, we're talking about a business plan here, not the Great American Novel. And chances are, the people who sit down to read it have plenty of other demands on their time.

In this chapter, we start by working with you on effective ways to introduce your company and the products and services you plan to offer. We help you examine and describe the various parts of your business, from research and development, operations, sales and marketing, and distribution and delivery to customer service, management, and the organization of your company. Finally, we show you how to focus on what you do best so that your company description really reflects what's most important to you and your customers.

Introducing Your Company

Imagine, for a moment, that you're at your high school reunion. A bunch of old pals ask you what you're doing. Naturally, you want to describe the new venture you're planning, and you also want to impress your classmates with what a cool idea you have.

Here's one example of what that particular conversation may sound like:

We're putting together a brand-new way to encourage people to contribute to worthy not-for-profit organizations. It all started when I began to think about the success of online gift certificates. It occurred to me that we could use the same idea for worthy causes — combining the Internet with not-for-profit gift certificates to provide a simple way for people to donate to charities instead of exchanging presents during the holidays.

> Here's how it works. Instead of planning a big holiday party and giving gifts to employees, a company can give each employee a $100 charitable gift certificate. When the employees go to our Internet site, they find a list of 100 hand-picked not-for-profits, ranging from environmental groups to medical research. The person who gets a gift certificate can then choose where he or she wants to contribute the money. He can contribute all $100 to one organization or divvy it up.
>
> And you can do the same thing with your family. Instead of giving everyone a $50 gift, you can give them a charitable gift certificate. The cool thing is that recipients get to direct the money to causes that really matter to them. And, of course, we're hoping that after they see the site, they'll think about giving charitable gift certificates instead of ugly ties or unwanted kitchen gadgets when the next holiday season rolls around.

Sound like an interesting venture? You bet it does. It also sounds exciting, because the speaker is so obviously enthusiastic about the idea. Now imagine his classmates asking a few questions. "So how will the company support itself?" Or, "How will people hear about the site?" Or, "How do you choose the charitable organizations featured on the site?"

Hitting the high points

You can see what we're getting at here. This chapter is about describing your company. And there's no better way to start than by imagining that you're talking to a group of high school or college chums. At least, it's the best way we know to make sure you get right to the point, explaining your idea — or your company — in the simplest, most persuasive language possible.

Take a few minutes now to imagine that you're talking with three or four friends about your new venture. Whaddya going to say? Jot down the first things that come to mind. (If you have a cassette recorder or Dictaphone handy, even better. Say it aloud and transcribe your words later.) Don't worry about polished prose here. The only way this little exercise works is to plunge in and hit the highlights.

If you're having trouble getting your creative juices flowing, revisit your company's mission statement. It should capture in a nutshell what your company is all about. Looking back at your vision statement can also help re-inspire you. (Don't have a mission statement or vision statement? Chapter 3 helps you put them together).

Keep the notes you've jotted down handy and refer to them when you sit down to write the Company Overview and the Company Description sections of your plan (flip to Chapter 2 for more on these sections). You may not use exactly the same words in your formal business plan, but make sure the key points are covered. And wherever possible, use language that expresses enthusiasm and excitement (without getting gushy, of course).

Describing exactly what you do

An entrepreneur we know was making a presentation to a group of potential investors. She was really excited about her idea, which involved summarizing the latest medical research into easy-to-understand capsule reports designed to encourage people to lead healthier lifestyles. She talked about the accelerating pace of medical research and the insights that behavioral science has made in understanding how people change. She waxed eloquent on the subject of preventive health care and gave detailed statistics about the aging of the American population. Ten minutes into her presentation one of the investors interrupted to ask the simple question, "What is it you're selling, anyway?" The answer: an online health newsletter directed at people over 50. In her excitement, she'd forgotten to state the obvious.

The moral of this tale is that, when describing your company, you have to explain exactly what products or services you'll be offering, who your customers are going to be, and what benefits they'll get. It's so important, in fact, that we've put together a product/service description checklist as a handy guide. Figure 6-1 shows how our friend with the health newsletter proposal would complete the checklist.

Use the checklist in Form 6-1 (on the CD-ROM) to describe your own products or services, the customers you plan to target, and the benefits your customers will receive.

PRODUCT/SERVICE DESCRIPTION CHECKLIST
1. Product or service summary: "Wellness Update," an online health newsletter for people over 50
2. Key product or service features: • Easy-to-understand summaries of key medical findings related to healthy lifestyles • Targeted e-mail updates tailored to specific diseases or health conditions • Personalized "health accounts" that allow users to keep track of exercise, diet, weight, and other lifestyle factors
3. Target customers: • People 50 years and over with an interest in maintaining a healthy lifestyle • HMOs and other health organizations with preventive health programs • Fitness centers interested in offering clients expanded services
4. Key customer benefits: • Getting the latest health-related news in easy-to-read capsule summaries • Advice and practical help on making lifestyle changes • Access to experts who will answer preventive health-related FAQs

Figure 6-1: Using a checklist to capture all aspects of a business description.

Include concise descriptions of the products and services you plan to offer in both the Company Overview and Company Description sections of your written plan (see Chapter 2), adding only as much technical detail as you need to make sense of them. Don't forget who your audience is here. (If you're not sure, Chapter 2 will help you identify who your plan is for.) Too much detail may simply confuse the very people you're hoping to convince. Features worth mentioning include size, color, shape, cost, design, quality, capabilities, and life span. And don't forget to describe the customers who will buy these products and services, as well as the benefits they'll receive.

Consider including a picture of your product or service as a part of your business plan, if you think it will help readers get a better idea of what you intend to offer. As the saying goes, a picture is worth a thousand words — and takes up less room.

Examining Your Business Capabilities

Every company has its own unique assets. Management gurus typically refer to these as *business capabilities.* Whatever you call them, they are the major attributes that help turn a great idea into a thriving business. They are also key elements of your company description. In this section, we take a closer look at the business capabilities that your business plan will likely touch on:

- Research and development
- Operations
- Sales and marketing
- Distribution and delivery
- Customer service
- Management
- Organization

The mysterious case of the vanishing winery

By any reckoning, $9.5 million dollars is a lot to pay for a small winery — no matter how sought after its wines are. When a brash entrepreneur bought Williams Selyem Winery in California's Sonoma County for that amount, he may have gotten even less than he bargained for.

The winery was famous for making pinot noirs, but it didn't own a single vineyard. Instead, the legendary winemaker purchased his grapes — some of the finest in the world — from a number of small growers in the area, many by way of informal handshake agreements. When the new owner took over, several of these growers decided they weren't going to sell to the winery any longer. What's more, the original winemaker, who'd agreed to work with the new owner for a short transition period, became disenchanted and left. Then came more trouble: Word got out that the winery planned to increase production of their coveted wines. Immediately, connoisseurs began to worry that the quality of the vintages would suffer. The worries threatened to seriously erode the winery's high reputation.

So what had the entrepreneur bought for his big bucks? A winery with no vineyards, a disgruntled winemaker, and worries that the new production may not live up to its reputation. The company's enduring business capabilities were, in fact, a lot fewer than they had once seemed.

The lesson? Know exactly what your company assets and business capabilities are before you take that big plunge into a new venture.

If the list looks familiar, it's because we use a similar rundown of capabilities when we discuss your company's strengths and weaknesses in Chapter 5. (Doesn't ring a bell? Flip to Chapter 5 for a detailed discussion of strengths and weaknesses and how they relate to the opportunities and threats your business faces.) In Chapter 5, we also include your financial condition as one of the essential business capabilities. Why not here? Because it's so important that we devote an entire chapter to it (see Chapter 7).

Acknowledge each of these capabilities in your written business plan. (Well, we may let you off the hook on one or two of them if you're in business all by yourself.) We can't stress enough how important it is to include a concise description of your company's assets in every one of the relevant areas. After all, these capabilities are the engines that drive you toward your business goals and objectives.

Research and development

When we talk about *research and development (R&D),* we're referring to your ability to design, develop, or enhance new products, services, or technologies. If you're a high-tech company, R&D is going to be number one on the list of capabilities crucial to your long-term success. In any case, your business plan should include a section that specifically addresses your R&D capabilities. Key points may include the following:

- The importance of R&D to your competitive success
- A concise description of your current R&D capacity (size and expertise of your engineering staff, for example)
- Your agenda for R&D over the next year
- Planned R&D expenditures over the next year
- Your long-term R&D goals

If you own a small business or a company that doesn't have much to do with high technology, don't assume that research and development isn't a part of your business. No matter what line of work you're in, your future success is probably tied to R&D of one sort or another.

Suppose you're starting a used bookstore. Not much R&D required for that, right? Think again. The Internet has created a whole new way to market used books of all sorts — from first editions and antique books to hard-to-find titles that sometimes sell for thousands of dollars. As an enterprising local bookstore owner, you may want to take advantage of this Internet network of booksellers to leverage your business and potentially create a nationwide client base of your own. And even if you decide not to sell books over the Internet, you can certainly use online resources to find out what people are paying for specific titles.

Are you in business on your own? For you, R&D can include all the steps you take to enhance your basic skills or enlarge the portfolio of services you offer customers. Take a few minutes to think about three ways you can develop your personal capabilities. Examples may include the following:

- Attending a trade show
- Taking a training course
- Completing a certification program
- Updating your computer skills
- Keeping up-to-date with trade journals
- Joining an industry group
- Enlarging your business library

Operations

In the business sense, the term *operations* describes how you get the job done and includes the resources and equipment you plan to have in place to produce the highest quality products or the very best services as efficiently as possible. How critical this capability is to your own company depends, of course, on the kind of business you're in. But take our word for it: Having a top-notch set of operations assets in place to actually carry out your business is essential, whether you're a sole proprietor or the CEO of a not-so-small company.

Your business operations typically include four key areas:

- **Location:** Where you do business
- **Equipment:** The tools you need to get the job done
- **Labor:** The human side of business operations
- **Process:** The way you get business done

Each of the areas will be more or less important to your operations, depending on the kind of business you're planning. Location is absolutely critical to a retail operation that lives or dies by walk-in customers. But for an Internet company, location may not matter a whit, because the Web is everywhere. Of course, even in the networked world, location can be important if a business depends on highly skilled high-tech talent that's clustered in places like Silicon Valley.

We've put together an operations planning survey to help you evaluate the four key operational areas as they relate to your own business. The survey is divided up into four parts — location, equipment, labor, process — that you can find, respectively, in Form 6-2, Form 6-3, Form 6-4 and Form 6-5 on the CD-ROM.

Growing pains

Even for a small company, operations can be critical to success. A talented San Francisco florist watched his small business blossom as the local economy boomed. At the beginning, he saw to all the designs and arrangements himself. He was the one who bought new inventory at the flower market early in the morning and finished the bookkeeping late at night.

That all changed as the company grew bigger. The florist found that he could no longer do everything himself, so he scrambled to hire and train employees. In the rush to meet growing demand, however, he failed to establish a clear set of operational procedures. The result: a business breakdown. Suddenly, his company had no mechanism for quality control. Flower arrangements were delivered to customers before they were approved. And no single person was put in charge of going to the flower market.

For a brief, rocky period, a number of influential and unhappy clients threatened to find other suppliers. Just in the nick of time, the florist sat down with a consultant and worked out a new way of doing business that was based on the larger staff size. The new operational procedures spelled out everyone's duties and responsibilities. They described the process of filling customer orders from the first telephone call to the last bill. To his surprise, the florist discovered that, thanks to the new procedures, he had more time to do what he did best — the creative end of the business — and still meet the growing demand.

Sales and marketing

Build a better mousetrap, the old saying goes, and the world will beat a path to your door. Ah, if only sales and marketing were that simple. First, of course, the world has to hear about your state-of-the-art contraption. And they have to know how to get their hands on it. (Will it be BetterMouseTrap.com? Mail order? Your local hardware store?) Only then will they be in a position to beat their path.

Getting the word out is what *sales and marketing* are all about — your ability to get your products or services into the marketplace and onto your customers' shopping lists. Whether you're involved in a one-person business or a future Microsoft, your plan needs to include a careful consideration of how you intend to market and sell your products or services. An effective marketing plan must answer two basic questions:

- **Who's your target market?** When you answer this question, try to be as specific as possible. One way to think about your target market is to describe your ideal customer, including information such as age, gender, geographic location, income bracket, buying habits — anything you can think of that helps fill in the details of who will be buying what you have to offer.

  If you're not quite sure who your customers really are, take a look at Chapter 4.

- **What's your strategy for communicating with that market?** After you describe your ideal customers — the ones who will beat that path to your door — explain how you plan to reach out to them. Depending on your size, your customer communications strategy may be as simple as a straightforward to-do list that captures your best advertising and promotional ideas.

As an example, here's what Rest Easy Baby Sitting Services' customer communications strategy consists of:

- Print and distribute flyers door-to-door
- Start a promotional campaign (two free hours for each referral)
- Place an ad in the local penny-saver newspaper

No matter how large or small your company is, take the time to come up with a list of three to five effective ways to communicate with your own target customers using Form 6-6 on the CD-ROM. Be as specific as you can. And be realistic. Sure, a TV ad during the Super Bowl may do wonders for your business — but only if you have a couple million bucks to spare on advertising.

Make your customer communications strategy a part of your written business plan. And if appropriate, include examples of your marketing materials (letterhead, business cards, brochures, and so on) in the Appendix of your plan.

Distribution and delivery

Distribution and delivery focus on how you plan to get your products and services into your customers' hands. Not all businesses have to be overly concerned with distribution and delivery, of course. If you're hanging up a shingle as a lawyer, creating a freelance design business, or starting a dog-walking service, a telephone, e-mail access, and a car may be all that you need. But if you manufacture a product or provide a service that's delivered to people's homes or offices, distribution and delivery are definitely important. In some cases, in fact, they're absolutely critical.

Every time the holiday season rolls around, catalog companies and online retailers face the same nail-biting challenge: How to ensure that customer orders reach their destinations in time for the big day. In the past couple of years, online retailers have had to absorb much of the extra cost of overnight express delivery in order to stay on schedule. Worse yet, a few have seen their reputations plummet — and their customers disappear — when they just haven't been able to get their toys to kids on time.

Distribution and delivery can be a matter of life or death for a business in other ways, as well. One of the biggest challenges that a new magazine faces, for example, is getting distributors to give the magazine valuable shelf space on newsstands. The same goes for food manufacturers. With grocery store shelves already overcrowded with thousands of products, getting a new breakfast cereal or snack chip distributed isn't an easy hurdle to clear.

Even businesses in traditional service industries sometimes have to focus on distribution and delivery. Management-training companies, for example, are often required to deliver training programs to thousands of managers at one time. But they can't get the programs to these customers unless they have trainers available in the classrooms when and where they need them.

Failing to plan for both the method and cost of distribution or delivery can prove fatal to your business. Consider the regional Internet grocery service that became famous for offering free delivery on orders of any size. Customers could call up and order a single frozen dinner, a bottle of wine, or even a candy bar. Trouble was, it cost the delivery service more than $10 to fill each order. You don't have to be a business guru to know it wasn't long before this particular business promise faded away — along with the company.

If distribution and delivery of your product or service are high on the list of key capabilities determining your business success, fill out the distribution and delivery survey in Form 6-7. Be as specific as you can, flagging those areas where you need to track down more information.

Customer service

While there may be a business out there that doesn't depend on keeping customers satisfied, we can't think of any at the moment. Customer service is usually the key to long-term success in almost any business. Happy customers, after all, are customers who tell their friends about your company — and keep coming back themselves to buy from you again and again.

One of the new buzzwords in business, in fact, is something called *customer-relationship management* (*CRM*). It's a fancy way to make sure you always keep the customer satisfied. Now you can find software programs, Web sites, and whole books devoted to CRM. For really big companies with complex customer interactions, the job of managing customer relationships can get pretty complicated, but when you get right down to it, the strategies aren't exactly rocket science.

DISTRIBUTION AND DELIVERY SURVEY
1. Outline the steps required in distributing and delivering your product or service:
2. Describe the extent of the geographic area you intend to cover, including any plans to expand:
3. Estimate the costs associated with the distribution and delivery of your product or service:
4. List the relationships and agreements you plan to forge with distribution or delivery companies in your industry:
5. Review any contingency plans you have in place in case your primary distribution or delivery services are interrupted:

Form 6-7: Distribution and delivery survey.

What are some of the things that really satisfy customers? They may include no-questions-asked return policies on anything purchased from a store or Web site and sales staff that's trained to recognize repeat customers and address them by name. They may consist of software systems that allow tracking of customer contacts to make sure no inquiry or question goes unanswered or sending thank-you notes after large purchases — along with discount coupons for future purchases.

The size and sophistication of your customer service function depends on what kind of company you run — and how often you make contact with customers. But whether you're a freelance graphic artist or the CEO of a fast-growing Internet start-up, make sure you keep track of the customer service issues you face in your own business.

Review the customer service checklist in Form 6-8, checking off the things that you already do and circling those that you'd like to consider starting. We've left room for your own additions to the list because creative customer service shows up in all sorts of ways.

CUSTOMER SERVICE CHECKLIST
☐ Follow-up e-mail or telephone call after an initial customer inquiry
☐ Mail or e-mail acknowledgement after an order is placed
☐ Mail or e-mail "thank you" after an order is filled
☐ No questions asked money-back return policy
☐ Extended warranty programs
☐ Hotline for customer questions or complaints
☐ Special frequent customer programs
☐ Follow-up customer satisfaction questionnaires
☐ Customer tracking software
☐ Birthday mailings and special offers
☐
☐
☐

Form 6-8: Customer service checklist.

Not sure where to begin? One place to start is to think about the companies or individuals you deal with that provide crackerjack customer service. You know who we mean: The automotive repair company that washes your car inside and out, the local restaurant that sends you a one-free entree coupon when your birthday rolls around, or the shop that allows you to return anything you purchase within 30 days, no questions asked. If you come up with any more ideas here, add them to your customer service checklist.

Management

The long-term success of many companies depends, above all, on the quality of the team that provides leadership, direction, and vision. In some cases, in fact, investors have been known to fund a start-up company purely on the basis of the people who will run it.

If you're going into business all alone, you don't have to spend too much time describing yourself in your plan — although it's not a bad idea to review your own education, experience, and accomplishments and write up a résumé. Sole proprietors are sometimes called upon to provide information about themselves to bankers, suppliers, and even prospective customers.

If you're running a small business, include biographies of your top managers in the plan. We recommend limiting your management team to no more than five people — individuals in senior posts who are involved in the day-to-day operations of the business. This includes all the big Cs, from CEO (Chief Executive Officer) and COO (Chief Operating Officer) to CFO (Chief Financial Officer) and CTO (Chief Technology Officer). Depending on the size of your company, you may also want to include brief descriptions of the members of your Board of Directors, Board of Advisors, or consultants who will play a major role in making your business a success.

When describing your management team, include everything that's relevant to the potential success of your business — but keep the descriptions brief and to the point. Keep biographical notes to a half page or less.

You can use the management team member profile shown in Form 6-9 to collect essential background information on each of your senior people.

Organization

Your company's success hinges on the quality of the people around you, but it also depends on having an organization in place that allows those people to work as effectively and efficiently as possible. A company's organization consists of the relationship of employees to one another — who reports to whom, for example. It also determines each employee's access to important company resources.

MANAGEMENT TEAM MEMBER PROFILE ON: ______________________
1. Title or position:
2. Describe duties and responsibilities (include the functions overseen and daily activities, where appropriate): • • •
3. List previous industry and related experience (include past employers, positions, duties, and responsibilities): • • •
4. List notable accomplishments (include successful projects, new product introductions, honors, awards, and so on): • • •
5. Education (certifications, degrees, and so on):

Form 6-9: Management team member profile.

All this may sound straightforward, and for small companies, it usually is. But in large firms, a flawed organization can undermine the efforts of even the best staff. Consider the ongoing saga of one of the biggest health-information and management companies on the Internet. Part of its early strategy was to gobble up smaller online information providers to acquire their assets and to eliminate competition. Trouble was, each of these small companies had its own organizational structure and editorial procedures. Before long, different groups within the larger organization were producing the same content, unnecessarily duplicating one another's efforts. No one was sure who was supposed to report to whom. And there was very little editorial control over the site. Content that should have taken only three weeks to produce began to require six and seven weeks. As a result, the company bled money. The moral: Organization matters.

The most successful organizations are tailored to a company's management team as well as the business it's in. An effective organization for a small magazine, for example, is different from the successful organization of a highly-profitable manufacturing firm. How do you choose what's best for you? To make the task a bit easier, consider the four basic organizational models, each most appropriate to a specific company size. Your job is to identify which model is best suited to you.

- **The pack:** In this structure, one person holds the top position, and everyone else in the company is an equal member of the pack. This organizational style works well in small companies — no more than 20 people — where everyone on staff has the training and the expertise to do almost any job required of them.
    - **The advantages:** A simple, flexible organizational structure allows the entire team to work together. This loose-knit arrangement is often effective when a small company needs to adjust quickly to changing business conditions.
    - **The disadvantages:** If the company gets too big, the top dog can no longer keep track of what the rest of the pack is up to. Also, people may end up doing jobs they've never done before, which can compromise both quality and efficiency.
- **Form follows function:** In this organization, people are divided into groups depending on what functions they perform. For example, a company may have an engineering department, a marketing department, a production department, and a finance department. Each department has its own manager, and a general manager typically takes on the role of coordinating the activities of the various functional groups.
    - **The advantages:** People are assigned to do what they do best, and everyone knows exactly what he or she is responsible for. If your business is medium-sized and markets only one type of product or service, this is probably the organizational structure for you.
    - **The disadvantages:** Without good communication and oversight from above, functional hierarchies can break down into separate little boxes that work well on their own but aren't very good at carrying out the company's larger strategies and goals.
- **Divide and conquer:** Companies that are big enough to be in more than one business often choose to organize around separate divisions. A firm that sells, installs, and services computer networks, for example, may separate those functions into independent divisions. In this organizational model, each of a company's divisions may be responsible for a particular product, service, market, or geographical area. And all of the divisions may have to justify themselves as independent profit centers. In some of the largest companies, each division consists of a strategic business unit (SBU) — almost a company inside a company. For more details on SBUs, check out *Business Plans For Dummies* by Paul Tiffany and Steven Peterson (Hungry Minds, Inc.).

- **The advantages:** Organization by division encourages the separate parts of a company to focus on the real business at hand — selling computers, servicing them, or installing them, for example. Managers within the division can zero in on their own sets of customers, competitors, and strategic issues.
- **The disadvantages:** Separate divisions may find themselves competing for the same customers. Overhead costs may be duplicated unnecessarily, and the company may end up becoming less efficient.

- **The matrix:** In a matrix organization, everybody has multiple bosses and does more than one job. Wearing one hat, for example, an employee may be involved in developing new content for the company Web site. Wearing another, the same employee may work with the marketing team on special projects designed to bring in new business.
  - **The advantages:** This structure creates a lot of flexibility in the organization by allowing different parts of a company to share talent, expertise, and experience. Companies with a matrix structure are often able to respond quickly to changing business conditions.
  - **The disadvantages:** When people wear two hats, managing employees can be a bit tricky. And employees sometimes feel a tense tug-of-war between the demands of different bosses. This structure can also lead to confused and conflicting business priorities unless a strong general manager makes sure that the company stays on track.

You won't find an absolute right or wrong way to organize your business, so use your own instincts — along with the preceding suggestions — to come up with an organizational plan that allows you and everyone around you to work at their best. And remember: An organization is a living thing that should grow and change as business circumstances change. In other words, reevaluate your organization on a regular basis, especially if your company is growing rapidly.

Your written plan will include a section on your company's organization. Charts or diagrams can sometimes help make a complicated organization a little clearer, so considering using a flow chart to show who reports to whom, for example, or using a series of boxes to show how the company's various divisions relate to one another. But don't get lost in the details. Remember that the goal is to present a coherent description of what the company looks like and why.

Focusing On What You Do Best

No business can be all things to all people. When companies try to do that, in fact, they usually find themselves becoming less effective at almost everything they do. We could make a long and scary list of companies that decided to build on their past success by expanding in new directions — only to lose the original focus that kept them sharp and successful in the first place. Your business plan needs to do more than simply describe who you are and what you intend to do. To be successful, your plan has to highlight what you do best.

Imagine for the moment that you own the local bookstore in town. Question: What's your business? Simple answer: You sell books. But if that's all you do, chances are, you won't be in business long. After all, big online bookstores also sell books, and they probably offer deeper discounts than you can afford to give. They also have huge inventories — certainly more titles than your little shop can ever stock.

But the fact is that despite these competitive limitations, you're doing pretty well, thank you very much. So what's going on here? What does this local bookstore of yours really have to offer? Here's what:

- Thanks to the easy chairs you added last year, you now offer a warm and cozy place for people to come and browse through books.
- You've invited a local acoustic guitarist to come in and play on weekends, adding to the overall ambiance.
- You pride yourself on a high quality selection of books, even if it's not the biggest in the world, and you special order any book requested.
- You've been careful to hire sales people who know and love books — so in a way, you're also in the business of recommending good books to your patrons.
- You've made a point of finding and featuring local writers and also of inviting leading authors to read at your bookstore.
- You've also arranged for free, same-day delivery of books within a 25-mile radius.
- Your bookstore is a major supporter of the local community Web page, and you spearhead the library book-donation drive.
- You've teamed up with the local coffee shop. They feature copies of your best-selling books, and you offer discount coupons on lattes and cappuccinos.

Selling books, you're beginning to realize, is only a small part of what your bookstore does. And it's only one of many ways that you provide value to your customers.

The business capabilities that provide the greatest value to customers deserve special attention in your written plan. After all, these capabilities represent the heart and soul of your business — and your strongest selling points as a company. Your business plan should include specific details about how you intend to make the most of them.

The capabilities that provide the greatest customer value also needs the most attention in your ongoing planning process, so make sure to reevaluate how well you're doing in these key areas on a regular basis. And use the time to brainstorm new ways to increase the overall value you provide.

Forms on the CD-ROM

The following forms on the CD-ROM are designed to help you come up with a clear and compelling description of your company and what you do.

Form 6-1	**Product/Service Description Checklist**	A checklist that helps you create a complete description of your product or service
Form 6-2	**Operations Planning Survey (Location)**	Key factors to consider in planning the location of your operations
Form 6-3	**Operations Planning Survey (Equipment)**	Key factors to consider in planning the equipment needs of your operations
Form 6-4	**Operations Planning Survey (Labor)**	Key factors to consider in planning the labor needs of your operations
Form 6-5	**Operations Planning Survey (Process)**	Key factors to consider in planning the process requirements of your operations
Form 6-6	**Customer Communications Strategy Checklist**	A checklist that helps you record good ideas for ways to communicate effectively with your target customers
Form 6-7	**Distribution and Delivery Survey**	A survey designed to help you get a handle on your distribution and delivery capabilities
Form 6-8	**Customer Service Checklist**	A checklist designed to generate new ideas on ways to improve your own customer service
Form 6-9	**Management Team Member Profile**	A questionnaire designed to collect relevant background information on top management team members

Chapter 7

Examining Your Financial Situation

In This Chapter

- Understanding income statements, balance sheets, and cash flow statements
- Looking into your financial future

Some people love adding and subtracting columns of numbers. They can spend all day happily filling in computer spreadsheets or poring over budgets. And then there are the rest of us. We balance our checkbooks and add up our credit card charges because we know we have to. Because if we don't, we realize, we won't know what we've spent, how much we have, and whether there will be enough money when the mortgage or rent comes due.

In this chapter, we ask you to do a bunch of adding and subtracting. If you love numbers, it'll be a breeze. If not, you may have to put a little extra effort in. Either way, one thing is certain: You can't plan and run a successful business without knowing exactly what your financial situation is. As the football player famously said in the movie *Jerry Maguire*: "Show me the money!" Entrepreneurs and business owners are being asked to show the money all the time — in their business plans, in their financial statements, and in their budgets and forecasts. Why? Because while there's certainly more to being in business than money, without the money you can't stay in business. Period.

So, in this chapter, we show you the money — or at least help you keep close tabs on yours. We help you master these three building blocks of financial planning, which paint a pretty complete picture of how you're doing:

- **Your *income statement:*** A form that starts with how much money you earned in a given period of time (most often, a year) and then subtracts all the costs of doing business over that same period to arrive at your *net profit.* Sometimes you may hear the income statement referred to as an *earnings report* or a *profit-and-loss statement.* Don't be confused, they're all one and the same.

- **Your *balance sheet:*** A form that captures a financial snapshot of your business at a particular moment in time, usually the very end of the year. The top half of your balance sheet tallies up your company's *assets,* all the things you own that have any monetary value. The bottom half combines all the money you owe (your *liabilities*) together with what your company is actually worth (your *equity*). The top and bottoms halves must always balance each other out, hence the name.
- **Your *cash flow statement:*** A form that tracks the money as it flows in and out of your business over any given period of time (weekly, monthly, quarterly, or yearly.) The top half of your cash flow statement looks in detail at the funds coming in and the funds going out of your company over the period. The bottom half shows the resulting changes in your cash position. Like the balance sheet, the top and bottom halves must match up.

Finally, in this chapter, we give you tips on how to use your current financial situation to gaze into the crystal ball and forecast your company's financial future.

Putting Together an Income Statement

Your company's income statement is designed to reveal your proverbial bottom line. By adding up all the revenue you receive from selling your products and services, and then subtracting all the costs associated with doing business over a certain period of time, the income statement comes up with your net profit for the period:

Net profit = Revenue – costs

It's really a simple calculation, no matter how complicated the financial experts out there sometimes make it seem, and it's a basic measure of how well your company's doing. The time period you choose for your income statement depends on the type of business you're in and what you're using the income statement for. The IRS, of course, is interested in your income statement for the taxable year. But you may also want to look over your profits by quarter if, for example, your business is seasonal. And you get a more complete picture of where your company's headed by reviewing your income statements over a number of years.

To get a better idea about how an income statement is constructed, take a look at the books for Broad Street Emporium, a gift shop specializing in handicrafts and hard-to-find items. The store has been in business for several years, and Figure 7-1 shows an income statement as of December 31st for the most recent year, as well as the year before that. By comparing two years in a row, the owners of the gift shop can see how revenues, costs, and profits are changing over time.

BROAD STREET EMPORIUM INCOME STATEMENT			
INCOME STATEMENT AS OF DECEMBER 31			
		Last Year	**Previous Year**
1	Revenue on in-store sales	624,000.	595,000.
	Revenue on catalog sales	+ 105,000.	+ 95,000.
	Gross Revenue	**$ 729,000.**	**$ 690,000.**
2	Cost of goods sold	– 448,000.	– 445,000.
	Gross Profit	**$ 281,000.**	**$ 245,000.**
3	Sales, general, and administration	– 126,000.	– 108,000.
	Depreciation expense	– 20,000.	– 20,000.
	Operating Profit	**$ 135,000.**	**$ 117,000.**
4	Dividend and interest income	+ 3,000.	+ 3,000.
	Interest expense	– 24,000.	– 25,000.
	Profit Before Taxes	**$ 114,000.**	**$ 95,000.**
5	Taxes	– 22,000.	– 19,000.
	Net Profit	**$ 92,000.**	**$ 76,000.**

Figure 7-1: An income statement helps determine profits for the year.

The income statement for the Broad Street Emporium is made up of five different sections. Each one says something important about the company's financial condition, so we take a look at them section by section.

Section 1: Gross revenue

Revenues are the sum total of all the money your company takes in as a direct result of operating your business. In the case of Broad Street Emporium, those revenues are broken down into two major sources: money taken in by the store itself and money collected on the store's catalog sales. Any time you have money coming in from different lines of business, you want to track the dollars separately so that you know at a glance where the revenues are really coming from.

Depending on the type of business you're in, revenues may be based on the sale of a single product, entire product lines, or the delivery of a whole array of services. Revenues can take the form of simple purchase transactions, leasing arrangements, subscription services, or any number of financing options. Together, these sources all get totaled up and entered on the income statement as *gross revenue*. Here, the word "gross" doesn't refer to a teenager's standard response. Instead, it means that the revenue is as large as it can get, without subtracting any costs whatsoever.

Section 2: Gross profit

In general, *profits* refer to the money from your revenues that you get to keep after all the bills have been paid. But as you can see from Broad Street Emporium's income statement, there are different kinds of profit. By taking time to analyze your profit at various stages of your business, you gain a clearer idea of where you're making money and where your costs may be too high.

The first stage profit is typically referred to as *gross profit.* Gross profit starts with gross revenue and subtracts only those costs that can be directly associated with producing, assembling, or purchasing what you have to sell. In the case of Broad Street Emporium, the *cost of goods sold* refers to the wholesale costs that the store must pay out for the gifts and handicrafts found on its shelves and in its catalog.

If you offer a service, your gross profit will subtract only the costs directly related to supplying or delivering that service. If your company actually produces a product from raw materials, your gross profit reflects only those material costs as well as the labor, utilities, and facilities needed to put the product together. As you can tell, you may have to make judgment calls as to which costs should or shouldn't be included here. No matter what you decide, be consistent over time. Otherwise you won't know whether you're adding and subtracting apples or oranges.

Section 3: Operating profit

All sorts of costs associated with doing business are not directly related to assembling your products or delivering your services. These costs include everything from the ads you run and the sales force you hire to travel expenses, telephone bills, and office supplies. No doubt, they also include your own office space if you rent and even the salary you pay yourself — at least the part of it that's often referred to as *overhead.* All of these indirect costs are usually lumped together into a category simply titled *SG&A (sales, general, and administration) expense*.

Keep a careful eye on all your SG&A expenses. Because they're not tied directly to your products and services, these expenses don't directly contribute to your revenue. If they should get out of line, your profits can rather quickly turn into losses.

In addition to your SG&A expenses, chances are you'll invest in at least one or two big-ticket items in the course of doing business. Maybe you need a car to call on clients, some sort of a computer system, and perhaps even a building or two for offices, a warehouse, or other facilities. When you think about it, each of these big purchases is really an exchange of one asset (cash in the bank) for another asset (the car, computer, or building). The business assets you acquire all have useful life spans, so one way to spread out the costs of these assets over the number of years they're actually in service is to calculate *depreciation expenses* each year.

Operating profit is the money you make from your actual business operations. It's calculated by subtracting your SG&A and depreciation expenses from gross profit. For Broad Street Emporium, the bulk of the SG&A expense is tied to the salaries of the sales staff, advertising, and the production and delivery of the store's catalog three times per year. In addition to SG&A expense, the company is taking depreciation expenses on its storefront building, the store's computer system, and a delivery van.

Section 4: Profit before taxes

Managing money is part of running almost every business. You're likely to have a business checking account, for example, maybe a business savings account, and perhaps even an investment portfolio to make sure that the cash your business keeps on hand is working for you. You may need to borrow money to finance a car, a building, business equipment, or your ongoing operations.

The money you make on your invested cash as well as the interest on any business-related loans you have must be included in your business income and expense tally. But you want to keep these amounts outside your operating profit because the income you make on investments isn't really a part of your business operations — unless you're an investment banker. And the interest expenses you pay out are different from other expenses you have. For one thing, interest payments depend on how you've structured your company financially, not on the business itself. And for another thing, they absolutely, positively have to be paid on a strict and unforgiving schedule.

Profit before taxes takes into account all the income your company makes on investments of any sort and subtracts any interest expenses you pay out. Broad Street Emporium has dividend and interest income amounting to $3,000 for the current year, but the company also paid out $24,000 in interest expenses, most of that going toward the mortgage for the store itself.

Section 5: Net profit

Net profit refers to your company's bottom line — the amount you have left after every last one of your expenses is subtracted from all the income available. Haven't we considered every conceivable cost you'll incur by now? Not quite. There's one important one left: taxes.

Depending on the structure of your company, your business may or may not have to pay taxes directly on the profits you've earned. If you're a sole proprietor or your business is structured as a partnership, for example, your business profits are funneled straight down to the individual owners for tax purposes, so no profit is left to be taxed. Of course, the owners can't escape the IRS so easily and must still pay individual income taxes on the money. Even if your business isn't taxed on its profits, you may still find yourself owing money to the city, county, or state through various licensing requirements or other forms of tax.

After Broad Street Emporium pays taxes for the year, the business is left with a net profit of $92,000. Good news. That amounts to a 21 percent increase over the year before.

All sections: Your turn

Now it's time to put together your own version of an income statement. Maybe you're already using accounting or financial software that does much of the work for you. That's great. We suggest, however, that you print out a copy of the most recent income statement to date and look it over carefully. Make sure that you understand each entry and are convinced that your overall financial picture makes sense.

Don't let a software program do all the number crunching for you and assume everything must be okay. In the end, you have to know what all the numbers mean. After all, you are responsible for knowing what the income statement says about the financial health of your company.

If you're not using a computer to track your company's finances, assemble all the relevant income and expense figures. Not yet in business? Never fear: The income statement is also used to project what you expect to earn in the future and, for this reason, is the basis for putting together budgets as your business looks ahead.

Form 7-1 provides an ideal template to develop an income statement for your own company. Each section of the form is meant to capture a profit figure at a different point in your business, starting with revenues and then coming up with gross profit, operating profit, profit before taxes, and net profit. The individual entries we include on the form are typical of an income statement, but because your individual situation may require additional items, we've left additional space.

An income statement is an essential part of your written business plan. If your venture is already up and running, include numbers for the last year or two for comparison purposes. No matter how long you've been in business — even if you're just starting out — use the income statement to show what you plan to do in the future. A year or two ahead is usually an appropriate projection to make, but even five-year forecasts aren't unheard of. Jump to the "Forecasting and Budgeting" section, near the end of this chapter, for more info on financial forecasting and budgeting.

COMPANY INCOME STATEMENT		
INCOME STATEMENT AS OF:		
	Year:	**Year:**
Revenue from ____________	+	+
Revenue from ____________	+	+
Other revenue ____________	+	+
Gross Revenue	=	=
Cost of goods sold	–	–
Other direct costs ____________	–	–
Gross Profit	=	=
Sales, general, and administration	–	–
Depreciation expense	–	–
Other expenses ____________	–	–
Operating Profit	=	=
Dividend and interest income	+	+
Interest expense	–	–
Other ____________		
Profit Before Taxes	=	=
Taxes	–	–
Net Profit	=	=

Form 7-1: Company income statement.

Creating a Balance Sheet

Your company's balance sheet gives you a snapshot of what your business is worth, captured at a particular moment in time. In order to make the calculation, you need to tally up the monetary value of everything your company owns and then subtract the money you owe to others. The stuff you own is usually referred to as *assets.* The amounts you owe are called *liabilities.* The difference — or what's left over — is what your company's worth, sometimes referred to as the *equity* in your business.

You can represent what your balance sheet is telling you about your company in a really straightforward equation:

Equity = Assets – Liabilities

In a bizarre attempt to ensure their job security, however, accountants have decided to confuse things further by rewriting the equation as follows:

Assets = Liabilities + Equity

It's the very same equation, only now it no longer makes common sense. Go figure. Anyway, the layout of your company's balance sheet is based on this second equation. The top half of the balance sheet is a list of all your business assets, divided into a number of basic categories. The bottom half of the balance sheet lists all your liabilities by category and then tacks on all of the equity in the business. Given the equation we just looked at, the top half's total and the bottom half's total must be equal. In other words, they must balance each other out. How they balance each other tells you a lot about your company's financial health.

How often should you create a balance sheet for your company? Well, you can do it as often as you like, of course. At the very least, put together a balance sheet on the last day of the year. This particular balance sheet can also show the numbers for the end of the previous year, so you can compare how your assets, liabilities, and equity have changed over the year.

To see how a balance sheet is put together, take a look at Broad Street Emporium, a specialty gift shop. Figure 7-2 shows the company's balance sheet on December 31st for the most recent year and includes the numbers for the end of the previous year for comparison purposes.

The top and bottom halves of the balance sheet for the Broad Street Emporium are each made up of four different sections. Each section totals up a different category of assets, liabilities or owners' equity. We take a look at them section by section.

Section 1: Current assets

Your company's *assets* are made up of all the things you own that have monetary value. On the balance sheet, you're interested not only in how much each asset is worth, but how long it would take you to sell it off, converting it into cold, hard cash. The length of time needed to dispose of an asset is often described in terms of *liquidity.* The more *liquid* an asset, the faster you can sell it off.

BROAD STREET EMPORIUM BALANCE SHEET			
BALANCE SHEET ON DECEMBER 31			
Assets		**Last Year**	**Previous Year**
1	**Current Assets**		
	Cash	45,000.	36,000.
	Investment portfolio	+ 20,000.	+ 17,000.
	Accounts receivable	+ 15,000.	+ 18,000.
	Inventories	+ 110,000.	+ 97,000.
	Prepaid expenses	+ 1,000.	+ 1,000.
	Total Current Assets	**$ 191,000.**	**$ 169,000.**
2	**Fixed Assets**		
	Land	100,000.	100,000.
	Buildings	+ 295,000.	+ 295,000.
	Equipment	+ 15,000.	+ 10,000.
	Accumulated depreciation	– 65,000.	– 45,000.
	Total Fixed Assets	**$ 345,000.**	**$ 360,000.**
3	**Intangibles (goodwill, patents)**	**$ 10,000.**	**$ 10,000.**
4	**TOTAL ASSETS**	**$ 546,000.**	**$ 539,000.**
Liabilities and Owners' Equity		**Last Year**	**Previous Year**
5	**Current Liabilities**		
	Accounts payable	4,000.	6,000.
	Accrued expenses payable	+ 12,000.	+ 11,000.
	Total Current Liabilities	**$ 16,000.**	**$ 17,000.**
6	**Long-term Liabilities**		
	Building mortgage	210,000.	214,000.
	Total Long-term Liabilities	**$ 210,000.**	**$ 214,000.**
7	**Owners' Equity**		
	Invested capital	200,000.	195,000.
	Accumulated retained earnings	+ 120,000.	+ 113,000.
	Total Owners' Equity	**$ 320,000.**	**$ 308,000.**
8	**TOTAL LIABILITIES and EQUITY**	**$ 546,000.**	**$ 539,000.**

Figure 7-2: Creating a balance sheet determines the company's worth.

Current assets represent all the items your business owns that are liquid enough to be converted into cash within a year, including the following:

- **Cash:** You can't get more liquid than cash. Cash can be anything from the bills and change in the cash register or the petty cash drawer to the money you have in a checking or savings account at the bank.
- **Investment portfolio:** Cash is nice, but it's even nicer to see your money working a bit harder for you as long as you have to keep it on hand. Your investments may include money market accounts, government bonds, or any other reasonably safe security. You probably won't want to make high-risk investments with these particular funds.

- **Accounts receivable:** This asset consists of the money your customers owe you for products or services you've already delivered to them. If you bill your clients, for example, you may give them 30, 60, or 90 days to pay. Keep an eye on your accounts receivable. One deadbeat customer, after all, can throw your numbers for a loop.
- **Inventories:** The equivalent cash value of the products or supplies you have on hand. It's often tricky to come up with a realistic number for the value of your inventories. Our advice: Stay on the conservative side. Your balance sheet should reflect what you can reasonably expect to receive if you should have to liquidate these assets.
- **Prepaid expenses:** At any given time, your company may have paid for services you haven't received yet. Maybe you've paid retainers or insurance premiums ahead of time, for example. These should be considered as part of your current assets.

Current assets, especially the most liquid ones, are extremely important to your business. They represent the readily available reserves you have to fund your day-to-day operations and to draw on in case of an unforeseen financial emergency. Broad Street Emporium had a total of $191,000 in current assets as of the end of the most recent year, including $65,000 in cash or securities.

Section 2: Fixed assets

Fixed assets are fixed in the sense that they're usually big, expensive, meant to last a long time — and not very liquid at all. Buildings, machinery, cars, and computers fall into this category. As a rule, expect to take a year or more to dispose of these assets, turning them into cash in the bank. In general, fixed assets include the following:

- **Land:** If your company happens to own land — the ground under your office building, for example — it's listed separately on the balance sheet. Unlike other fixed assets, land can't be depreciated over time, so its value remains the same on the books year after year.

- **Buildings:** As far as your balance sheet is concerned, the value of the buildings your company owns is equal to the original price you paid for them plus whatever you've spent on improving them over the years.
- **Equipment:** Equipment includes anything and everything you buy for the business that's meant to last more than a year. Machinery, cars, office equipment, computers, telephones, and furniture all fall into this category. Their value is the original price you paid for them. If, for some reason, you didn't pay cash for one of these fixed assets, you should assign a reasonable value to it and include it on your balance sheet.
- **Accumulated depreciation:** All the big-ticket items you acquire as part of doing business each have a useful lifespan. *Depreciation* measures the decline in the useful value of these fixed assets over time. Don't worry, you don't have to come up with the numbers here. The IRS has a standard set of depreciation schedules, depending on the kind of assets you own. *Accumulated depreciation* sums these numbers up over all your assets and your years of ownership, and then reduces the total value of your fixed assets accordingly.

The value of a fixed asset is really quite arbitrary, at least as far as it's defined on your balance sheet. After all, the amount is based on the original price you paid minus any accumulated depreciation according to a general depreciation schedule. The resulting figure may in fact have very little to do with the market value you could receive if you decided to sell the asset or the price you'd have to pay if you needed to replace it for some reason.

Broad Street Emporium now has fixed assets valued at $345,000 after accumulated depreciation is taken into account. During the most recent year, the company spent an additional $5,000 on equipment. At the same time, the book value of all its assets was reduced by $20,000 because of depreciation. That same $20,000, by the way, shows up and is taken as a depreciation expense on the income statement in Figure 7-1.

Section 3: Intangibles

Intangibles are assets that, by definition, are hard to get your arms around. They can turn out to be extremely important to your business, however. Intangible assets include things like an exclusive contract to supply services, a franchise ownership, or a hard-to-get license or permit to do business. An intangible asset can also be a patent protecting some invention, software technology, or production process. All these assets are clearly valuable to the company that owns them, but the question is, what are they really worth?

Some companies don't even try to place a monetary value on their intangible assets. Instead, they allocate a symbolic $1 toward them on the balance sheet, indicating that these assets are there and are valuable, but aren't measurable.

Sock puppet lives on

Sometimes, a company's intangible assets prove to be worth more than anyone would have expected — in one case, a lot more than the company itself. After a wild ride on the roller-coaster of e-commerce, the pet supply Web site called Pets.com closed down. But its advertising mascot, the familiar Sock Puppet of television commercials, lived on, spawning its own line of dolls and boasting its own licensing agent. The cuddly puppet turned out to be more valuable than any of the company's products or services. Go figure.

Under the category of intangible assets, you find an item with an odd name: *goodwill.* Now we're as big on treating one's colleagues well as the next guy, but that's not the kind of goodwill we're talking about here. Goodwill represents the amount of money your company may pay for something above and beyond its fair market value. Why would anyone do that? In fact, entire companies are often purchased at prices above market value, simply because they're worth a lot more to the buyer than to anyone else.

Broad Street Emporium bought an existing gift shop a number of years ago and paid $10,000 more than what was considered the fair market value of the business at the time. The company now carries that goodwill entry on its balance sheet.

Section 4: Total assets

The *total assets* entry on the balance sheet sums up the total value of all the assets your company owns including current assets, fixed assets, and intangibles. This completes the top half of the balance sheet. In the case of Broad Street Emporium, the company has increased its assets over the most recent year by $7,000 to $546,000.

Section 5: Current liabilities

Your company's *liabilities* are the various amounts of money you owe to creditors in the form of bills that are due, bank loans you've taken out, and bonds or warrants you may have issued to raise money. Many of these so-called financial instruments can get quite complex. The basic idea is always the same: You receive money or something else of value in exchange for the promise to pay the money back over a certain period of time (usually with interest, of course.) Sometimes these debts are secured by an asset that you own. (If you don't pay back as promised, the creditor can come in and take that asset away from you.) Sometimes the debts are unsecured. Sometimes the payback period is very long; other times, it's very short.

Current liabilities represent the short-term debts your company takes on that have to be repaid within one year. These liabilities are closely tied to your current assets listed on the top half of the balance sheet, because your current liabilities have to be paid off using those assets. In most cases, current liabilities fall into two groups:

- **Accounts payable:** At any given moment, your company typically owes money to various providers and suppliers that you do business with on a regular basis. The liabilities are usually in the form of outstanding bills that are due but haven't yet been paid for such things as utilities, telephone service, office supplies, professional services, or raw materials or wholesale goods that you resell to customers.
- **Accrued expenses payable:** In addition to outside accounts that come due, your business is continuously accruing liabilities related to salaries or wages (if you have employees), insurance premiums, interest on bank loans, and taxes you owe. To the extent that these current obligations are unpaid at the time your balance sheet is put together, they're grouped together here.

What's left over after you subtract your current liabilities from your current assets is typically called *working capital:* It's the money you have to work with on a day-to-day basis to keep your business up and running. On the balance sheet, Broad Street Emporium has a strong working capital position of $175,000.

Section 6: Long-term liabilities

Long-term liabilities usually represent the large financial obligations you take on either to get your company up and running or to expand your business operations. As such, these liabilities are often at the very heart of your company's financial structure. Perhaps you've taken out a ten-year business loan directly from the bank. Or you've issued bonds to a group of investors to be repaid in 15 years. Or maybe you have a real estate mortgage on the buildings you use.

Broad Street Emporium has only one long-term liability: A mortgage of $210,000 on the building housing its store, which will be completely paid off in 26 years.

Section 7: Owners' equity

When you own something, it's all yours, isn't it? Well, not always. Lots of people say they own their own homes, but what they really mean is that they own a piece of their own homes and banks or mortgage companies own the rest. In the same way, lots of people own their own businesses — or at least a part of their own businesses.

A company's owners can come in any number, from a single individual to tens of thousands of investors in a large, publicly traded company. How much the owners actually own is referred to as their *equity.* The equity in a company can be distributed in all sorts of ways and have various strings attached concerning when it can be sold or how it can be used. When you strip away all the complexity, however, you're left with two basic sources of equity: money coming from outside investors and money generated from profits that are kept inside the company:

- **Invested capital:** The money that's invested in your company comes from various sources, including the cash you put up as a principle owner of the business. You can also raise cash by selling off small pieces of the company to outside investors. The stock those investors receive in exchange represents their equity in your business. This outside equity may be privately held, or when you get big enough, you may decide to go for an IPO (Initial Public Offering). As part of an IPO, shares of your company are offered for sale to the general public. These shares are then traded on a public stock exchange. No matter how you exchange equity for cash, it's all lumped together as invested capital.
- **Accumulated retained earnings:** If you're lucky enough to make a profit on your business (meaning that the revenues you take in during the year exceed all the costs and expenses you incur), you're in the happy position to decide what to do with all the excess dough. You may decide to give some of it back to the owners and investors: That's what *dividends* are for. Or you may plow some of the extra cash back into the business so that you can grow bigger and, as a result, create more equity for everyone who has a stake in your company. Accumulated retained earnings represent all the profits you've poured back into the business year after year.

Total owner's equity sums up invested capital and accumulated retained earnings to come up with the value of the part of the company that all the owners actually own. The owners of Broad Street Emporium have invested $200,000 in the business and have poured another $120,000 of profits back into growing the company over the years.

Section 8: Total liabilities and equity

Total liabilities and equity sums up the total value of all the liabilities your company is responsible for, including both current and long-term liabilities, and then adds on the total owners' equity. This completes the bottom half of the balance sheet. As you can see, the top and bottom halves of the Broad Street Emporium balance sheet are in balance at $546,000 at the end of the most recent year.

All sections: Your turn

You guessed it: You need to make a balance sheet of your own. If you're using accounting software of any kind, you can probably push a button to create an instant balance sheet out of financial information you've already entered into the program. But don't assume that that's all you have to do. Your computer-generated balance sheet is only as good as the numbers you put into it in the first place. So print out a copy and make sure it makes sense.

If you want to get a head start on your company's balance sheet and don't yet have business software in place — or you just want to understand what the darn thing really means — think about putting together your own version the old fashioned way: on paper. Even if you're not in business yet, you can use the basic balance sheet format to total up the set of assets you think you'll need to get your business off the ground, as well as the liabilities and equity capital you'll require to get your hands on those assets.

Use the handy template in Form 7-2 to develop a balance sheet for your own company. Each section of the form is meant to capture a different category of assets, liabilities, and owners' equity. While the individual entries we've included on the form are typical, your individual situation may require additional items, so we've left additional space.

Your company's balance sheet will appear in your written business plan as another important part of your financial picture, producing a snapshot of what you own, what you owe, and what you're worth. If you're already in business, include year-end numbers for the most recent two years as a useful comparison. And no matter how long you've been in business — even if you're just starting out — use the balance sheet to show exactly how you plan to grow to meet the income statement projections you've developed. Flip to the "Forecasting and Budgeting" section, later in this chapter, for more information on financial forecasting and budgeting.

Constructing a Cash Flow Statement

Especially for companies that are small or have just started out, the cash flow statement can be as important as the income statement and balance sheet combined. Why? Well for one thing, it shows you where the money is. Paper profits and a healthy balance sheet, after all, don't necessarily mean that you have money in the bank. And you can't do business very long without cash.

The cash flow statement monitors the money flowing into and out of your business over a given period of time. The typical statement is divided into two halves: the top half keeps track of where the money comes in from and what it goes out for. The bottom half traces where the funds end up after they're inside your company. Just like the two halves of the balance sheet, the top and bottom halves must be in balance.

COMPANY BALANCE SHEET			
BALANCE SHEET ON DECEMBER 31			
Assets		**Year:**	**Year:**
1	**Current Assets**		
	Cash	+	+
	Investment portfolio	+	+
	Accounts receivable	+	+
	Inventories	+	+
	Prepaid expenses	+	+
	Other____________	+	+
	Total Current Assets	=	=
2	**Fixed Assets**		
	Land	+	+
	Buildings	+	+
	Equipment	+	+
	Other____________	+	+
	Accumulated depreciation	–	–
	Total Fixed Assets	=	=
3	**Intangibles (goodwill, patents)**	=	=
4	**TOTAL ASSETS (add totals 1-3)**	=	=
Liabilities and Owners' Equity		**Year:**	**Year:**
5	**Current Liabilities**		
	Accounts payable	+	+
	Accrued expenses payable	+	+
	Other____________	+	+
	Total Current Liabilities	=	=
6	**Long-term Liabilities**		
	Business loans	+	+
	Bank mortgages	+	+
	Other____________	+	+
	Total Long-term Liabilities	=	=
7	**Owners' Equity**		
	Invested capital	+	+
	Accumulated retained earnings	+	+
	Total Owners' Equity	=	=
8	**TOTAL LIABILITIES and EQUITY (add totals 5-7)**	=	=

Form 7-2: Company balance sheet.

If the cash flow statement is so important, how often should you look at it? If you're starting up a business, you probably can't look at it too often. At the very least, you review your monthly cash flow report. A well-designed cash flow report presents side-by-side numbers for two periods, so you can easily track changes in your cash position.

To see how a cash flow statement is constructed, we check in with Broad Street Emporium, the gift shop. Figure 7-3 shows the cash flow statement as of December 31st for the most recent year, as well as the year before that. By comparing two years in a row, the owners of the gift shop can monitor how their cash positions have changed over time.

BROAD STREET EMPORIUM CASH FLOW STATEMENT			
CASH FLOW AS OF DECEMBER 31			
Inflow and Outflow		**Last Year**	**Previous Year**
1	**Funds Provided By:**		
	Receipts on in-store sales	626,000.	596,000.
	Receipts on catalog sales	+ 106,000.	+ 96,000.
	Dividend and interest income	+ 3,000.	+ 3,000.
	Invested capital	+ 5,000.	+ 10,000.
	Total Funds In	**$ 740,000.**	**$ 705,000.**
2	**Funds Used For:**		
	Cost of goods acquired	461,000.	442,000.
	Sales, general, and administration	+ 127,000.	+ 109,000.
	Interest expense	+ 24,000.	+ 25,000.
	Taxes	+ 22,000.	+ 19,000.
	Buildings and equipment	+ 5,000.	+ 1,000.
	Long-term debt reduction	+ 4,000.	+ 3,000.
	Distributions to owners	+ 85,000.	+ 65,000.
	Total Funds Out	**$ 728,000.**	**$ 664,000.**
3	**NET CHANGE IN CASH POSITION**	**$ +12,000.**	**$ +41,000.**
Changes By Account		**Last Year**	**Previous Year**
4	**Changes in Liquid Assets:**		
	Cash	+ 9,000.	+ 28,000.
	Investment portfolio	+ 3,000.	+ 13,000.
	Total Changes	**$ 12,000.**	**$ 41,000.**
5	**NET CHANGE IN CASH POSITION**	**$ +12,000.**	**$ +41,000.**

Figure 7-3: Creating a cash flow statement helps monitor where the money is.

The two halves of Broad Street Emporium's cash flow statement are divided into sections. The top half lists where the cash funds come from and what they are used for over the statement period. The bottom half looks at where the money ends up, tracking changes in the company's liquid asset accounts. We look at each section individually.

Section 1: Total funds in

The cash flow statement keeps track of all the money coming into your company, no matter where it originates. That's why you find more entries listed in this section than just the revenues reported on your income statement. You may notice another important difference, too. The cash flow statement is more honest than the income statement. You can show the revenue on sales, for example, only when you actually have the money in hand. Yes, we really are talking about the flow of cash here. Take a look at the list of sources for funds coming into the company:

- **Receipts on sales:** The money you take in from sales of your products or services belongs in this section, but only when it's actually deposited in the bank. While billing a customer may be enough to generate revenue on your income statement, the amount of your invoice won't be included here until you have the deposit slip to show for it.
- **Dividend and interest income:** The interest income you make on the money in your business bank accounts and your investment portfolio earnings are recorded on your company's income statement. As long as you receive the money during the period covered by the cash flow statement, the funds appear here, as well.
- **Invested capital:** The money that's invested in your company shows up on your balance sheet as owner's equity. Because this may represent an important source of cash, it also makes an appearance on the cash flow statement when you receive it. This invested capital has nothing to do with the revenues your company generates from business operations, however, so you won't see these amounts appearing anywhere on your income statement.

When totaled together, the funds in this section of the cash flow statement represent every last dollar that comes into your company during the period. Broad Street Emporium took it $740,000 cash during the most recent year. The receipts on sales entry includes all the revenue recorded on the income statement, as well as $3,000 in accounts receivable (see the "Section 1: Current assets" section, earlier in this chapter) that were paid off. Along with the dividend and interest income, an additional $5,000 of equity was put into the company by its owners, bringing the total owners' equity as recorded on the balance sheet to $200,000.

Section 2: Total funds out

When you're in business, you can spend money in a lot of ways. In this section of the cash flow statement, you can see where all that money goes. Only the money that's actually spent is included here. You may notice a number of entries that don't appear as expenses on the income statement. That's because certain cash outlays aren't directly related to the cost of doing business. The following is a review of the complete list:

- **Cost of goods acquired:** The difference between this entry and the cost of goods sold on your income statement has to do with when you actually spend the money. For example, the cost of goods sold on the income statement includes only the items you actually sell and may include items out of inventory that you may have paid for years ago. Cost of goods acquired, on the other hand, covers all the products and materials that you actually purchase and pay for during the period that's covered by the cash flow statement, whether or not they are sold or go into inventory.
- **Sales, general, and administration:** These are the so-called *overhead expenses* that you write checks for day after day, including everything from paperclips to payroll. These are close to the same expenses that appear on your income statement, differing only if you put off bill-paying or decide to pay down your accounts and expenses payable. The difference is based on timing — when the money actually leaves your hands.
- **Interest expense:** Interest expense also shows up on your income statement. The amount here, however, reflects the interest you actually pay during the cash flow statement period.
- **Taxes:** Taxes are an unavoidable part of doing business, so they show up on your income statement. Again, the amount here reflects the taxes you actually pay during the cash flow statement period.
- **Buildings and equipment:** Any big-ticket item that you purchase and pay for shows up on the company's cash flow statement. It also shows up on the balance sheet. However, you won't find it as an expense on your income statement. Why? Because you're really just trading one asset (cash) for another. Your business expense shows up when this brand new asset begins to lose its value over time. To account for that, you're allowed to take a depreciation expense on your income statement every year that the asset's in service, reflecting the slow decline in its value.
- **Long-term debt reduction:** You need cash to pay down any of the business debts you owe and reducing your liabilities often makes for a healthier balance sheet. You can't include these debt reduction payments as business expenses, however. That's why they don't appear on your income statement.

- **Distributions to owners:** If your company makes a profit and your balance sheet is strong, you're probably in a position to give some of the financial rewards back to the owners of the business. For any outside owners, these distributions are the dividends they receive as return on their equity in the business. For small business owners and companies of one, these funds often represent the only paycheck for working long and hard hours. In either case, the distributions come out of your business funds but aren't a cost of doing business, so you won't find them referred to on your income statement.

The funds tallied up in this section of the cash flow statement represent absolutely all the money that goes out of your company coffers over the period. Broad Street Emporium used up $728,000 cash during the most recent year. The cost of goods acquired entry includes all the cost of goods sold on the income statement, plus an increase in inventories of $13,000. Sales, general, and administration reflects a pay down of $1,000 in current liabilities. $5,000 was spent on equipment and $4,000 on long-term debt reduction, increasing equipment assets and decreasing long-term liabilities on the balance sheet. Finally, $85,000 was distributed back to the owners of the gift shop over the year.

Section 3: Net change in cash position

If you subtract all the funds going out of the company from all the funds coming in, you end up with the net change in your cash position over the period. Broad Street Emporium increased their cash position by $12,000 during the most recent year.

Section 4: Changes in liquid assets

The bottom half of the cash flow statement monitors where the money ends up while it's inside your company, including everything from the petty cash box and the business checking account to the investment portfolio you may set up to manage your funds:

- **Cash:** Whether in a cash register or a checking account, this is the place you go first to receive payments and pay your bills. Cash is an asset, so you can find a similar entry on the balance sheet. Here, however, the cash entry tracks only the total change in your cash reserves over the period.
- **Investment portfolio:** If your company owns money market accounts, government bonds, or other securities, they represent assets and can be found on the balance sheet. The entry here tracks only the change in the value of your investment portfolio over the period.

By adding up the individual changes in all your liquid asset accounts, you can determine the net change in your company's overall cash position. Broad Street Emporium increased its cash account by $9,000 and its investment portfolio by $3,000 for a total increase of $12,000 in the most recent year. By the way, if you look at the previous and last year's entries under current assets, you see these changes reflected on the balance sheet.

Section 5: Net change in cash position

Because the top and the bottom halves of the cash flow statement must be in balance, Section 5 should be identical to Section 3. In other words, a net change in cash position can be determined either by subtracting money going out from money coming in, or by monitoring changes to the accounts where the money is coming and going from.

All sections: Your turn

As you begin to assemble a cash flow statement of your own, you may notice that many of the entries are based on the figures that appear on your income statement and your balance sheet. That's not surprising. After all, your company's cash flow is closely tied to your revenues and costs, as well as the assets you own and the debts you've taken on.

If you're already using an accounting package to manage your business finances on the computer, find the appropriate menu and create a cash flow statement. Now that you know how to read it, you can find out all sorts of important information about where and when the money comes into and goes out of your business.

You may find out even more by putting together a cash flow statement from scratch — at least one time. Use the basic template in Form 7-3 to create a cash flow statement for your own company. Each section of the form focuses on a different aspect of your cash flow situation. We've included standard entries on the form, but we've also left space for you to add additional categories.

When Ford teetered on the brink

Big-spending dot-coms aren't the first companies to see their dreams threatened by sudden cash flow problems. When Henry Ford started manufacturing his pioneering automobiles in 1903, he quickly burned through $19,500 in seed money. Where did it all go? $15,000 for motors and other parts, $640 for 64 rubber tires, $31.40 for office furniture, and $7 for fenders. By July 10, 1903, Ford's total cash on hand was down to an alarmingly low $223.65. The 25-day-old company looked as if it was about to sputter to an untimely end.

Then, on July 11, the treasurer recorded a deposit of $5,000 — a life-saving infusion of funds from an investor. Four days later, the company sold its first car. Ford's cash on hand soared to $6,486.44. And the rest, as they say, is history.

COMPANY CASH FLOW STATEMENT			
CASH FLOW AS OF DECEMBER 31			
Inflow and Outflow		**Year:**	**Year:**
1	**Funds Provided By:**		
	Receipts__________	+	+
	Receipts__________	+	+
	Dividend and interest income	+	+
	Invested capital	+	+
	Other__________	+	+
	Total Funds In	=	=
2	**Funds Used For:**		
	Cost of goods acquired	+	+
	Sales, general, and administration	+	+
	Interest expense	+	+
	Taxes	+	+
	Other__________	+	+
	Buildings and equipment	+	+
	Long-term debt reduction	+	+
	Distributions to owners	+	+
	Total Funds Out	=	=
3	**NET CHANGE IN CASH POSITION (Total Funds In – Total Funds Out)**	=	=
Changes By Account		**Year:**	**Year:**
4	**Changes in Liquid Assets:**		
	Cash	+	+
	Investment portfolio	+	+
	Other__________	+	+
	Total Changes	=	=
5	**NET CHANGE IN CASH POSITION (Total Funds In – Total Funds Out)**	=	=

Form 7-3: Company cash flow statement.

In your written business plan, the cash flow statement shows how you intend to manage your one indispensable resource: cash. If your business is already up and running, include year-end numbers for the most recent two years. If you're just getting started, the balance sheet becomes a particularly important piece of evidence to show exactly how you plan to grow to meet the income statement projections you've developed.

Forecasting and Budgeting

After your business is in operation, you can use the three basic financial building blocks — your income statement, balance sheet, and cash flow statement — to paint a financial portrait of your company. By definition, this picture captures only what you once were — and maybe what you are today. It says almost nothing about what your finances will look like tomorrow, next month, or next year. And yet the future is where we're all headed.

There's nothing quite as hard as peering forward and constructing a financial portrait of what your business will look like at some point down the road. Ever heard the saying, "The future ain't what it used to be?" That's exactly why forecasting is so important. Unfortunately, if you're just starting up a business, the task can be especially difficult, because you don't have a financial history to look back on as a guide. We're not going to be able to fill in the numbers for you, but we can outline the steps you have to take as you start to look ahead.

Your financial forecast is constructed around the same three financial building blocks covered in the preceding sections of this chapter. Only this time, the numbers are projected into the future. Based on what you see in your financial future, you can then develop a master budget for your company. This budget sets out the major guidelines for where and how you plan to spend all the money you seeing coming in. But it's more than just a set of spending limits. Your budget is really a financial blueprint for carrying out your business plan, allocating your company's resources in directions that are most likely to see your business succeed.

Your financial forecast

The financial forecast you put together will end up containing all sorts of numbers — revenue predictions, expense projections, and cost estimates. Sound familiar? These are the same kinds of figures that appear on the financial forms covered in the preceding sections of this chapter. But in this case, the numbers aren't really real. Instead, they're based on your best guess about the future — based on a set of assumptions about what you expect to happen down the road.

We can talk about two kinds of assumptions here: assumptions that are right out there on the table and assumptions that remain in the shadows, barely noticed. The first kind are good assumptions, not because they're necessarily correct, but because at least we know what they are. The second kind of assumptions may or may not be right, but because they're hidden, they can be dangerous.

Carefully consider all the business assumptions that go into your financial forecast. Make sure you know what each is based on. For example,

- If you're assuming that the economy will grow at a given rate, state it.
- If you believe you can raise the cash you need from at least three different funding sources, be specific.
- If you're almost certain that a new technology is going to completely change the way your industry does business, explain your reasoning.
- If you think competition will increase in a certain segment of your market, say so.

In other words, spell out what's behind the numbers, because the assumptions you make are just as important as the financial forecast itself.

In the three following sections, we go over exactly what your financial forecast should look like. In addition to the assumptions you make, the forecast consists of three basic financial forms.

Pro forma income statement

Pro forma is one of those strange Latin phrases that sound pretty fancy but actually means something quite simple; in this case, it refers to anything you're going to estimate in advance. So your pro forma income statement is meant to estimate your business revenue, expenses, and profit ahead of time — looking out one, three, or even five years. In fact, you may want to subdivide the first two of these years into quarterly projections, if you can. It's a big undertaking, so take time out to prepare for it by doing the following:

- If you've been in business for awhile, get together your company's income statements for the last several years. If your history doesn't go back that far, use whatever financial information you can get your hands on. Your past income statements can serve as a starting point for the pro forma income statements you're about to create.
- If you're just starting up your business and don't have a company history to fall back on, think about other sources of information in your industry. Search out people in similar businesses, go to trade shows, get on the Internet, and find out if consultants can give you guidance. You may have to invest some real effort here, but if your financial projections end up close to the mark, the results will definitely be worth it in the end.

As you begin to put together your estimates, think about using the company income statement template in Form 7-1. You may also want to review the description of each of the entries on the income statement by referring to the "Putting Together an Income Statement" section, near the beginning of this chapter. When you're finished, your pro forma income statements should look quite similar in format to their real counterparts. That way, you'll have an easy time comparing the future you projected with the future as it really happens.

Remember, the more of these projections you make, the better you'll get at them. To learn from your previous attempts, take time to go back over you pro forma income statements after the quarter or the year is finished. Make notes on where you were right as well as those areas where you need to work on your crystal ball.

Estimated balance sheet

An estimated balance sheet looks very similar to the real thing, which is discussed in the "Creating a Balance Sheet" section, earlier in this chapter. Rather than taking a snapshot of your company at some point back in time, however, the estimated balance sheet tries to take a picture of what your company will look like sometime in the future. In other words, your estimated balance sheet attempts to project what you will own, what you will owe, and what your company will be worth year-by-year — looking ahead four or five years. We know it sounds tough, and it is. But make a stab at this estimate, anyway: Even if it proves to be less than perfect, your estimated balance sheet will provide you with a financial roadmap into the future.

While a pro forma income statement tells you something about what you expect to earn over the next few years, your estimated balance sheet lays out how you expect the company to grow so you can meet those income projections. To put it together, you first look at what assets you think you'll need to support the growth you're looking forward to. Then you have to make some decisions about how to pay for those assets. That means you have to consider how much debt you're willing to take on, what company earnings you'll be able to plow back into the business, and how much equity you need to invest in the future. Needless to say, these are all major decisions.

As you work on your estimated balance sheet, think about using the company balance sheet template in Form 7-2 (see the "Creating a Balance Sheet" section, earlier in this chapter). You may want to review the individual entries on the balance sheet. Form 7-2 works as well looking ahead as it does looking back.

Projected cash flow

As the lyrics of a famous Broadway tune tell us, "Money makes the world go around." That's certainly true in the business world. After the money's gone, the company stops. It's as simple as that. The projected cash flow statement will help you ensure that you'll always have money around when you need it.

Your projected cash flow statement is put together just like a normal cash flow statement. But rather than focus on what happened to the cash last year or the year before, the projection tries to predict where the cash will come from and how it will be used looking ahead anywhere from three to five years. If you can make your cash flow projections quarterly, so much the better. And if your business has built-in seasonal variations, you may want to make your projections monthly.

When you start looking closely at your future cash needs and sources, you may want to take advantage of the company cash flow statement template in Form 7-3 (see the "Constructing a Cash Flow Statement" section, earlier in this chapter). That way, you're able to compare your projected cash flow with your actual cash flow statements.

Your business plan wouldn't be a plan at all without some sort of a financial forecast. So make sure to include your pro forma income statement, estimated balance sheet, and projected cash flow statement along with the business assumptions that go into them. Be prepared to review and revise this financial forecast on a regular basis. Your financial forecast just happens to be one of the most important — and fragile — parts of a business plan, and you have to be able and willing to change it when the business circumstances around you change.

The master budget

The various parts of your financial forecast create a moving picture of your company as it goes forward into the future. While this picture is clearest in the near-term, it can get extremely fuzzy the farther you look out ahead. Fortunately, you can use the sharpest parts of your financial forecast to create a master budget — a detailed spending blueprint that not only reflects your financial picture, but also reinforces what you would like to see happen.

The master budget you put together for your company allows you to do two extremely important things:

- **Live within your means.** When the rough outlines of your company's budget are defined by your projected cash flow statement, your spending guidelines are based on the most realistic financial picture you have. The budget, of course, fills in all the details.
- **Use your money wisely.** The master budget allows you to plan your spending so that it's in line with both your strategy and your business plan. That way, you make sure that funds are allocated in the most efficient and effective way possible to achieve your larger, long-term goals.

To begin your own budgeting process, start with copies of your projected cash flow statements for the next year or two. In particular, review the section that shows where you expect the cash to be used. (Flip to Form 7-3 in the "Constructing a Cash Flow Statement" section.) The categories in your projected cash flow statement are very broad, including cost of goods acquired; sales, general, and administration expenses; buildings and equipment; and distributions to owners. Your job is to break down these broad categories into more manageable pieces, as you begin the process of assigning exactly how much money should be spent on what service or what piece of equipment.

If your company is large enough, you may want to get a few of your colleagues involved in the budgeting process at this point. After all, it's a big job. Working with the key people around you not only spreads some of the effort around but also improves the odds that your management team will buy into the master budget you finally come up with.

While your master budget is a key operational part of your business planning efforts, you have to decide whether you want to include it as a formal part of your written business plan. For the majority of your readers, your financial forecasts — the pro forma income statement, estimated balance sheet, and projected cash flow statement — are usually enough to make them feel comfortable with your future finances.

Forms on the CD-ROM

The following forms on the CD-ROM are designed to help you examine your financial situation.

Form 7-1	**Company Income Statement**	An income statement template that helps you determine your business profits
Form 7-2	**Company Balance Sheet**	A balance sheet template that helps you figure out how much your business is worth
Form 7-3	**Company Cash Flow Statement**	A cash flow statement template that shows you where the money is

Part III

Adjusting Your Plan to Fit Your Needs

The 5th Wave By Rich Tennant

"This is a 'dot-com' company, Stacey. Risk-taking is a given. If you're not comfortable running with scissors, cleaning your ear with a darning needle, or swimming right after a big meal, this might not be the place for you."

In this part . . .

Different kinds of businesses pose different kinds of planning challenges. Starting a not-for-profit organization is a lot different from creating a for-profit company, after all. And putting together a freelance business isn't quite the same as planning a company with a staff of hundreds.

In the four chapters in this part, we help you adjust your business plan to fit the particular business situation you're in. Chapter 8 covers planning issues for self-employed entrepreneurs. Chapter 9 takes on the challenges of small-business planning. And because many new business ventures are based on the Internet and its opportunities, we devote Chapter 10 to planning in the new economy. Finally, in Chapter 11, we take a look at the special planning issues faced by not-for-profit organizations.

Chances are, you'll recognize your own situation in one of these chapters. But we encourage you to browse through all four, because they contain advice and information that you may find useful no matter what kind of business you're planning.

Chapter 8

Planning for the Self-Employed

In This Chapter

- Understanding why you need a business plan
- Choosing where to focus your business planning efforts
- Putting a price on what you do

Almost everyone who's ever felt trapped on the corporate treadmill — or stuck in a long commute — has dreamed of working on their own. "Be Your Own Boss!" the advertisements promise. And what could sound better? No more having someone else tell you what to do. No more having to punch a time clock. No more being at the mercy of supervisors who don't know what they're doing.

The dream of going into business for yourself is even closer now that the Internet makes it possible to work from almost anywhere — whether from a cabin in the Michigan woods or a beach shack on Nantucket Island.

In this chapter, we help you understand that writing down a business plan is really important, even if you're self-employed and the only one who ever reads it. We look at which parts of your business plan are most important. And as part of your financial review, we help you figure out how much to charge for your product or services. Because it's not always easy to go it alone, we point you toward resources that will make your job easier.

Understanding the Benefits of a Written Plan

Suppose you've carefully weighed all the pluses and minuses of working for yourself, and you've decided that the self-employed life is for you. Before you take another step, we want to warn you about the biggest mistake many free-lancers make at this point — a mistake that often comes back to haunt them. You guessed it: They don't create a formal business plan. By formal, we don't mean long and complicated. But we do mean a written document that addresses everything of importance to the business you plan to go into.

The pros and cons of a solo career

Seems like people working on their own have it made. They work when they want to work. They don't have to worry about performance reviews or incompetent bosses. And no one tells them when to start work or when to knock off for the day.

The reality isn't quite so enticing. Oh sure, if you're self-employed, you get to set your own hours. But in our experience that usually means solo careerists work longer and harder than the majority of employees to make their businesses successful. And believe us, that takes a lot of self-discipline. It's true, they don't have to answer to incompetent or unfriendly bosses. But they often have to deal with difficult clients. And frankly, they have to be willing to put up with a system that's stacked against people in business for themselves. Take a look at the pros and cons.

If you work for yourself, you get to:

- Be your own boss
- Determine your own schedule
- Control your own economic fate
- Choose the kinds of work you want to do

But you don't get:

- A regular paycheck
- Employer-provided benefits
- Unemployment insurance and workers' compensation
- Protection under labor laws

We don't want to discourage you from going out on your own — far from it. But we do want you to know exactly what you're getting into. If you're not quite sure whether you're ready to take the big leap, fill out the survey in Form 8-1 (on the CD-ROM). If you answer yes to five or more of the statements, you probably have the discipline to be self-employed. If not, you may want to spend more time mulling over your options.

You may be tempted to rush in without a written business plan. If you're working for yourself, after all, who's going to read the dang thing anyway? So why bother taking the time and effort to put one together in the first place? Because putting together a few good ideas in your head and jotting down a few numbers on the back of an envelope doesn't create a business roadmap you can trust. A written business plan is important for the following reasons:

- The plan represents a formal contract with yourself describing what you intend to do and how you plan to accomplish it.
- A business plan results in a serious business to-do list for putting together the necessary resources you need to get underway.
- A business plan provides you with a set of goals and objectives that you can use as benchmarks to measure your future success.

- Going through the planning process gives you added confidence, and that's key to making a solo career work.
- Having a written plan in place can help you if you run into financial trouble down the road.

Still hoping you can get started without a business plan in place? Take a moment to look at Chapter 2, where we go into even more detail about the real benefits of a business plan. Maybe we can convince you yet!

Knowing What Your Plan Is For

Naturally, the most important target audience for your business plan, if you're self-employed, is you. But if you're like many people we know who work for themselves, you may be surprised to discover that your plan comes in handy for a variety of different purposes — and a variety of different audiences. Here are just a few:

- **If you need a business loan:** Your business plan, especially the financial projections, helps convince a banker or other potential investors that you're serious about a serious business.
- **If you decide to put together a marketing brochure:** Your business plan, with its description of your products and services, your target markets, and your customer benefits, can serve as a guide for what you want to say to potential customers.
- **If you hire an employee or outsource work:** Your plan's perspective gives a new hire or an outside resource person easy access to what you do, what kinds of customers you serve, and how you run your business.
- **If your one-person show grows bigger:** The mission and vision statements in your plan (see Chapter 3) help convey your company's potential to future investors and colleagues alike.

We're sold on the idea of a business plan — even if you're self-employed. But that doesn't mean your written plan needs to be big and complicated. In fact, it may turn out to be no more than a few pages long. Remember, it's mainly there for you.

Defining "independent contractor"

An *independent contractor* is someone who performs specific services for other companies, usually on a project basis. For example, a corporate trainer who contracts with a company to deliver a series of training programs works as an independent contractor. So does a technical writer who works on a project basis to deliver corporate training manuals. On the other hand, a computer programmer who bills by the hour but works onsite for one company almost all the time may not qualify as an independent contractor.

In general, you're an independent contractor if you do the following:

- Furnish your own equipment and materials for your work
- Are paid by the job, not by the hour
- Work for more than one firm at a time
- Pay your own business and travel expenses
- Control how you do your own work
- Set your own working hours

You're probably not an independent contractor if you:

- Work for only one company
- Work at the company's location most of the time
- Are provided company equipment and materials
- Work with other employees on a day-to-day basis
- Are told exactly what to do and when to do it
- Receive company training

The Internal Revenue Service makes a strict distinction between employees and independent contractors — and they don't want companies confusing the two.

Reviewing the Essential Parts of Your Plan

A business plan is almost always divided up into a number of sections. If you need a refresher on what they are, check out Chapter 2 where we describe each component. Fortunately, if you're self-employed, you can skip a few of them:

- You can ditch the executive summary completely.
- You don't have to say much about your company's organization.
- Your company description can be short and sweet.
- The financial review can be basic, as long as it's clear.

Here's some additional encouragement, especially if you're one who breaks into a cold sweat at the thought of writing: You don't need to polish your prose until it's perfect. After you get the key ideas down on paper, you've done what really matters.

We've told you what you don't need to include in your business plan. Now we want to go over the five components of a business plan that are especially important if you plan to go into business on your own. We highlight them because they represent the nuts and bolts of self-employment planning. Along the way, we'll give you some tips on what to focus on in each section.

Company overview

When you're in business for yourself, it's especially important to spend time developing your mission and vision statements. Freelancers and independent contractors tend to assume that they already know what business they're in and what they intend to do. Unfortunately, fuzzy thinking as you start a business can mean that all the work you do later on lacks direction and focus. A strong mission statement clarifies exactly what you hope to achieve, and a clear vision statement can give your new business real direction. For more details, check out Chapter 3.

Well-defined goals and objectives are equally important. For most people, becoming self-employed means entering uncharted waters. You're the captain, the first mate, and the entire crew. So developing practical goals and specific objectives can help keep your business afloat and on course. In the absence of a boss to push you, specific objectives serve as great motivators. And because you'll also be doing your own performance reviews, a practical set of goals serves as an important yardstick to measure your forward progress. For more about setting goals and objectives, see Chapter 3.

Business environment

Self-employed types usually don't find themselves locked in the fierce live-or-die competitive struggles that larger companies sometimes face. Typically, there's room in the regional economy for plenty of construction contractors, self-employed accountants, and freelance editors. But that doesn't mean you can ignore the competition entirely. In fact, your long-term success could depend on knowing who else is out there doing the same kind of work you do. If you're thinking of going out on your own as a tax accountant, for example, you'd better know how many accountants already practice in your part of the world — and whether there's enough business left over for you to get your freelance business off the ground.

Developing a business network

When you're self-employed, the working relationships you establish outside your company can be just as important as the work environment you create for yourself inside the company. So include a discussion of your extended business network in your written plan, highlighting the ways you intend to maintain and expand your most important external relationships.

One way to create your own network is to keep track of all your business contacts and make a point of being in touch at least once a year ("Season's Greetings," anyone?). Try calling associates from time to time just to say hello, see how business is going, and make small talk. Many freelancers find that friendly calls like this often yield new business. If appropriate, consider creating your own newsletter — either in hardcopy or online — as a way to communicate on a regular basis with customers, suppliers, and just about anyone else who may be interested in your business.

Don't be afraid to make contact with people who may, strictly speaking, be your competitors. In fact, these are likely the folks who can be most helpful to you. Typically, you have more to gain by networking with people in your industry than you have to lose. In fact, many freelancers and independent contractors end up referring business to one another — jobs they can't do themselves or don't have time for. And these mutual referrals are a great way to develop a network and build your own business at the same time.

Think about joining a business support group if you want to become part of an instant network. You can find hundreds of them out there. Some represent people involved in the same kind of business, such as writers' unions or editors' guilds. Others may be loose alliances of businesspeople working in the same area. Still others represent specific interest groups, such as women, minorities, or gay businesspeople. If you're not sure how to find a business support group in your area that's appropriate to the work you do, use the checklist included in Form 8-2 (on the CD-ROM).

Tracking key trends in your industry can be just as important. If business is booming in your area, lucky you: Odds are, you can find plenty of work to support your new career. If economic trends don't look so hot, however, you may need to focus additional time and energy on coming up with strategies to attract new customers or clients in a slowing market.

We know a tax accountant who moved into a new and expensive office space at a time when there was more work around than she could possibly take on. What she failed to pick up on, however, was the fact that business growth in her area was actually slowing. What's more, many of her traditional clients — individuals and small businesses — were increasingly turning to tax software programs rather than to her services. With her sky-high office rent and a declining client base, she soon found herself in a real financial crunch. If she'd only taken the time to evaluate the business environment beforehand, she could have saved herself months of anxiety and some difficult business decisions later on.

For more details on assessing your business environment and sizing up both your customers and your competitors, check out Chapter 4.

Company description and strategy

Some parts of your company description and strategy are more important than others when you're self-employed. For example, you shouldn't need to take up too much space describing your organization. If it's appropriate, however, spend a little extra time describing the way your company will operate — how you plan to work with customers, deliver your products and services, get new business, and so on. (And don't forget to talk about the parts of your business you plan to outsource to others.) Check out Chapter 6 for more details.

A big part of your company description and strategy should probably focus on describing your strengths and weaknesses, both personal and business. Why? Because when you're on your own, you may have difficulty being completely honest with yourself about where you shine — and where you fall short. And because you *are* the entire management team and staff, defining your own capabilities and shortcomings is an essential element of effective business planning. If you need some guidance here, look at the personal strengths and weaknesses discussion in Chapter 1 and check out the section on company strengths and weaknesses in Chapter 5.

Let someone else do it: The outsourcing option

You don't have to do it all, of course. Even if you work for yourself, you can still outsource certain parts of your business, getting someone else to take over your bookkeeping, for example, or a piece of your marketing. We know this sounds rather obvious, but it bears repeating: Make sure you have enough time to do what you do best — the very heart and soul of your business. If the time you spend doing accounting gets in the way of the time you need to make money in the first place, hire a bookkeeper.

Some tasks are easier to delegate than others. Bookkeeping is a cinch. You can find plenty of freelance accountants who will spend a couple of hours a week doing the numbers for you. The same goes for tax preparation. On the other hand, outsourcing your marketing activities can be a little more complicated. Even so, if you have better things to do, find a company that will take over for you. Just remember one thing: When you outsource important business functions, you still have to oversee them. After all, you're the boss. If things go wrong, you have no one else to blame.

Your business plan should include a rundown of the business activities you plan to outsource, whom you intend to use, and how much it's likely to cost you. Because outsourcing represents a part of your operating expenses, the estimates should also appear as part of your financial review.

Financial review

This section doesn't have to be long, but it does have to be complete. If you're going to make a success of your solo venture, after all, you have to know how much you plan to make, and how much you plan to spend to get started and keep yourself in business. That means you have to know how much to charge for your products and services, how to budget your expenses, and how to keep up-to-date financial records. In the "Putting a Price on What You Do" section, we take a look at how to put a reasonable price on what you do. For more information on financial statements, forecasting, and budgeting, check out Chapter 7.

Action plan

Creating well-defined goals and objectives is the first step in creating your action plan. But your business plan should also describe, in detail, what you intend to do right off the bat to work toward those goals and objectives. The action plan is just what the name suggests — a nuts and bolts plan of action, step by step, to move your business ahead.

To make sure your action plan covers the most important bases, take the time to describe how you intend both to capitalize on the strengths and to compensate for the weaknesses you've identified. If you're a bit thin in the marketing area, for example, you may include a plan to sign up for a marketing class at the local junior college. If you're a little wobbly when it comes to accounting, your action plan may be as simple as hiring an outside accountant.

Why emphasize the action plan if you're going into business alone? Because, you don't have a supervisor or a boss telling you what to do next. You're the one who has to set the direction, steer a course, and measure your progress. A detailed action plan is one more way to make sure your company stays on track.

Putting a Price on What You Do

Pricing a product or service may seem straightforward at first, but the process can be quite complicated after you get involved in it. On the one hand, you have to figure out what costs go into providing your service or making your product. On the other hand, you have to make sure you're competitive, charging roughly what your competitors charge for similar products or services. And finally, of course, you don't want to short-change yourself.

Knowing how to charge

If you provide a service, for example, the main ways most self-employed professionals charge are as follows:

- By the hour (you establish an hourly rate and keep track of the hours you spend)
- By the project (you and your client agree on a fixed price for a defined amount of work)

We also know of self-employed people who combine these two approaches. A freelance building contractor may bid on a set of plans and establish a fee for the project, for example. But he may also stipulate that any additional work not covered by the contract is to be paid at an hourly rate. You can set up other payment schemes, as well. Freelance authors are often paid royalties every time a copy of one of their books is sold. And some self-employed professionals are paid retainers in return for agreeing to be available to do work whenever they're needed.

If you're unsure about which approach may work best for you, take the survey shown in Form 8-3. Your answers will give you a good idea about how you spend your time and how much time you spend on each business activity. And that should help you determine what kind of pricing structure makes the most sense.

Sometimes freelancers work out innovative payment plans. Consider Stephen King, the best-selling suspense writer. He recently experimented with a novel Internet distribution plan. King invited online readers to download each new chapter of his new book as he finished it — as long as they voluntarily agreed to turn around and send him a few dollars. To keep his readers honest, King stipulated that he would continue writing the book only as long as at least 75 percent of the people who downloaded his chapters coughed up the dough.

The plan worked for a while. But when the ratio of payments to downloads fell to only 46 percent, King was true to his word: He closed the book on his online publishing experiment and stopped writing. But hey, the experiment wasn't a complete bust. The wildly-popular author still made more than $500,000. Not bad for a freelancer. And if and when King gets around to finishing the book, he'll probably sell it to a publisher and start making money all over again.

TASKS AND TIME SURVEY		
Activity	Estimated Hours Spent (Week)	(Month)
Developing new products and services		
Producing your product or service		
Marketing and business development		
Distribution or delivery		
Customer service or client management		
Office management		
Bookkeeping and accounting		
Other:		
Other:		

Form 8-3: Tasks and time survey.

You don't have to be a famous writer to try out an innovative payment scheme. We know of a computer network expert who charges his client companies a monthly retainer. In return, he agrees to keep their computer systems updated and up-and-running. If a client needs him, he's available 24/7. If not, he enjoys his free time. The monthly fees provide him a steady income, month by month. And his clients couldn't be happier. They view the monthly fee as a computer insurance policy that's always in effect.

Knowing what to charge

Whatever payment arrangement you settle on, you still have to figure out exactly how much to charge. If you provide a service of some sort, the easiest way to start is to establish an hourly rate — even if you end up charging by the project or product. After you have an hourly rate in mind, you can estimate the number of hours a job will take, multiply that number by your hourly rate, and come up with the project or product fee.

How to establish an hourly rate? One way involves a little digging to find out what other people doing similar work charge for their services. Suppose you freelance edit. If you check with other freelance editors, you're likely to find that their rates range from about $30 to, say, $100 an hour, depending on where they live and work and how much experience they have. To be competitive, you probably need to stay within that range. If you're just starting out, you may decide to begin at the lower end of the scale. If you already have a long list of credentials and rave reviews from previous clients, you can shoot for the upper end.

Another way to come up with what to charge is based on adding up the following:

- How much you personally need to make each year
- How much it costs to run your business
- How much profit you think your business should make

Divide this total number by the number of hours you expect to work each year, and you'll have a good idea of what you need to charge per hour.

Sound complicated? It's not really, but it does require some basic math. Because the numbers can get a little involved — but just a little — we use, as an example, a custom jeweler setting up a business of her own. Based on her income needs, the jeweler decides that she should earn about $42,000 a year. If she works 40 hours a week, 50 weeks a year — allowing herself a luxurious two-week vacation — she'll put in about 2,000 hours. Of course some of those hours will be spent marketing herself, billing customers, and doing other business chores not directly related to making jewelry. (And any self-employed person with a grain of sense will take off the occasional sunny afternoon for a long walk with the dog or a shopping spree.) So she figures that she's likely to put in about 1500 *billable hours* a year actually making jewelry.

To earn $42,000 working 1500 hours, she'll need to charge around $28 an hour. But that doesn't cover everything. The jeweler must also calculate what it costs her to run the business — everything from telephone charges and postage to the rent on her workshop and the gold going into the gold earrings she fashions. Adding all the expenses together, she figures that running her business costs her about $9,000 a year. If she puts in 1500 hours a year making jewelry, she'll need to add about $6 an hour to cover those costs. She's up to $34 an hour.

But there's one more calculation to make. Like any good business person, she wants her venture to make a profit — extra money that she can use to buy better equipment or even open a studio. She would like to set aside about $4,500 a year toward her long-term business goals. To reach that, she needs to add $3 an hour to her hourly rate. The grand total: $37 an hour. At that rate, the jeweler will make the salary she needs, cover her expenses, and set aside some profit she can put back into the business.

Of course, a jeweler doesn't usually charge customers by the hour, but rather by the finished piece. But using her hourly rate, all she has to do is estimate the number of hours she puts into a piece of jewelry to set its price. A set of original designer gold earrings requiring ten hours of her work, in other words, will cost $370. Now if our jeweler is a good businessperson as well as a good designer, she'll do a reality check at this point: Given her market and her competition, are the jewelry prices she's come up with reasonable? If they are, great. If not, she's going to have to think a little harder about her business model. For more information on business models and other strategies, flip to Chapter 5.

Even if you're self-employed, expect your company to make a profit above and beyond what you pay yourself. After all, this profit is your reward for taking the risk of going into business in the first place. Your company's profit will allow you to expand and develop your business when times are good. And the profits you set aside can also be an important safety net, should your business experience an unforeseen setback.

Take some time out, grab the back of an envelope (a sheet of paper will do), and put together an hourly rate for the work you plan to do. You may want to use Form 8-4 to make sure that you take into account all your business expenses. Check off the categories that apply to you and use the extra space to jot down the rough amounts you expect to spend.

If you provide a service, use the hourly rate you come up with as your initial billable rate. If you provide a product, the hourly rate will help you determine what to charge for each item you produce. In either case, don't forget to do a quick reality check by looking into what your competitors are charging and what your market is expecting in terms of price. You can get a pretty good sense of the price range by talking to prospective clients, customers, and other business owners in your industry. If your hourly rate is way out of line — either too high or too low — review either your income and profit expectations or your estimated business expenses.

Your plan should include all the relevant financial calculations you can make, including how much you intend to charge for your service or product and your projected revenue over the next year or two. (Turn to Chapter 7 for all the information you need on managing the financial end of your business.)

SELF-EMPLOYED EXPENSE CHECKLIST	
Expense Category	**Estimated Cost (week, month, year)**
☐ Rent	
☐ Utilities	
☐ Equipment costs	
☐ Maintenance costs	
☐ Office supplies	
☐ Postage and delivery costs	
☐ Automobile expenses	
☐ Travel expenses	
☐ Business-related meals	
☐ Advertising and marketing	
☐ Clerical or office help	
☐ Accounting and tax fees	
☐ Legal expenses	
☐ Other	
☐	
☐	

Form 8-4: Self-employed expense checklist.

Stay home and get rich fast 'n' easy

Chances are you've seen ads that say you can earn $5,000 to $10,000 a month working at home. Some of them even say *"in your spare time."* Don't believe a word of it. Most of these get-rich-in-your-spare-time schemes are bogus and even downright fraudulent. They seem to be created by the same people who say you can lose 25 pounds in a week.

But that doesn't mean that you can't make good money working for yourself. In fact, according to The Wall Street Journal, independent contractors are typically paid 20 to 40 percent more per hour than employees doing the very same job. Why? Because the hiring firms don't have to pay them additional benefits, including health insurance, sick leave, workers' compensation, and so on. Not only that, the companies have absolutely no obligation to their outside contractors. It's no wonder they can afford to pay higher hourly rates. The only drawback: If you're in business for yourself, you need to think seriously about providing yourself with the most important of these benefits, including a good health plan.

The ranks of the self-employed can also come out ahead by taking advantage of various business-related tax deductions. These include any and all necessary expenses related to your work — as long as the expenses are both reasonable and usual for the type of business you're in. You can even deduct the expenses of running a home office. Check out Form 8-5 on the CD-ROM to help you decide whether working out of your home is right for you, and then take a look at IRS Publication 587 (Business Use of Your Home), which you can get from the IRS Web site at `www.irs.gov`. If you're self-employed, you can also establish your own retirement plan, which can offer significant tax advantages.

Getting paid

Employees have the luxury of picking up a paycheck every week or two. Not so, the self-employed. When you're in business for yourself, you typically send out a bill and then wait — thirty to sixty days is not uncommon. And, of course, you count on your clients to hold up their end of the bargain and actually pay you. Most do, we're happy to report. But sometimes things go wrong. A company (or an individual) may be slow to pay. Worse yet, they may be unable to pay. There's no surefire way to avoid trouble. But the following tips may help:

- Make sure that everyone agrees on the fee. And get it down in writing. A contract signed by all parties will help you later if you have trouble collecting what you're owed.
- Send your bills out on time. The more promptly you bill, the more quickly you'll get paid.
- Get personal. Don't rely on e-mail or letters if you need to push a client to pay. Call on the telephone. Ask to speak to your contact for the project. Get the names of the people in accounts payable or purchasing and call them. Make appointments to visit in person.

- Be persistent. The squeaky wheel gets the grease, as the saying goes. If other creditors are trying to get money, the more persistent you are, the closer you'll get to the front of the line.
- Use small claims court. If all else fails, take your case to court. Small claims courts are designed to resolve disputes involving small amounts of money — usually under $10,000. You can represent yourself, and the process is relatively quick and inexpensive. And if it's any comfort, you won't be alone. Debt collection is the most common case heard in small claims court.

Setting some money aside

A degree of financial insecurity is the price self-employed people pay for the luxury of being out on their own. A fact of life for many independent contractors and freelance professionals is that there are times when the work dries up — and when it does, the cash stops flowing, too.

We can't emphasize this enough: Plan to sock away some money for the dry times. Decide how much you need to provide a financial cushion in case work slows down or a client doesn't pay on time — enough to carry you through a month, two months, six months, whatever. And be conservative! Then try to arrange your business finances so you can build up your cash reserves. And we don't mean in your personal account, either. We mean in a business savings account, where the money's less likely to be raided around the holidays or vacation time.

Giving yourself praise (even a raise)

Being self-employed means that you don't have to put up with a difficult boss or frustrating performance reviews, because, of course, you're the only one evaluating the job you do. But that can also be tricky. It's hard to be genuinely objective about what you do. Sometimes you can be too easy on yourself — or way too hard. That's why having specific business goals and objectives is so important when you're out on your own. You can use them to get an objective sense of what you've done well — and what still needs attention.

Keep in mind that no one else around will pat you on the back and say, "Job well done." So remember to reward yourself when you've worked hard and excelled — either with that gold watch you've always wanted, a trip to a sunny resort, or even a well-deserved raise.

Some people who are self-employed actually tie their raises directly to their own goals and objectives. It's a great way to motivate yourself. Make a pact: If, say, you reach one of your more ambitious goals, give yourself a cash bonus out of the business profits. This may sound a little silly — it's your own money, after all. But many freelancers and independent contractors we know say that similar kinds of incentives help keep them focused and on track.

Forms on the CD-ROM

If you're self-employed, check out the following forms on the CD-ROM to help you plan.

Form 8-1	**Is Self-Employment Right For You?**	A survey that helps you identify the traits needed to be successfully self-employed
Form 8-2	**Checklist of Business Networking Resources**	A checklist of resources you can turn to in order to track down business networking groups in your own industry
Form 8-3	**Tasks and Time Survey**	A survey designed to help you estimate how much time you spend on each area of your business as a self-employed person
Form 8-4	**Self-Employed Expense Checklist**	A checklist to help you get a handle on the various business expenses you can expect when you're self-employed
Form 8-5	**Evaluating Your Home Office Options**	A questionnaire to help you evaluate your home office options

Chapter 9

Planning for a Small Business

In This Chapter

- Creating a plan especially for your small business
- Choosing where to focus your business-planning efforts
- Planning to grow your small business — or not

The big guys like IBM, Ford, General Electric, Microsoft and AT&T may get all the attention in the press. But the real powerhouses driving the nation's economy are — you guessed it — small businesses. Places like Giovanni's Pizzas, Ye Olde Gift Shoppe, Woody's Custom Furniture Studio, and Eye of the Needle Fine Tailoring. Together, small businesses make up well over half of the United States gross domestic product and employ a majority of the country's workforce.

How small do you have to be to be a small business? As far as we're concerned, if you're big enough to be publicly traded on the NASDAQ or the NYSE, you're too big to be a small business. On the other hand, if your company consists of you and you alone, you're self-employed — and we give you your very own chapter (see Chapter 8). The official definition, direct from the Small Business Administration (SBA), is any business that is "independently owned and operated and that is not dominant in its field of operation." So if your company employs fewer than 100 people and has only a few locations, you're a small business.

Does size matter? In many ways, it really does. For example, a large company has to pay a lot of attention to how its many divisions are organized. The organization of a small business is usually pretty straightforward. And while a self-employed person doesn't have to worry about managing employees, the staff of a small business can be one of the major keys to success.

In this chapter, we show you why a business plan is essential to the success of any small business venture — and we point out which parts of the plan are most important to you. We also give you some advice on how to grow your small business bigger.

Recognizing the Importance of a Plan

Big companies wouldn't dream of starting a new fiscal year — or introducing a new product or service — without a detailed business plan. In fact, the largest companies have staffs that do nothing but business planning.

Well, listen up: Business planning is just as critical to the success of a small business as it is to a giant corporation. In fact, according to the Small Business Administration (SBA), *planning ability* is one of the four key components to small business success. (The others are *sound management*, *industry experience*, and *technical support* — find out more at the SBA Web site at www.sba.gov.) So why is planning important to a small business? We could write an entire book, of course. But here are just a few good reasons:

- **Having the necessary resources:** One of the major reasons small companies go out of business is that they don't have the resources they need when they start out. A detailed business plan gives you a good idea of your requirements for time, cash, and people. As part of the plan, you establish your equipment needs, the space you want, and the staff you have to hire. Taken together, these elements determine how much money you'll need upfront, as well as how long you have to wait before your business turns a profit.
- **Getting a small business loan:** Unless you're planning to borrow a bunch of money from your cousin Sylvia, you need a convincing business plan to get a loan from a bank or to attract small business investors. According to the SBA, a good business plan is "a crucial part of any loan package." We second that statement.
- **Shaping a successful business strategy:** The business-planning process requires you to think clearly about your potential customers and your competitors. It also gives you the opportunity to think about your own strengths and weaknesses — and the opportunities and threats you face in your industry and marketplace. If you do all this ahead of time, you can shape a business strategy that has the best possible chance of success.

If you're still not sure you want to take time out to put together a business plan, we suggest you take a look at Chapter 2, which includes even more reasons why business planning is so important.

Knowing What to Focus on in Your Plan

Perhaps you've already started to put together the pieces of a business plan. And if you're like most small business owners, you're probably wondering what you should focus on. After all, we're talking about a small business here. Does the business plan really have to be a big deal?

How to figure out how much you need

If you've never run a company before, you may have trouble guessing how much money you need in the bank to start up a small business. And even if you have some past business experience, unknowns are all around you, whether you branch off in a different direction or decide to start something entirely new. So figuring out how much cash you need to succeed is tough, no matter who you are. In calculating the money you need to get your own small business off the ground, consider two kinds of spending:

- **One-time start-up costs:** No matter what kind of small business you go into, you'll encounter a whole bunch of items that you have to spend money on one time, just to get up and running — everything from the building and equipment you need to a business license and that Grand Opening promotion you've planned.
- **Regular monthly expenses:** After you're open for business, you have all sorts of expenses to deal with, from paying salaries to buying supplies. Over time, of course, you expect that the money coming in will be greater than expenses, creating a profit for your business. But that won't happen overnight. So you have to set aside money to cover your expenses at the beginning. How long? Well, that depends on the business you're in. But a three- to six-month cushion is a good place to start.

To get a better idea of what you should expect when financing your own small business, use the worksheet in Form 9-1 (on the CD-ROM). For a quick, ballpark answer to the big money questions, take the total one-time start-up costs you come up with and add them to the total regular monthly expenses you expect multiplied by the number of months' cushion you think you should have. That number represents the cash that you probably need to lay your hands on if you want to get your business started with some reasonable chance of success.

You can use the figures you come up with in Form 9-1 as a starting point for developing the financial statements that you include in your written business plan (see Chapter 7). Just don't forget to include the assumptions you make as you put the numbers down on paper.

No, it doesn't have to be a big deal. But if it's going to help you be successful, it should cover all the major issues that determine the resources you need, your financial situation, and the strategy to make it all work.

In our experience, we've found that certain parts of a business plan are worth emphasizing if you're a small business. In the following sections, we share the five that deserve the most attention — and why.

Business environment

Your business environment covers everything around you that affects your company, from the industry you're in to your customers and your competition. Now when real estate agents talk about the housing business, the three most important factors they come up with are location, location, location. The same goes for many small companies when considering their business environments: Location often determines who your customers are and who you compete against.

Location is especially important to small retail businesses. It's true: Mail-order or Internet businesses can put their headquarters wherever they want. After all, who the heck cares where kitchensink.com is located, anyway? But if you're planning to sell to a local clientele, where you place your shop or office — on a busy thoroughfare or on a less-traveled alleyway — can mean the difference between success and failure. So make sure you spend serious business-planning time considering where you intend to locate your business, and then weigh the pros and cons of the location you finally choose. For more details on evaluating your location as well as other aspects of your business operations, check out Chapter 6.

Even if you aren't in retail, location can be critical to a small business. Suppose you're starting a small software company, and you know you need highly-trained software engineers. You have to locate your company in a place where these kinds of people live — or at least are willing to move.

Uncle Sam's helping hand

The Small Business Administration (SBA) has a mandate from Congress to help small businesses with their financial needs. In other words, the SBA loves to hand out money to small companies just like yours. The SBA does its good deeds through four specific programs. These include:

- **The 7(A) program:** Providing financing for a variety of general purposes, this is the most flexible loan program the government offers to small businesses. The money can be used to acquire or to start up a business or to meet special financing needs such as a specific contractual obligation or mandatory export financing requirements.
- **The 504 program:** Also known as the Certified Development Company, this program has been established to help finance the purchase of big-ticket items by small businesses using fixed interest loans in combination with additional outside financing and equity.
- **The micro loan program:** This is where you go to get very small loans, usually under $25,000. The SBA provides funds to an outside micro lender who then makes the actual loan to a small business.
- **The Small Business Investment Company (SBIC):** The SBIC program supports the creation of independent investment companies that provide equity capital to invest in small businesses as well as long-term loan financing when required.

To find out more about any of the Small Business Administration programs, check out the agency's Web site at `www.sba.gov`.

Company description

Your company description is the component of your business plan that states, as clearly and succinctly as possible, what kind of business you're in and what you look like as a company. If you succeed here, anyone reading your plan will know exactly what you intend to do, how you intend to do it, and what's going to make you special.

Why is this so important for a small business? Usually it has to do with one word: Money. Most small companies have to take out business loans or enlist the help of outside investors to round up the cash they need to get started. And the best way to convince a loan officer or an investor that your business idea can be turned into a business reality is to describe what you intend to do so persuasively that they can't say no.

There's another reason why it's absolutely essential to spend serious time on your company description. Many small business owners begin their adventure with nothing but a dream. Maybe it's the dream of running a small surf-and-ski shop. Or of turning a hobby like collecting baseball cards into a retail business. That's how it should start, of course. But to go forward, you also need at least one foot grounded firmly in business realities. Describing your business in a business plan forces you to face those realities — and in the end, that can help you keep your dream alive.

Company strategy

Your company strategy needs to lay out exactly how you intend to accomplish your key business goals. A big piece of that strategy centers around the marketplace. No matter how big or small you are, you have to figure out how to communicate with customers — understanding what they want and fulfilling their needs. But as a small business owner, you have to pay special attention to the details, because you'll probably end up doing much of the work yourself. So spend a little extra time during the planning process to make sure you have a marketing strategy in place that you and your small business can actually carry out.

Another reason we focus on marketing strategy is that it's too often overlooked completely by small businesses. We know you may assume, in the excitement of starting up a small company of your own, that customers will simply appear after you turn on the lights and open the door. But hey, they still have to hear about you somehow. And not all of them will be as excited as you are. Your marketing strategy offers the chance for you to explain how you plan to reach customers in the first place, and then how you plan to convince them to buy what you sell.

Financial review

Finances are almost nobody's idea of a good time. But a complete financial picture of your company — including planned income, estimated balance sheet, and cash flow projections — are absolutely critical if you're a small business.

Too many small businesses go belly-up either because they don't have the necessary financial resources upfront, or they don't have the cash flow required to sustain themselves down the road. And that's a shame. We could tell sorrowful tales of promising small businesses with everything going for them except enough money to really get going in the first place — businesses that could be prospering today if only they'd planned their financing better or small companies that were sailing smoothly along, only to be capsized by a sudden cash flow problem they just hadn't planned for.

We'll spare you the details here. For a step-by-step guide on how to put together your financial picture, flip to Chapter 7.

For the IRS's view on financial and tax matters, go to the horse's mouth. Check out Business Expenses (IRS Publication 535), Tax Guide for Small Business (IRS Publication 334), and Small Business tax Workshop Workbook (IRS Publication 1066). The three publications are available on the IRS Web site at www.irs.gov.

Action plan

Your action plan includes all the steps you intend to take to carry out your business plan, focusing first on the most immediate and pressing tasks at hand. After you have your financial house in order, the biggest challenge you often face as a small business owner has to do with putting together a top-notch staff. Especially if your company depends on skilled labor — and most businesses do these days — your action plan should pay particular attention to how you plan to find and keep the very best employees out there.

A perfectly good business can fail simply because the owners can't hold on to skilled workers. We're not talking about people with advanced degrees here, either. A high-end restaurant had better be able to attract and keep good waiters and waitresses — or customers won't come back. And a small custom print shop can't survive for long without people with the technical background to get the job done right the first time around.

Putting together a winning team

If getting and holding onto top quality employees is absolutely crucial to your small company's long-term success, your written business plan should describe exactly how you intend to keep a top-notch team in place. Of course, this requires you to make a few organizational decisions right up front. For starters, decide on the number of employees you need to operate your business and determine precisely what each of them will do. You can use Form 9-2 (on the CD-ROM) to fill in the duties, responsibilities, experience, and qualifications for each position you come up with.

After you have your job descriptions in hand, how can you find the top-notch employees you need? Well, be prepared to work at it. We've put together a checklist of some of the most common ways to search for qualified people in Form 9-3 (on the CD-ROM): Check off those that seem most appropriate to your own situation.

Finding qualified employees is only half your battle. The other half is figuring out how to keep them onboard. Top salaries and good benefits are great ways to win loyalty, of course. But other intangible qualities in a company can increase job satisfaction — things that don't necessarily require additional resources. We've included the most common strategies that small businesses use to retain good employees in Form 9-4 (on the CD-ROM). As you begin to think about ways to make your own work environment more rewarding and satisfying to all your employees, look over the checklist and make note of the ones you may want to consider.

As a small business, you have to do more that just hire and keep good people — you have to make a team out of them. Employees in a small organization end up working closely together: They share tasks and responsibilities, and they pitch in when someone else is unavailable. That means that individuals who are motivated and groups that can really collaborate with each other are key to making your business work. If you think you need to focus more on teamwork, take a look at the tips we've put together in Form 9-5 (on the CD-ROM). Sure, many of them are just plain common sense, but taken together, they can go a long way toward promoting a healthy, productive workplace environment for your small business to thrive in. For more details on developing an organization and working with employees, check out Chapter 6.

Growing Your Small Business

Rome, as the saying goes, wasn't built in a day. (Heck, it's still not done!) The same goes for many companies, including your own. You need time to grow your business — to improve products and services, reach more customers, attract new clients, and create an effective organization to support everything. And growing bigger can be tough, especially if you start out really small.

As a small business owner, you face all sorts of obstacles when you try to get a bit bigger. The highest hurdles typically include getting noticed by a wider audience, and then managing all the changes that come along if you actually succeed in getting noticed.

Making a name for yourself

If you plan to set up shop along the busiest street in town, maybe customers can't help but stumble through your doorway. But even then, you have to spend a little time and money getting the word out about your business if you want to grow bigger. In other words, you'll have to do some marketing — figuring out how to bring more customers in and then keep them coming back.

Marketing is important to any kind of business, large or small. But it's especially important for a small company to think carefully about the ins and outs of reaching customers as part of a business plan. Why? Larger companies can afford to hire experts to create a marketing strategy. The big guys can also afford to spend big bucks on promotions and advertising to get their name and products out in front of customers. Small businesses usually can't — so they have to rely on careful planning and clever marketing strategies.

As a small business owner, you will probably end up doing most of your marketing all by yourself. Unfortunately, it's all too easy to put business development at the bottom of your daily to-do list because marketing isn't often a burning issue, and you always have another business fire to put out first. But you neglect this part of your business at your own peril. After all, if you don't reach out to your customers and communicate with them on some level, you're going to lose their business over time.

What do you need to consider when you're in change of marketing plans? First, spend time thinking about who actually buys your product or service — and why. For details on describing your ideal customer, take a look at Chapter 4. Then think of clever ways (ways you can afford) to reach those customers and promote what you have to offer. Form 9-6 (on the CD-ROM) provides a checklist of the most common ways that small businesses promote themselves and develop new business. Of course, not all of them work for every company. Take time to check off the promotional ideas that seem most promising to you.

Make sure your written business plan includes a section on marketing or business development that describes who your ideal customers are and how you intend to reach out to them. In particular, if you have any promotional plans or new business initiatives in the works — an ad on TV during the Super Bowl (nice try) or giving out mugs with your logo on them during a local Super Bowl party — put them in your plan, as well.

Managing change

Petaluma, California — population 50,000 or so — isn't exactly a bustling metropolis. Fifty miles north of San Francisco, it began life as the egg capital of America more than a century ago. Until recently, through economic ups and downs, it has remained a charming little town. But as the California economy has boomed, whole new housing developments have sprung up, seemingly overnight. There's a growing telecom industry on the outskirts of town. A dozen shops in the historic downtown have gone out of business and new shops have come along. The old shoe repair shop and the family-run men's clothing store are gone — but a new high-end gift shop and a chic gallery just opened, a couple of day spas are thriving, and it's hard to get reservations at the half a dozen new restaurants.

The point of our little story, of course, is that change is an inevitable part of the economic landscape, whether you're in a big city or a small town. And change is coming faster than it used to. A small business is especially vulnerable to change. Imagine a luxury ocean liner: When it encounters a little squall, the passengers barely feel it. The same is true for large companies. They can weather economic downturns or changes in the marketplace. Small businesses, however, are like small boats — and small towns. The winds of change can bounce them around pretty hard and, sometimes, capsize them completely.

If you want to be successful over the long haul, you have to navigate through all the changes that are bound to happen. How do you do it? First, keep an eye on the horizon, watching out for what may be coming along. Second, be ready to change course or shift position to avoid trouble or take advantage of good winds and strong currents.

Okay, enough with the nautical metaphors. In the real world of business, change can take on many forms. But most of the changes you're likely to see fall into one of five main areas:

- **The economy:** *Economic change* refers to the state of the larger marketplace and is usually measured in terms of the ups or downs of interest rates or inflation, or changes in the value of one currency in relation to another.
- **Technology:** Changes in technology may mean the introduction of a brand new technology or new ways of using an old technology. While a change in technology can result in a new product or service, it may also lead to process improvements — better ways of manufacturing a product or delivering a service or new ways to better serve customers.

- **Business trends:** Changes in the business climate may result from new competitors coming into an industry or area, or companies getting out. Business trends may open new markets and close off others.
- **Cultural change:** Everything from a change in the *demographics* of an area — population shifts, age differences — to social and lifestyle changes affect industries and markets. While these changes are often gradual, they can be extremely powerful and almost impossible to escape.
- **Government affairs:** The government's influence over business often takes the form of new regulations, legislation, or court rulings, and may be based on longer-term shifts in federal, state, or local political agendas.

If you feel you need more information on any of these areas, pick up a copy of *Business Plans For Dummies* by Paul Tiffany and Steven Peterson (Hungry Minds, Inc.).

After you identify the trends and changes that are most likely to affect you, begin to keep track of the specific issues and events that could well play a significant role in the future of your small business — a pending legal case, an emerging technology, or an upcoming regulatory decision. And make sure you address each of them in your written business plan.

Growing or not growing

One reason the Small Business Administration (SBA) exists is that so many small businesses exist. They not only dominate in terms of sheer numbers, they're responsible for a large chunk of the world's economic activity, as well.

Some businesses will always remain small: The gift shop featuring the works of local artists, for example, or the Laundromat around the corner, or the deli and diner down the street. Other businesses start small and grow up to become big — sometimes very big. Starbuck's began as a local Seattle coffee shop. Apple Computer's first headquarters was in a garage. When a small business grows into a giant corporation, it's not by accident. Behind that growth is a well-thought-out business plan along with the drive and the resources to get there. And it's not for everybody.

An entrepreneur we know started a stereo shop in a small Illinois town a few years back. The store was just the kind of friendly, cluttered, slightly disorganized place you'd expect to see in a college town. But the salespeople who worked there really knew and loved audio equipment. And by keeping his overhead very low, the young owner was able to offer great components at very competitive prices. That unbeatable combination soon made the store a huge success — and our friend began to dream of turning his solo shop into a chain of stores throughout the Midwest.

We'd like to say that this idea sounded good on paper. But the guy never even put his business plan in writing. He began building inventory and leasing storefronts without once thinking about how he would find knowledgeable sales teams, promote the new stores — or create an organization that could manage the jump from one shop to half a dozen. The laid-back, disorganized style worked okay for a single store with a garage-worth of inventory. But it turned out to be a disaster for the small chain. The original store's profits were soon eaten up by losses from the new outlets. Six months later, our friend went back to school, even though he already had a brand new business degree from the school of hard knocks.

A well-crafted business plan may have helped this young entrepreneur avoid disaster. But even before the planning, he should have asked himself one simple question: Do I really want to grow my business? As we've said, some small businesses are meant to remain small. And some business owners are meant to run small companies. In this case, our friend loved audio equipment, worked well with his sales team, and had a great rapport with the customers who came through his door. But he wasn't particularly well organized or good at delegating — the two main characteristics he needed to run a larger operation.

Before you make plans to grow your own small business into something bigger, take time to ask yourself whether you really want to manage a larger company:

- How will the day-to-day operations of the company have to change?
- How will my own duties and responsibilities be different?
- What additional skills will I need to make the growing business work?
- What weak points or limitations do I have that may get in the way?

Don't be discouraged if your answers make you think twice about growing your business into something bigger. Not every business is suited to expand — and not every small business owner really wants to manage a big organization. Many are perfectly happy and successful staying small. However, if your answers give you confidence that growth is a smart move, it's time to buckle down and really start planning. Turn to Chapter 5 for more details on the ways that companies typically grow — along with a checklist of critical resources you'll need as your own company begins to grow.

Forms on the CD-ROM

If you're part of a small business, check out the following forms on the CD-ROM to help you plan.

Form 9-1	**Start-up Costs Worksheet For Small Business**	A worksheet designed to give you an idea of how much cash you need upfront to get a small business off the ground
Form 9-2	**Job Description Profile**	A template designed to capture all the relevant information that should be included in a job description
Form 9-3	**Job Recruiting Checklist**	A checklist of places small businesses can go to find qualified employees
Form 9-4	**Employee Retention Checklist**	A checklist of strategies to help you improve overall employee job satisfaction
Form 9-5	**Tips on Promoting Teamwork**	A list of ways you can promote a sense of team spirit and teamwork in your own company
Form 9-6	**Ways to Promote Your Small Business**	A checklist of ways you can promote your small business

Chapter 10

Planning in the New Economy

In This Chapter

- Planning an Internet-based business
- Making e-business work for you
- Sticking with your business in tough times

When you asked experts in the early 1980s what the future had in store, they envisioned everything from mining colonies on the moon to micro-robots that could travel through our bloodstreams, diagnosing disease along the way. But the one thing almost none of them predicted was the real revolution that was just around the corner: the emergence of a vast global network of interlinked computers we now fondly refer to as *the Net.*

In an astonishingly short time, the Internet has become a household word and a part of life from New York City to Bombay, India, transforming the way we live and work in profound ways. Who would have thought you'd be able to zap a letter instantaneously from Athens, Georgia to Athens, Greece — and not just a simple note, but a packet including pictures of the kids, important business documents, even your favorite music? And who could have imagined that you'd be able to track a package, step by step, as it makes its way across the country? Or that you could specify the exact computer system you want, down to the last peripheral, and submit your order from your bedroom with a click of the mouse? For that matter, who would have imagined a mouse in every house?

With change coming along so quickly, business gurus started talking about more than just new technologies. They envisioned a whole new economy, with brand new rules and revolutionary ways of doing business. Well, in some ways there really is a new economy out there, but many of the old rules still apply, even on the Internet. Rules like, investors in a business eventually expect to see some profits or at least the possibility of profits. And to become profitable, a company first needs a source of revenue. And for that, you gotta have a business model that makes clear exactly where the money will come from. Basic stuff.

Don't get us wrong: Opportunities on and around the Internet are everywhere, for traditional bricks-and-mortar companies and Web-based ventures alike. But now that the first wild-west days of Internet speculation are over, the old-timers have a more realistic sense of what it takes to succeed in the new economy. And success, almost everyone agrees, begins with an old-fashioned business plan.

In this chapter, we help you plan an Internet business or add on a Web-based component to your existing business. Because speed is of the essence, we show you how to streamline the business planning process and zero in on what really matters.

Planning at Internet Speed

Ask most high-tech entrepreneurs to tell you what sets the new economy apart from the old economy, and they're likely to give you a one-word answer: *speed.* (That's assuming you can catch them running between a meeting with venture capitalists and a pow-wow with the engineering folks.) Ever since the first dot-coms debuted, speed to market has been seen as the key to success on the Internet. If you're not the first to get your Web site up and running, the first to get your name up on billboards, or the first to exploit a new technology, look out. Chances are, you'll be playing catch-up with one of your competitors.

Why all the rush? For one thing, the technologies that drive the new economy continue to change at lightning speed. In addition, because the barriers to creating an Internet presence are low — anyone and his mother, it seems, can start a Web site, and probably already has — competitors appear overnight and out of nowhere. The Internet is still a business frontier, with extraordinary opportunities and grave risks. Those companies that succeed will be the ones that are nimble, flexible, and fast.

Another reason business seems to be changing so fast is uncertainty. Everyone assumes the Internet will transform retail business. But how? No one really knows. You can find widespread agreement that the publishing, music, and movie businesses will be radically altered. But which way and when are anyone's guess. The Internet is transforming the ways that businesses do business with each other. But it's far from clear who will benefit and who won't.

So the rules of doing business on the Internet change as quickly as the stock price of the latest IPO (initial public offering.) This rapid change has made life in the world of e-business as exciting and fast-paced as a shoot-'em-up western. And for some companies, just as dangerous.

Reviewing four lessons from the wild west

By now, the new economy has been around long enough that a few basic lessons have emerged. You can avoid some of the pitfalls that other e-businesses have fallen into by taking them to heart.

Planning is critical in a fast-changing environment

We're the first to admit that making plans when everything around you is changing isn't easy. You can't necessarily rely on your customers to behave like they used to in the old economy. You can't assume that you understand what your competitors will do next. And you can't always count on the tried-and-true business models that have guided traditional businesses in the past.

But these truisms make the need to plan all the more important. The simple fact remains that the more thoroughly you assess your current business environment, focus on the competition, and try to understand your customers, the better chance you have of anticipating the future — rather than falling victim to it.

A clear mission and vision help set a steady course

Creating a strong sense of mission and a compelling vision for your company (see Chapter 3) will help you reach your long-term business goals. Sure, being flexible and ready to adapt as conditions change is absolutely essential. But you still have to know who you are and what you plan to do as a company, or you risk getting blown way off course. Plenty of big players have lost their focus, only to find themselves directionless and dead in the water.

Silicon Graphics, for example, began its life as a developer of animation and 3-D imaging software. Then it transformed itself into the maker of powerful computers that could create the complex 3-D images its software produced. Next came a detour into the TV cable-on-demand delivery business. When that went nowhere, the company tried to turn itself into a general computer workstation manufacturer. Now Silicon Graphics is trying its luck once again, this time by making workstations that run on Linux, an open-source operating system that competes with Microsoft Windows. We can't help but think that a strong and compelling sense of mission would have helped the company avoid a few of its highly-publicized zigs, zags, and dead ends.

A plan can support quick, well-informed decisions

The short history of e-business is chock full of stories about canny entrepreneurs who sensed that change was afoot, repositioned their business strategy — and then hit it big. Take Yahoo!, for example. The venerable Internet giant began life as a simple Web site listing service. Then it began to review and rank those Web sites. Now it's a full-service Internet portal with its own suite of content developers. Given the extraordinary pace of change, major strategic decisions like the ones Yahoo! has made often have to be made on the fly, relying on intuition, experience — and a strong business plan. A solid and carefully researched plan can provide the foundation for making quick, well-informed decisions when time is of the essence and change is everywhere.

Business planning is no longer a once-a-year task

The most successful e-businesses make planning a continuous process. They constantly scan the business environment and monitor their company's own performance. They continuously assess new technologies and their impact on the marketplace. They listen to customers all the time. And they're ready and willing to adjust pieces of the business plan whenever the need arises. Luckily, many of the same technologies that drive e-business also make easy work of tracking all sorts of information in real time — how many people visit your Web site, for example, what they do there, who looks at what, who buys what. To stay agile, the best e-businesses are finding ways to incorporate this wealth of data into an ongoing business-planning process.

Zeroing in on what matters most

Maybe you're convinced that a business plan is not only nice to have but absolutely essential in the new economy. Perhaps you've already started to put together a written plan of your own, knowing it's a requirement to raise the cash you need. At the same time, you know the clock is ticking. That window of opportunity isn't going to stay open for long. So how can you streamline the planning process?

The best advice we can offer you is to concentrate first on what really matters — and then fill in the details later on. That's why we put together Form 10-1 (on the CD-ROM). It's a checklist of the key steps in e-business planning. Going through these steps forces you to think seriously about the special issues, opportunities, and hurdles presented by the new economy. As you complete each step, use Form 10-1(on the CD-ROM) to keep track of your progress.

If you get stuck along the way, consider the following as food for thought:

- **Evaluate the business environment.** In the early days of e-business, online entrepreneurs assumed that if they built a Web site, visitors would find their way to it. Well, that just doesn't work anymore. With the proliferation of Web sites (over 100 million and counting), getting customers to visit yours turns out to be a real challenge. Getting them to buy something is even harder. That's why you must assess the competitive forces at work in your own particular corner of the Internet. Chapter 4 is all about assessing your business environment.
- **Estimate your upfront costs.** One of the biggest mistakes many e-businesses make is underestimating how much it will cost to develop (or purchase) the necessary software, set up the hardware, develop the

content, and get their Web sites up and running — not to mention how much they'll spend maintaining those sites after they're off the ground. To create a realistic budget, you need to do your financial homework. If you need more help in putting together a budget that doesn't leave anything out, flip back to Chapter 7.

- **Fine-tune your business model.** You can't expect your e-business to succeed in the long run if you're not quite sure about revenues. You absolutely have to know where the money's going to come from. And that means having a workable business model in place well before you start burning through your start-up dough. Identifying a successful business model hasn't been all that easy in the new economy. Luckily for you, the experiences of other companies on the Net — good, bad, and ugly — are beginning to provide some useful guidelines. Take a look at Chapter 5 for an overview of business models.
- **Create a realistic business timeline.** Wouldn't it be nice if you had all the time in the world to plan your e-business and make it work? Sure it would, but you don't. After all, we're talking about the Internet. Yet even at Internet speeds, you need time to create a business, find customers, generate revenues, and make a profit. A realistic business timeline lets everyone know exactly what to expect, from investors to employees. We could list plenty of failed e-businesses that may have succeeded if only they'd had a little bit more time. Their mistake: Failing to create an honest timeline that laid out how long their start-up cash would last and how much time they needed to be successful. For a general look at business time frames, flip to Chapter 2.
- **Build flexibility into your plan.** Most business plans include contingencies — "what if" scenarios that provide alternatives in case something goes wrong. Contingency planning is especially important for an e-business. For one thing, the e-marketplace is still in its infancy, and experts are still trying to figure out what really drives Internet buying behavior. Even the basic business rules of the new economy are still shaking out. So these days, a business plan that depends on Internet advertising revenue must also include a contingency, just in case those ad dollars don't come rolling in as expected. And a Web site that's betting on customer loyalty for return business better have an alternative in place, on the off chance that those online customers are more fickle than you think.
- **Plan for the people you need.** A top-notch staff is important, whether you're opening a hair salon on Main Street or a financial Web site on the Internet. But experience tells us that a strong staff of highly committed employees is essential to the success of an e-business. Given the pace of new Internet ventures, employees are often asked to work long hours under some pretty fierce pressure. What's more, high-tech companies usually need highly trained technical people — a scarce commodity these days. So if your business venture requires top-flight software engineers or skilled content providers, make sure your business plan addresses exactly how you intend to find them, recruit them, and keep them onboard.

Create an online customer profile

Whether you're planning a brand new Web-based business or simply adding an Internet extension to a more traditional business, it's important that your business plan describe the kinds of customers you hope to attract — and how they'll behave after they get to your Web site. In fact, it's not just important, it's *essential.* If you hope to start a B2B (business-to-business) e-company that brings together printers, designers, writers, and graphic artists, for example, you better include something about what these people do, how they think, and what they expect when they go online. And if you're planning an online consumer magazine, you'd better talk about what your prospective readers (and consumers) are looking for when they turn to the Internet.

We know this sounds rather obvious. But it's not as easy as you may think, so don't be surprised if you don't come up with all the answers right away. Even the thousand pound e-gorillas, like Amazon, are still trying to figure out exactly what makes their online customers tick (or click).

If you need some help, take a look at the questionnaire we've put together in Form 10-2 (on the CD-ROM). Your answers should capture the key characteristics of your most likely online customers, and begin to fill in the outlines of an online customer profile. For additional details on how to size up your customers, flip back to Chapter 4.

Building a Stand-Alone Internet business

For a while during the late 1990s, people thought we would all end up spending our lives in cyber-cafes and cyber-boutiques doing cyber-shopping and cyber-chatting and being entertained by cyber-sports and cyber-music. Well, enough already.

In reality, very few new economy businesses operate entirely out there in cyberspace, conducting all their operations and business over the Internet. Amazon.com is perhaps the most famous e-business in the world — and an awful lot of its operations don't have anything to do with cyberspace — stocking warehouses, for example, or filling orders and seeing to it that the goods get delivered to customers the old-fashioned way, by truck or plane. In fact, Amazon.com recently began printing catalogs — real ink and paper catalogs, just like the old Sears catalog, for heaven's sake — and sending them along with their shipments. You can't get much more old economy than that!

Perhaps a purer form of e-business may be just down the road. E-books, for example, offer a possible glimpse into the future. Sooner or later, these digital tomes may really catch on and completely transform the way books are sold and distributed. A few pioneers are already selling digital books that are delivered directly over the Internet. And, of course, you can download plenty of music straight from the Net — even as judges, lawyers, and politicians argue over copyright infringement. Movies, too, will eventually be sold and delivered directly to your digital entertainment system. But for now, anyway, most online businesses find themselves using a business model that combines the latest technologies with more traditional operations — trying to figure out, on the fly, exactly where the true value of the Internet lies as they attempt to satisfy today's customers.

Fine-tuning your value proposition

To increase the odds that your e-business model is going to come through for you, think about approaching it from a brand-new direction. Step back and consider your business model from your customers' point of view: What's in it for them? What are you really providing your customers, and what value do they place on it?

Business types combine the answers to these questions into something they call the *value proposition* — fancy jargon for a simple idea. Now you'd think a company's value proposition would be pretty obvious:

- Wal-Mart offers the cheapest prices around on a wide range of merchandise.
- Rolls-Royce offers unparalleled luxury and the ultimate in snob appeal.
- Travelocity.com offers cheap airline tickets to anywhere in the world.

But there's often more to the real value proposition that a company provides its customers than first meets the eye — even more than many businesses themselves realize.

Think about Amazon again. The Internet company sells its books and other merchandise at a discount, so part of its value proposition is clearly based on low prices. But Amazon also happens to stock one of the largest inventories of books anywhere in the world. Thus, having a wide selection is also part of its value proposition. And Amazon's appeal to book lovers doesn't stop there. The online bookseller invites readers to review and rate books — a feature that many customers like so much that they wouldn't dream of shopping for books anywhere else. In addition, customers can read recent book reviews from magazines, newspapers, and other media with the click of a mouse. They can also usually look over the first chapter of many of the books on sale. Each one of these features represents additional customer value.

What does all this have to do with your own business model? Plenty. Customers are willing to pay what they place value on. So the more clearly you understand the real value your e-business offers, the better sense you'll have of what customers are actually buying — and what they're paying for. And that, of course, is what your business model is all about.

To help you zero in on the real value your e-business will offer customers, we've put together a simple value proposition worksheet. Before you fill it in, however, take a look at Figure 10-1, which shows how a brand new travel-related Web site we'll call Cultural Escapes completed a similar questionnaire.

E-BUSINESS VALUE PROPOSITION WORKSHEET

1. Write a one-sentence description of your e-business:

Cultural Escapes offers visitors to its Web site personalized travel information packages tailored to their specific cultural interests, from arts and music to language studies and culinary adventures.

2. Describe three or four of the most important features on your Web site:

- A personal profile that allows visitors to describe the kinds of information they want to see presented about travel destinations under consideration
- A customer feedback feature that allows users to give their own reviews of restaurants, hotels, museums, performances, tours, cruises, cities, and countries
- An online "classified lodging" section that allows travelers to arrange short-term rentals or house-swaps with people in other parts of the world
- E-mail alerts and travel reminders highlighting special events, exhibits, performances, and limited-time travel offers

3. List three or four benefits customers receive when they visit your Web site:

- The most comprehensive and up-to-date cultural information about travel destinations available anywhere
- The ability to tailor information to meet personal interests, such as concert schedules, gallery openings, and well-reviewed restaurants in a given destination
- The chance to hear what other like-minded travelers are saying about popular and undiscovered travel destinations

4. Looking back at #3, describe the essential value that customers take away:

- Access to timely, reliable, personalized travel information
- Time-savings when it comes to the travel planning process
- Peace of mind about major travel-related decisions

5. Think about your ideal customers. What's the best thing they can say about your e-business?

They can count on us to provide them complete, reliable, and up-to-date information about travel destinations that's tailored to their own personal needs and interests.

Figure 10-1: Using the e-business value proposition worksheet to discover why customers come to your Web site and what they take away.

The mystery of the abandoned shopping cart

Imagine someone going into a store, taking the time to fill a shopping cart full of all sorts of things, and then abruptly walking away, abandoning the cart and leaving the store without purchasing a single item. Strange? It certainly would be at your local grocery or department store. But it turns out that this sort of thing happens all the time at online retail stores. At BooksAMillion or LetsBuyIt, for example, customers routinely prowl around the online aisles, select this and that, fill up their shopping carts — and then all of a sudden, they vanish. Poof.

Understanding why this sort of thing happens is just one of the goals of a new research facility at Vanderbilt University. It turns out that researchers don't really know much about how people interact with Web sites as they surf around the Net. Which is where eLab comes in. The new facility will be used to create Web sites and then closely monitor visitors to see how they behave. The sites on eLab may even sell products so that researchers can learn more about the behavior of e-consumers — including why shoppers load up their carts with all sorts of goodies, only to abandon them in cyberspace.

The value proposition worksheet shown in Figure 10-1 allows Cultural Escapes to capture some of the most important benefits that it can offer customers as it tries to create value. The worksheet also points out some of the challenges the company faces in putting its business together. Customized information will be the hallmark of this company. But to be useful — and to keep customers coming back — that information absolutely, positively has to be right on the mark. One bad meal at a favorably-reviewed restaurant, in other words, and the site loses one of its principle values to customers.

By zeroing in on its unique value, Cultural Escapes can begin to select the kinds of features its customers may be willing to pay for. Consider the traveler who's planning a trip to Barcelona and happens to be passionate about great food and culinary culture. He may be willing to pay a small fee for a customized package of information that includes hot new restaurants in the city, cooking school courses available, and a bit about the city's culinary history. This same customer may also be willing to pay for a subscription to a monthly newsletter that highlights upcoming culinary events in major cities around the world. In addition, the Web site can attract ads from cooking schools and the sponsors of food-related events — even cookbook publishers — if it can successfully reach out to people interested in food and culture.

As you can see, Cultural Escapes' business model is beginning to emerge. And hey, it looks promising. Like many successful business models, it includes more than one revenue stream: fees for personalized travel information packages; subscription fees for special interest travel newsletters; and promotional fees from select advertisers.

Compressing your business plan

A written business plan is an absolute must for an Internet venture. You'd be hard-pressed to find a serious investor who'd let you past the receptionist without a detailed plan down on paper — but not too detailed. The watchwords for a business plan you submit to a venture capitalist: short and sweet. Some old hands in the game swear that ten pages is the absolute limit.

Consider a few other tips when tailoring your plan for investors:

- Avoid technical jargon in favor of plain, everyday language.
- Emphasize the expertise of your management team.
- Include a complete analysis of the marketplace — not just the easy, obvious markets but also the tougher markets to break into.
- Describe your competitors and distinguish your company from the rest of the pack.
- Include a thorough overview of the financials and summarize what they mean.
- Emphasize your company's growth potential.

Of course, keep your full-blown business plan, complete with all the gory details, close at hand — just in case your investors want to see more.

Take time to fill out your own value proposition worksheet, using Form 10-3 (on the CD-ROM). If you're still in the early planning stages of your e-business, be as creative as you can. Include core features that you definitely plan to offer, as well as a wish-list of features that you may be able to introduce down the road. The point here is to come up with a variety of ways for your Web site to offer real value to customers who click their way in.

If your company's value proposition still feels a bit shaky at this point, take a look at Chapter 1 and think about doing some high-level brainstorming to see if you can refine your basic business idea.

Putting together a workable business model

Coming up with a business model is one thing. Coming up with a model that actually works can be quite another. You need to take what you've learned from your value proposition and put it to good use, answering the following no-nonsense business question: How can you turn the value you provide online customers into cold, hard cash (or at least plastic)? That's your business model in a nutshell.

To help you think through your answer, we've put together an e-business model construction worksheet. Take a look at how Cultural Escapes, the online travel information Web site, used the worksheet to put together its business model in Figure 10-2.

Use Form 10-4 (on the CD-ROM) to help you construct a workable e-business model of your own. One word of caution here: Some of the entries may be more relevant to your situation than others. Focus on coming up with potential sources of revenue that can be supported by Web site features adding real customer value. If you're in the early stages of planning your e-business, think of this as a brainstorming exercise and be creative. If you need more info on business models, check out Chapter 5.

The business model you settle on will shape much of what you do in planning your e-business. But in particular, make sure a discussion of the model itself is prominently featured in your written plan as part of your overall company strategy.

Adding an Internet Extension to Bricks and Mortar

If you're thinking about using the Internet simply to support your traditional business — providing product information, for example, or customer support — you must still calculate the overall costs of developing and running your Web site, and then wrap those expenses into your budget.

We probably don't need to tell you that estimating start-up costs for a Web site is notoriously difficult. We've seen companies that have underestimated their actual expenses by five- and ten-fold. Part of the problem is that nobody has a long history of previous experience to point to. And, of course, every Web site is different, with its own features and unique challenges. Finally, Internet technology is changing so quickly that many companies find themselves spending far more on updating equipment and software than they ever imagined they would.

How can you get a handle on what your actual costs will be? First, do a little digging and find out what businesses similar to yours have spent in the past — and are currently spending — to run their online operations. The business press, including magazines and newspapers, continues to publish all sorts of useful stories about companies and their experiences with Web development. You'll also find a treasure trove of information online, naturally. The registration statements for companies that are going (or have already gone) public are all available on the Internet. These statements provide detailed pictures of the companies, their financial positions, and the risks they anticipate.

E-BUSINESS MODEL CONSTRUCTION WORKSHEET
1. List three key value-added features that your Web site offers: • Personalized travel information packages • Monthly newsletters focused on specific interest areas • Customized email alerts and travel reminders
2. Given your key Web site features, identify potential sources of revenue: • Sale of travel information packages • Subscriptions to special interest newsletters • Merchandising of select travel products
3. Is your Web site attractive to advertisers? If so, list at least three examples: • Tour companies • Travel industry (airlines, hotels, cruise lines) • City and institutional sponsors • Publishers
4. Will you capture useful demographic information on your Web site? Are there additional ways to leverage your customer database? • Merchandise tie-ins • Event ticketing opportunities • Direct market travel offers
5. Identify at least one up-and-running e-business with a similar business model: 2AHealthyU.com is a Web site that provides customized disease prevention and health maintenance information based on an online questionnaire format.
6. How does your business model resemble the one above? How does it differ? Both Web sites offer customized information to consumers. But our model allows us to learn more about our customers and offer more personalized products and services. We are also in a better position to match up our clients with targeted advertisers.
7. Describe what you see as the key strengths of your business model: • Strong and growing market for travel services • Information with high value-added content • Multiple revenue sources
8. Describe major concerns or uncertainties inherent in your business model: • Strong competition among online travel resource Web sites • Challenges of maintaining reliable, up-to-date information • Internet advertising rates and demand still quite uncertain

Figure 10-2: Using the business model construction worksheet to create a workable e-business model.

Ain't no mountain high enough

So you think putting up a Web site for an existing business is easy, eh? Well it is, according to Matt Hyde, an avid mountain climber and vice president of Internet sales at the venerable outdoor outfitter Recreational Equipment Inc, or REI. It's about as easy as climbing a 23,000-foot mountain, that is. "You do it because it's a challenge," he told *the New York Times* not long ago, "not because it's fun."

REI.com is one of the few real success stories on the Internet. The company's Web site has become the number one online seller of outdoor equipment. Better yet, it's turning a tidy profit — proof that an e-business can actually make money. But on the way to profitability, REI had to climb past more than a few of the prevailing myths about the new economy. Here's what they discovered:

> **Myth #1: Running a retail Web site is cheaper than running a physical store.** Not so. True, the start-up costs may be less. But given the need to continuously upgrade equipment and technical staff, the operating costs of the REI.com Web site have consistently gone up — including frequent computer overhauls to the tune of over half a million dollars a pop.
>
> **Myth #2: Internet retailers can save a bundle on personnel costs.** Forget it. Automation may allow an e-business to hire fewer sales people than a bricks-and-mortar store requires. But the technical people needed to maintain a Web site are much harder to find — and far more expensive to hire and retain — than retail sales people.
>
> **Myth #3: Online retail companies can maintain a more extensive selection than a catalog business or a storefront.** Well, maybe. But REI.com has discovered that creating digital images of the many items it carries is unexpectedly expensive. And maintaining the online catalog is also costly. In addition, the more items an Internet retailer carries, the more complex the job of filling orders becomes. That's especially true if some of the vendors — the people who actually make the products — don't have the state-of-the-art distribution systems that Internet shoppers have come to expect.

So how did REI succeed where so many other retail e-businesses have failed? Part of their success has hinged on the reputation that the company's bricks-and-mortar outlets already have among customers. And although Internet-related costs have been high, the company, which is privately held, has kept a watchful eye on achieving bottom-line results. Finally, REI has worked closely with its many vendors to continue to improve and expedite the order-fulfillment process — thus avoiding delivery problems that have brought some high-flying online retailers down.

Creating an online presence is a lot like remodeling your kitchen — it almost always costs more than you expect. To give you an example — of a company, not a kitchen — consider the outdoor equipment retailer Recreational Equipment, Incorporated, or REI. In 1996, the company spent $500,000 to get its Web site up and running. By 2001, it had tallied up more than $15 million in additional costs related to online upgrades and redesigns. Although the total outlay has been far greater than the company or its Internet business director ever anticipated, REI still considers all the money well spent.

To zero in on what your own Web development bill is likely to be, consider both the development costs you foresee and the ongoing expense of maintaining your Web site. If you need help in putting together a quick financial projection, flip to Chapter 5. In addition to the standard costs and expenses, make sure your calculations include the following:

- **Development costs**
  - Computer hardware
  - Communications equipment
  - Systems installation
  - Web site design
  - Web site content development
  - Testing and launch
- **Maintenance costs**
  - Web site administration
  - Web site content updating
  - Communications services
  - Hardware servicing and upgrades
  - Software upgrades and support

Before you go ahead and install your own Internet computer servers, complete with all the associated network communications links you require, think about having an outside company host your Web site for you. They can provide you with all the hardware and software infrastructure you'll need and guarantee that your site is up-and-running 24/7, often at a very competitive price.

After you've estimated what the final tab is likely to be for your new Web site, take a deep breath and tick off the business benefits you hope to gain from your presence on the Internet. If some of the benefits add revenue, make sure that they appear in your financial projections. Don't be surprised, however, if you have a tough time attaching hard numbers to all the benefits you expect. In the end, you're going to have to somehow weigh those benefits — hard and soft — against very real costs before deciding when and how to proceed with your Internet development plans.

Keeping the Faith

In its first several years, the new economy has experienced both boom and bust. Talk about Internet speed! It's been a real roller coaster ride for many online companies. But Internet companies have found a silver lining to all that's happened: These days, entrepreneurs have a much more down-to-earth sense of what makes an e-business succeed. Companies that want to create an online presence realize that they have to do more that hire a programmer or two and buy a few modems. Cyberspace has grown up, and everyone involved is a little older and a little wiser.

Unfortunately, all this new-found wisdom means that it's harder than ever to raise money to start an Internet venture. Everyone from bankers to VCs are scrutinizing the business plans they see more carefully than ever before. Don't be discouraged, though. This extra scrutiny simply means that you have to spend more time and effort hammering together a rock solid plan of your own. And that's not a bad idea, in any case.

Talking the talk

Venture capitalists (VCs) come in all shapes and sizes, from small, independent operators to large VC firms that evaluate thousands of new business proposals every year. They aren't the only funding game in town. Another source of startup cash can be found in so-called angel financing. Angels are high net-worth individuals (that is, rich people) who are interested in getting richer by investing in promising new companies. As you may expect, the world of VCs and angels has generated its own little glossary of jargon. Here's what you need to know to talk the talk:

- **Seed financing:** The money you need to prove that your basic business concept is a solid one. It may go into building a prototype of your very cool new technology or conducting market research to show that customers really what you have.
- **Start-up financing:** The initial level of investment required to get your business off the ground. The funds will be used for everything from assembling your business team to developing your product or service, testing it, and bringing it to market.
- **First-stage financing:** Additional money that comes in after your initial start-up funds run out. The funds are often used to support further growth by ramping up new product development, production, marketing, or your sales efforts.
- **Second-stage financing:** Money raised further down the road after your business has initially proven itself. The funds are typically used to allow the company to expand even more quickly by supporting growth in all areas of the companies operations.
- **Mezzanine financing:** We're not talking about theater tickets here. Mezzanine means in between, and this financing falls in between an equity investment and a standard bank loan. The money allows your company to expand in a particular direction without having to give up additional ownership in the business.
- **Bridge financing:** Like a bridge over troubled waters, this kind of financing can help your company over temporary rough spots. For example, bridge loans are sometimes used before an Initial Public Offering (IPO) to smooth out any cash shortfalls that may occur before the IPO is completed.

After you have your business plan in place and a management team all lined up, you're going to need something else to turn your vision into reality: perseverance. After all, it's a competitive world out there — especially online. The majority of start-ups struggle to get funding and then really struggle to be successful. Those that make it are usually led by people who absolutely believe in what they're doing — people who manage to shrug off setbacks and keep pushing forward against all odds.

A serious business plan can provide the momentum you need to keep on going when — you knew this was coming — the going gets tough. Truth is, we know entrepreneurs who return to their written business plans time and again to recapture the inspiration, the spirit, and the direction that started them out planning a business in the first place.

Forms on the CD-ROM

If you're planning to be on the Internet, take a look at the following forms on the CD-ROM to help you plan your business.

Form 10-1	**Checklist of Key Steps in Planning an e-Business**	A checklist of the key steps in e-business planning to help you streamline your own planning process
Form 10-2	**Online Customer Profile**	A questionnaire that's designed to capture the key characteristics of your most likely online customers
Form 10-3	**E-Business Value Proposition Worksheet**	A worksheet designed to capture the key benefits your Web site offers along with the value customers place on them
Form 10-4	**E-Business Model Construction Worksheet**	A worksheet to help you create a workable e-business model that combines customer value with revenue-generating opportunities

Chapter 11

Planning a Not-for-Profit Organization

In This Chapter

- Being a businessperson — even in your not-for-profit
- Using your plan to explain your purpose

We've all heard the joke about the company that loses money year after year: In an attempt to better meet their goals, they decide to become a not-for-profit organization. Seriously, though, if these organizations didn't exist, the world would be a colder and harsher place. Not-for-profit organizations (sometimes called nonprofit organizations or NPOs) do good in hundreds of ways — aiding disaster victims, protecting the environment, offering childhood vaccinations, preserving history, protecting individual rights, providing meals to the elderly, and the list goes on. By the latest tally, more than one million charities are registered with the Internal Revenue Service. Doing good deeds, we're happy to say, is alive and well.

At first, you may think that not-for-profits don't have much in common with the kinds of for-profit businesses we talk about in this book. After all, making money is the bottom line for most companies. Not-for-profits, on the other hand, aren't *supposed* to make money. Sure, an NPO needs to raise cash in order to do its good deeds, but as a not-for-profit organization, you're really in the business of providing services — whether that means alerting people to the hazards of toxic chemicals around schools or helping people with AIDS find housing.

Why should a not-for-profit organization have a business plan? For one thing, business planning helps hone an organization's mission and vision — and what could be more important to an NPO? Planning also helps you zero in on the people you hope to serve. And here's another reason: The more businesslike your not-for-profit organization — by which we mean carefully planned, well organized, and efficiently run — the more money you'll be able to raise and the higher the percentage of funds you'll be able to devote to the good work you want to accomplish.

Talking the talk

In many ways, for-profit and not-for-profit companies are very much the same. But when you enter the world of not-for-profit organizations — informally known as NPOs — you're likely to hear a different language being spoken. Here's how to translate for-profit jargon into not-for-profit lingo:

For-Profit Jargon	*Not-for-Profit Lingo*
Balance sheet	Statement of financial position
Profit-and-loss statement	Statement of financial activities
Customer	Client
Investor	Funder
Product or service	Programs or services
Market analysis	Needs assessment

In this chapter we take a look at the special considerations of business planning for not-for-profit organizations. We begin by talking about how to run an NPO like a business. We walk you through the parts of a business plan that deserve special attention — things like mission and vision statements, as well as measurable goals and objectives. Finally, we help you think through how you plan to get the job done, including everything from how you'll operate to how you'll keep the books.

Running Your Not-for-Profit Like a Business

How does a business spell success? If you're part of a for-profit company, the answer is M-O-N-E-Y. If you're involved in a not-for-profit organization, the measures of success are usually more intangible, having to do with how well you serve those in need or advance the causes you champion. Beyond the obvious differences, however, the two kinds of organization are run in very much the same way.

For-profits and not-for-profits alike have to manage staff, market themselves, deliver products and services, set goals, stay within budget, and measure progress. The business rules are pretty much the same whether you're providing meals to shut-ins or turning your mother's cookie recipe into a million-dollar enterprise. Follow the rules, and you have a good chance of success. Ignore them, and you probably won't be around very long, no matter how lofty your mission.

The same goes for business planning. The steps that go into creating a plan are important no matter what kind of venture you're starting — big or little, service or retail, old or new economy, for-profit or not-for-profit. If you're part of a not-for-profit organization, however, certain aspects of and approaches to business planning — and certain parts of a written plan — are more important than others.

Fine-tuning your mission and vision

The typical business plan includes a clear and concise mission statement along with an inspiring and compelling vision for the company: The mission statement describes who the company is, what it does, and what it hopes to achieve; the vision statement, in turn, captures its enduring purpose. Many companies also include a set of values in their plan: a list of the underlying beliefs and principles that guide their business decisions. If you need more information on any of these, flip to Chapter 3 for details on how to create your own mission, vision, and values statements. We mention them here because they are especially important to not-for-profit organizations. A mission statement, in fact, is really the driving force behind a not-for-profit:

- A big pharmaceutical company may hope to find cures for all sorts of diseases, but the real reason it's in business is to make money. In contrast, a not-for-profit organization dedicated to providing breast cancer treatments to the uninsured, for example, is guided solely by its mission to assist women in need.
- A bookshop owner does what she does because she loves books — but she also wants to make money. A lending library, on the other hand, is solely in the business of encouraging reading and promoting knowledge.

Here's a practical reason you should give your mission, values, and vision some extra polish if you're part of a not-for-profit organization: The more compelling these statements are, the more easily you can attract contributors — those people who make all your good works possible. Many NPOs use their mission statements again and again as they write grant proposals and develop fundraising literature. It makes for better reading and keeps their messages on track and on target.

Consider the National Wildlife Federation, which publishes a magazine for its supporters called — you guessed it — *National Wildlife.* What do they place at the very top of the magazine credits, above the name of the publisher, the CEO, or the editor-in-chief? That's right: a mission statement.

> **National Wildlife Federation Mission:** To educate, inspire and assist individuals and organizations of diverse cultures to conserve wildlife and other natural resources and to protect the Earth's environment in order to achieve a peaceful, equitable and sustainable future.

Pretty good, as mission statements go. It's clear, to the point, and lofty enough to be inspiring. Anyone reading these brief 34 words will have a pretty good idea of what the organization stands for.

For more examples, take a look at Chapter 3, where we put together twelve real-life mission statements from both the for-profit and not-for-profit worlds. And because mission statements are so central to the work of not-for-profit organizations in particular, we include a dozen more in Form 11-2 (on the CD-ROM). These additional statements give you a good idea of how a variety of not-for-profit organizations describe their missions. Take a moment to evaluate what you like and don't like about each mission statement.

Look over the mission statements that caught your attention. Use them as models to help you shape a polished version of your own mission to include in your business plan. Remember: Your mission statement should be clear, concise, and compelling. It should give anyone who reads it a sense of who you are and what you do. It should communicate the value you provide to the people you serve. And most important, it should convince anyone who reads it that the work you do is absolutely essential.

Do what you believe in

The first test of a not-for-profit idea is a simple one: Is it something you really believe in? A driving passion isn't the only qualification for success, but it sure helps. The fact is, most people who start, run, or work with not-for-profit organizations make less money than they would out in the private sector. What motivates them isn't the money, but doing something that they really care about.

The next test of your not-for-profit idea is also pretty straightforward: Is your organization needed? In other words, do you see a real need that you can fulfill? The process of planning, after all, is all about making sure your venture — profit or not-for-profit — makes sense, so that it's given the best possible chance of succeeding.

To jumpstart your own not-for-profit idea, fill out the not-for-profit planning worksheet in Form 11-1 (on the CD-ROM). Remember, it's just a worksheet, so you don't have to agonize over the wording just yet. But give the questions serious consideration, jotting down as many ideas as you can come up with. The worksheet will come in handy when you begin putting together your mission, your goals, and your plan.

Make sure that you and your board of trustees review your organization's mission statement periodically to make sure that it still reflects the environment you work in. If the profile of the clients you serve or the causes you champion change over time, consider revising your mission statement accordingly.

Creating the appropriate structure

The more than one million not-for-profits operating in the United States come in all shapes and sizes — from small groups like the Walk on the Wild Side hiking club to large national charities like Volunteers for America. The kind of legal structure you choose for your not-for-profit depends both on your size and the kind of work you plan to do. The following represent your basic options:

- **Informal not-for-profits:** As the name implies, these are loose-knit groups of like-minded people who typically get together for pleasure or service to the local community. Examples may include a local book club, a self-help support group, or a graffiti clean-up patrol. Informal not-for-profits have no legal structure and typically manage only small sums of money. They aren't big enough to fall under the watchful eye of the IRS.
- **Not-for-profit corporations:** Incorporation allows a not-for-profit organization to protect its directors and staff from certain types of liability, providing the same shield offered to for-profit companies. Incorporation also ensures that the organization will be able to continue its activities even when the founding members are no longer around. To get the details on incorporation in your state, check with your state's attorney general's office.
- **Tax-exempt not-for-profits:** Not-for-profit corporations with charitable, educational, scientific, religious, or cultural purposes can file for tax exempt status under section 501 of the Internal Revenue Service Code. (Sounds like bedtime reading to us.) Who actually qualifies for this exemption? The major types of tax-exempt organization include the following:
    - **Charitable organizations:** Religious, educational, scientific, and literary organizations
    - **Social welfare organizations:** Civic leagues and community groups
    - **Labor and agricultural organizations:** Labor unions and farm bureaus
    - **Business leagues:** Trade associations and Chambers of Commerce
    - **Social clubs:** Country clubs, fraternities, and sororities
    - **Fraternal organizations:** Lodges and other clubs
    - **Veterans' organizations:** Armed forces groups

- **Employees' associations:** Employee-benefit groups
- **Political organizations:** Campaign committees, political parties, and political action committees (PACs)

- **Qualified not-for-profits:** Tax-exempt not-for-profits — in which donations to the organization may also be tax deductible — are referred to as qualified not-for-profits. For your contributors, needless to say, this can make a big difference — especially when it comes to how much they plan on giving. Qualified organizations include religious, educational, scientific, and literary groups as well as child and animal welfare organizations, certain veterans' organizations, fraternal societies, and more.

For information on whether your organization may qualify for tax-exempt status, check out IRS Publication 557. For a current list of qualified not-for-profits, look at IRS Publication 78. Both publications are available from the IRS Web site at `www.irs.gov`.

Setting clear goals and objectives

Most not-for-profits want to make the world a better place. That's great, of course, but it's not enough. In fact, too many not-for-profits think that their lofty ideals are a substitute for specific goals and measurable objectives. And unfortunately, many of them end up being much less effective than they could be.

If you need information on setting up goals and objectives, flip to Chapter 3, where we offer some really good tips. We emphasize the importance of goals and objectives again here for this reason: Contributors and grant-makers want hard evidence that a not-for-profit organization is actually accomplishing its mission. And the best way to convince them that your own not-for-profit is doing its job is to set goals and objectives that measure the value you provide.

Suppose you create a not-for-profit group that matches unemployed people in your area with employers who have entry-level positions to fill. How do you gauge your effectiveness? Well, one way to measure success is to count how many clients you serve each year. But that tells only part of the story. A better measure of your value may be how many clients you actually place in jobs. But even that doesn't go far enough. Your organization places a premium on preparing people to work by teaching them simple job skills and helping them deal with issues like child care. So in fact, the best measure of your success may be how many people you place in jobs that they can keep.

Imagine, then, that one of the enduring goals you come up with is to continue to expand the number of clients you successfully place in long-term job situations. Another goal may be to raise the funds necessary to expand your services by increasing your donor rolls. Your next task is to break each goal down into objectives; that is, the specific steps you plan to take in order to achieve the goal. For example, the objectives that will help you reach your first goal — expanding the number of clients you successfully serve each year — may include the following:

- Enlisting ten new employers into the job placement program over the next six months
- Finding jobs for an additional 75 unemployed people in the coming year
- Increasing the percentage of clients who actually remain employed for at least six months from 60 percent to 85 percent

As you can probably see, goals and objectives provide the road map that allows you to keep the organization on track. And they help ensure that you provide the greatest value possible to the clients you hope to serve.

For-profit companies can always point to the money they make during the year to convince investors that they've done a good job. Not-for-profits have to measure their progress in other ways, which is why clear goals and measurable objectives are critically important. They help convince contributors, both large and small, that you make a real difference in the world. Beyond your lofty ideals and big-hearted intentions, they create a real bottom line: how much value you provide.

You can also use your goals and objectives to develop fundraising campaigns that are right on target. For example, take a look at the solicitation letter the job-placement organization put together:

Last year, **Jobs For All** placed 350 unemployed people in productive and meaningful positions in our community. This year, with your help, we plan to make that number 425. What's more, we're committed to increasing the percentage of our clients who remain on the job for at least six months from 60 percent to 85 percent.

> How will we do it? First, we plan to expand our job placement program. But that's only the beginning. We're working with the community college to offer basic computer-skills classes. And we're creating a job assistance hotline to provide immediate help to our clients when they encounter problems at home or on the job.
>
> But to do any of this, we need your help. This year's fundraising goal of $500,000 represents a 20 percent increase over last year's target. We know that's ambitious. But we also know that with your generosity, we can change people's lives for the better.

Putting a value on doing good

How do you place a value on a child who finds a warm and loving home, thanks to a not-for-profit adoption agency? Or a homeless person who manages to find and keep a job for the first time? Or a woman with breast cancer who gets the treatment she wouldn't otherwise be able to afford?

You can't, of course. At least not with the precision that you can put a price on a widget. But many charitable organizations — including the United Way — have instituted tough new standards to help them assess the real value of what they provide. And a foundation in San Francisco is taking this to a new level. They're using higher mathematics to estimate the social return on investment of the good works that not-for-profit organizations do.

The Roberts Enterprise Development Fund (REDF), started by The Roberts Foundation, analyzes a not-for-profit's financial data and then uses a complex formula to measure the benefits that the not-for-profit provides to its clients — including tangibles like reduced cost of social services and intangibles like increased self-esteem. By dividing the value of these benefits by the not-for-profit's costs, the REDF comes up with a ratio it calls the *social return on investment,* or SROI.

For example, here's how the benefits add up for the Pedal Revolution, a not-for-profit enterprise that trains homeless kids to repair and sell used bicycles. According to the REDF, each of the newly-employed kids ends up with an average income of $18,768 a year, saving the public $9,839 annually in social service and public assistance expenses. When combined with other intangible benefits along with low overhead and operating costs, the Pedal Revolution scores an impressive SROI of 95.26. What does that mean? For every dollar invested, the organization returns over $95 back to society over time. Now that's inspiring.

Make sure your written plan includes your organization's goals and objectives. As a not-for-profit, think about these goals and objectives from the standpoint of both your clients and your contributors:

- What goals are most meaningful to the people you serve or the cause you're fighting for? How can you best meet those goals through a series of specific objectives?
- What goals would best persuade your contributors that the work you do is important and makes a difference? What specific objectives would help convince them that you are meeting those goals?

Explaining How You'll Get the Job Done

The best intentions in the world are only as good as your ability to bring them about. Even a not-for-profit, in other words, has to be well run. And that requires a skilled staff, an efficient organization, a well-conceived operation — and the financial resources and expertise to make it all happen.

Describing what you do

The qualities that make a not-for-profit organization successful in raising funds and building financial support are the same ones that make a for-profit company attractive to investors. The qualities typically fall under the category of Company Description in a standard business plan. For a general overview, take a look at Chapter 6. Here, we highlight four pieces of the company description that are particularly important to not-for-profit organizations: operations, organization, management, and R&D.

Operations

In the for-profit world, operations have to do with how companies carry out their business — the day-to-day goings-on that enable them to produce products and provide services. Of course, a for-profit company tries to deliver its products and services as efficiently and cost-effectively as possible in order to maximize profits. But what about a not-for-profit organization? Efficient operations are just as important, although for different reasons. The more efficient your operations, the less you have to spend to deliver the same level of service or support for your causes. That means you get a greater bang for your donors' bucks. In other words, you end up reaching more people, doing more good, and having an easier time raising funds in the future.

The four areas that make up a for-profit company's operations — location, equipment, labor, and process — are also relevant to most not-for-profit organizations, so include a discussion of each one in your business plan. Consider the following situations:

- **Location:** If you plan to offer food to homeless people, for example, you need to find a suitable location, one that's close to homeless shelters or other social services.
- **Equipment:** If you plan to reach potential donors through a Web site, you may need to acquire a computer server, modems, software, and other equipment.
- **Labor:** No matter what you plan to do, you need people — either paid staff or volunteers — to make it all happen.
- **Process:** Describe the way you plan to operate your organization. A food bank, for example, needs a process in place to gather food contributions, sort them in a central location, and deliver them to people in need.

Serious contributors and grant-making institutions usually take a keen interest in the operations of the not-for-profit organizations they support. Most grant applications, in fact, require a detailed description of your organization's operational procedures. The good news: You may be able to cut and paste directly from your business plan — or at least borrow from the main points.

Make sure the procedures you set up as part of your operations include a detailed record-keeping system. If your not-for-profit is incorporated, for example, official corporate documents, board meeting minutes, financial reports, and other records must be preserved over the life of the organization. For more information, check with the Secretary of State or your state's Attorney General's office.

Organization

One thing that sets not-for-profits apart from for-profit companies is the central role that volunteers play. Indeed, some not-for-profit groups manage to do their work entirely through the services of unpaid volunteers. Hats off to them.

After a not-for-profit reaches a certain size, however, the organization usually retains a core staff of paid employees who work closely with volunteers. The professional staff is typically headed by a chief executive, sometimes referred to as a CPO, or Chief Professional Officer. Some not-for-profits also appoint a senior volunteer to the position of CVO, or Chief Volunteer Officer. The CPO's role is to manage the organization's paid staff; the CVO oversees volunteer activities.

Spend time early in the planning process developing a basic organizational chart for your not-for-profit that clearly indicates the paid positions you intend to have as well as the opportunities for volunteer assistance. Assign titles to the positions that describe responsibilities — director of programs, for example, or director of fundraising. Make sure your written business plan outlines your organizational structure and includes a summary of key job descriptions and responsibilities. For more information, check out Chapter 6.

Because the overriding purpose of most not-for-profits is to promote a worthy cause or serve people in need, salaries and compensation can be delicate issues. It's easy to assume, after all, that the money you spend on your staff is money not being spent on your mission. But that's not really how it works. If your organization is set up right, everybody plays a vital role in making it as efficient and effective as it can be, and they deserve to be compensated. Most people who choose to work for not-for-profits aren't really in it for the money. Employees typically don't make as much, on average, as they would make doing similar work in the for-profit world, but they should be paid fairly for what they do.

If you're not certain how much to pay your own permanent staff members, check around to see how much employees in similar positions are paid at other not-for-profits in your area.

Management

Most states require incorporated not-for-profit groups to have a Board of Trustees in place — a group of people who help raise funds, guide the organization, and shape its programs. (Contact your state's attorney general's office for details.) In this case, the Board is the official governing body of the organization, providing oversight and direction. Even if you don't plan to be a not-for-profit corporation, however, consider creating an informal advisory board to help steer your organization.

Who should you choose to be on your board? First, make sure the people you select are as passionate as you are about your not-for-profit's mission. They should also be ready, willing, and able to go out and raise money for the organization. And it certainly doesn't hurt if they have experience in the for-profit world of business. Retired businesspeople are often tapped to serve on not-for-profit boards for this very reason.

Form 11-4 (on the CD-ROM) provides a checklist of some of the major duties that not-for-profit Boards of Trustees often assume. Take time to select the ones that are relevant to your own organization and its particular requirements. You can use your list to get an idea of the kinds of capabilities your board members need to have. It will also come in handy when you're evaluating the overall makeup of your board.

Opening hearts and minds (and wallets)

Fundraising is so crucial to the health and well-being of most not-for-profit organizations that it will probably play a starring role in your own plan. You should begin by describing who will head up your fundraising efforts and how your fundraising activities will be organized.

For-profit companies spend a lot of time — and money — doing market analysis and customer profiling to decide how best to target their sales efforts. The same goes for successful not-for-profits. Not-for-profit organizations get the bulk of their contributions from one or more of the following sources:

- Individuals
- Corporations
- Private foundations
- Community foundations
- Government agencies

Individuals are by far the biggest contributors of all. In fact, most not-for-profit fundraising campaigns receive 70 to 80 percent of their money from individuals. People who have given in the past are the most likely candidates to give again — as long as they have a sense that their money is being well spent, of course. People who somehow benefit from the programs you offer are usually receptive contributors, as well. A person who knows someone with Parkinson's disease, after all, is more likely to write out a check to support related medical research than someone who knows very little about the illness.

What's the best way to reach individual donors? The answer depends, of course, on the nature of your organization and the kinds of contributors you plan to target. Door-to-door solicitations are great for local not-for-profits or for large organizations with strong grassroots networks. If you can tell your story clearly and compellingly in print, a direct mail campaign can be cost-effective and generate results, too. To help you begin crafting your own fundraising plans, fill out Form 11-3 (on the CD-ROM). It's a questionnaire designed to gather information about your ideal individual donor.

Snare that grant

Thousands of foundations and government agencies are just waiting to give their money away. All you have to do is convince them that your organization is best suited to turn that money into good deeds. To do that, put together a strong grant proposal — a written description of your not-for-profit organization, the specific programs you hope to run, how much they're going to cost, and exactly how you plan to carry them out.

We won't pretend that writing a grant proposal is anyone's idea of a good time. But we can assure you that it doesn't have to be agony — as long as you have a good solid business plan in place. A lot of the stuff you'll be asked to include in your grant proposal is already in your written plan — your mission statement, for example, and a bit about your philosophy and vision, plus a description of how your organization is set up and how you operate. If you've done your homework, it's all right there, ready to be copied and pasted — or at least waiting to serve as useful background material.

Form 11-5 (on the CD-ROM) provides a checklist that outlines the typical parts of a grant proposal. As you put together your own proposal, make sure to include the information highlighted in each of the major sections listed. We also include a rough idea of how much space you should allocate to each part.

Your written plan should list the members of your Board of Trustees along with their affiliations. If you don't have a board yet, make sure your plan describes the kinds of people you hope to recruit and how you plan to go about approaching them.

Research and development (R&D)

R&D? Wait a minute: Isn't research and development something high-tech companies and pharmaceutical firms have to worry about? Why in the world would a not-for-profit need to conduct research and development? Well, for the same reason for-profit companies need R&D. In a word: Change. Just as the markets for products and services in the for-profit world are constantly changing, the needs and causes that not-for-profits address change over time.

Changes in the for-profit marketplace are pretty hard to miss. Customers stop buying whatever a company is selling, and unless the firm adapts, it's history. Not-for-profit organizations, on the other hand, are a bit more insulated from competition, which means that they typically have to work harder to monitor changes in their own environment. And that's precisely why we think conducting a little R&D is important. A robust research program can help your not-for-profit to stay one step ahead of change, which, in turn, helps ensure that your services continue to meet real needs.

Of course, we're not talking science or engineering R&D here. We're talking about research that delves into the particular issues your not-for-profit hopes to address through its programs. That may mean conducting a simple survey of the client groups you currently serve or poring over government reports. It may mean analyzing statistics like the rate of domestic abuse in your area, the continuing loss of regional open space, or the changing face of local homelessness. Many large not-for-profits hire outside specialists to conduct studies and write reports on the key issues they address. But often, you can do it yourself. Whatever the focus — and whoever carries it out — the goals of your research should probably include the following:

- Understanding basic issues and root problems
- Tracking major trends and external changes
- Identifying unmet program and service needs
- Weighing the pros and cons of alternative solutions
- Evaluating the effectiveness of existing programs

Include key research findings in your business plan that underscore the importance of the work you intend to do. Also, describe how you plan to conduct ongoing research in order to stay abreast of the changing needs of your clients, your causes, and your organization.

Keeping the books

Not-for-profits may not be in the business of making money, but if they don't keep track of the money they handle in a businesslike way, they may find themselves in hot water — even out of the picture entirely. The rules of accounting are pretty much the same for profit-making companies and not-for-profits alike. You can find everything you need to know about the basics in Chapter 7. In this section, we mention just a few special financial considerations your need to think about as a not-for-profit organization.

Where the funds come from

Unlike traditional for-profit companies, most not-for-profits don't fill their coffers from the sales of products and services — at least not entirely. (Proceeds from the museum shop, concert ticket sales, and door-to-door cookies do help a few organizations stay afloat). Typically, not-for-profit groups take in the money they need to operate from the following sources:

- Donations from companies and individuals
- Government or private foundation grants
- Income from endowments and trusts
- Fees from specialty product sales or specific services

Running on hope

Founded in 1971, Milwaukee's *Esperanza Unida*, or "United Hope," is working to better the lives of inner-city residents by training people to take on higher-wage jobs. The group trains about 450 people a year in skills that include car repair, welding, printing, construction, customer service, and child care. Half of the organization's $3 million annual budget comes from the sale of products that are built or renovated by *Esperanza Unida*'s clients, who make trash bins, recycle donated cars, and run a print shop, among other projects. The rest comes from individual donations, grants from foundations and corporations, and support from the city of Milwaukee.

Many not-for-profits are supported through a mix of these sources. National Public Radio, for example, is made possible by donations from listeners like you, corporate sponsors and — at least the last time we looked — a little bit of help from Uncle Sam.

Because fundraising is so crucial to many not-for-profit organizations, your written plan needs to explain exactly where you intend to get the money to support your group and how much you expect to raise.

What percentage goes to overhead

For-profit companies can spend as much money as they want on their offices, advertising, promotions, sales-force events, you name it — as long as they can generate revenues and profits in line with investor expectations. Even though not-for-profits don't have investors, they also have to be careful about expectations, especially when spending money on fundraising. Why?

Well, imagine the not-for-profit group that spends 80 percent of its revenue on fundraising events (and thus only 20 percent on supporting its causes and clients). At a certain point, donors are likely to ask whether this is really a charitable group — or just a fundraising engine. The National Charities Information Bureau requires its organizations to spend at least 60 percent of the money they raise directly on program activities, keeping overhead to less than 40 percent. As a rule, your own not-for-profit should shoot for spending no more than 25 percent of its budget on fundraising and other kinds of overhead.

How much cash is kept around

Just like for-profit companies, not-for-profits should have a cushion of cash or other liquid assets on hand. You never know when times will get lean, after all. But keeping too much money in the bank can be a touchy subject for a not-for-profit group. People donate money to further a good cause, and most contributors don't want their money sitting around in a bank account somewhere. They want it to go to work helping people, saving the environment, supporting concerts — in short, fulfilling their mission. (The exception, of course, are endowment funds, which are set up specifically to generate interest income, which is then used to fund not-for-profit programs.)

How much you plan to set aside in reserve depends on the nature of your not-for-profit and the kind of programs you support. For example, a relief agency that responds to unforeseen disasters needs a large bank balance in reserve. A not-for-profit that runs a community food bank probably doesn't need anywhere near as much. As a rule, the National Charities Information Bureau requires that organizations keep cash reserves no larger than twice their annual operating expenses.

If you do plan to keep a sizeable reserve fund in place, remember that donors have the right to expect that the money they contribute will eventually be used for the kinds of work they had in mind when they made their donation. Your organization should have a procedure in place to earmark funds for the appropriate programs.

Who's accountable

Not-for-profit organizations are founded on trust. Donors trust that the money they give will be used wisely. Grant-makers trust (and usually verify) that the funds they provide are used for the purposes described in the grant application. It's up to the Board of Trustees to make sure the organization lives up to that trust. And that means accountability: keeping track of where, when, and how each dollar is spent.

Home run hero runs afoul

In 1998, after his extraordinary season vying for the Major League single-season home run record, Chicago Cubs outfielder Sammy Sosa founded the Sammy Sosa Foundation. To launch the not-for-profit organization, he donated a $2.7 million building in his home town in the Dominican Republic. A few months later, a major hurricane hit the island, causing widespread damage. Thanks to Sosa's high profile image, disaster relief money poured into the new foundation.

There was only one problem. Poor financial accounting on the part of the foundation somehow allowed foundation funds to find their way back into Sosa's personal accounts. In one case, foundation money was mistakenly used to pay for moving Sosa's yacht from Florida to the Dominican Republic.

Don't throw away your baseball cards, though. Sosa's still a hero. The mistakes were all unintentional. And the great home-run hitter moved quickly to correct the accounting errors that were made. But the story carries an important lesson: Not-for-profit organizations must keep precise records, with all donations strictly accounted for and business and personal accounts kept completely separate.

Your business plan should include provisions for an annual audit of the organization's finances. Many not-for-profits hire professional accounting firms to conduct the audit in order to make sure it's independent and objective. If you're a small or relatively new not-for-profit group, you may be reluctant to spend the extra money on an outside audit. In that case, create a volunteer committee of people with experience in accounting to review the records, verify bank balances, and produce a written report of their findings. In order to ensure that there's no conflict of interest, this committee should operate completely independently of the Board of Trustees.

Forms on the CD-ROM

If you're part of a not-for-profit organization, take a look at the following forms on the CD-ROM to help you plan.

Form 11-1	**Not-for-Profit Planning Worksheet**	A worksheet that helps you develop your not-for-profit idea
Form 11-2	**Examples of Real-World Not-for-Profit Mission Statements**	A selection of actual not-for-profit mission statements along with space to record your own impressions
Form 11-3	**Ideal Individual Donor Questionnaire**	A questionnaire to help you gather information about your ideal individual donor
Form 11-4	**Checklist of Responsibilities For a Not-for-Profit Board**	A checklist of common responsibilities to help determine the capabilities your Board of Trustees members should have
Form 11-5	**Checklist of Typical Grant Proposal Sections**	A checklist of the typical sections you should think about including in your grant proposal

Part IV
Making the Most of Your Plan

"You bought what? You know we're on a budget. Now take Hughes Electric back to General Motors and see if you can get your money back."

In this part . . .

All your hard work in shaping a business idea, analyzing the opportunity, creating a strategy, and putting together a plan of action finally gets distilled in a written business plan. This is really where the rubber meets the road. Your business plan is likely to be the most powerful single document you ever create for your company: It can help you get funded, stay on track, grow bigger, make money — and get you out of trouble if things go wrong — which is why this part of the book is so important.

In Chapter 12, we give you insider tips on how to organize all your efforts into a comprehensive and convincing business plan. We also share some clever ways to address a variety of different audiences with the plan. In Chapter 13, we show you how to use your written plan to organize your staff, develop a strong sense of teamwork, operate your business efficiently and effectively, and troubleshoot problems if and when they arise. We also give you some pointers on how to keep your business plan as vital and up-to-date as it can possibly be.

Chapter 12

Putting Your Plan Together

In This Chapter

- Making sure you're ready
- Knowing where to turn for additional help
- Creating a business planning team
- Addressing important audiences
- Reviewing your finished plan

In this chapter, the real excitement builds: Here's where we help you put together your formal business plan. Of course, we assume you've completed most of the necessary business planning spadework: You've already laid down some ground rules (Chapter 3), assessed your business environment (Chapter 4), considered your strategy (Chapter 5), thought about what you want your company to look like (Chapter 6), and likely struggled with finances (Chapter 7).

After you've assembled all the raw materials for a business plan, a written document is your next order of business — that's right, we said *written.* All the hard work you've done already shouldn't go to waste: It deserves to find a place in print. We know that, for many people, the idea of writing ranks right up there with paying taxes. Putting one word in front of another can seem as excruciating as rolling boulders up a hill, one by one. But keep in mind that you get a big payoff for all your literary efforts. Writing down your ideas forces you to confront them in black and white — do they hold water or don't they? Some ideas won't measure up. Other ideas may look even better after you get them down on paper.

You may discover another important benefit to writing a formal business plan. If, like many entrepreneurs, you have dozens of ideas rattling around in your head, organizing them into a written plan forces you to think about how they all fit together. It also gives you a chance to decide which ideas are most important so that you can begin to set priorities. A written plan, in fact, is the first serious test of your new venture. If your budding business doesn't make sense on paper, after all, what are the odds that it will pass muster in the cold, cruel, competitive world of business?

In this chapter, we start by making sure that you have all the pieces in place to begin assembling your written plan. We also talk about additional planning resources that are available, just in case you need some extra assistance. Next, we help you put together a planning team. And because most business plans should address a variety of audiences, we help you target your plan to the different kinds of people who will be reading it. Finally, we help you make sure all the components of your plan fit together to create a cohesive sense of who you are and what you plan to do.

Doing Your Homework

Putting together your written business plan is a bit like taking a final exam at school. You want to make sure that you're well-prepared and that you have all the resources you need at your finger tips.

To help out, we've put together a complete checklist (see Form 12-1) of the items you may want to include as part of each of the major components found in a typical business plan. Check off the items that you already have in hand, at least in a rough form. (Don't worry about the Table of Contents and the Executive Summary at this point. These are the last two components of your business plan to put in place, and we get to them in the "Addressing more than one audience" section later in this chapter.)

Even after skipping the first two, odds are good that you haven't checked every box. That's okay. Not every business plan contains every item on this list. Still, take a moment to look at the items you *haven't* checked, just to make sure you're not leaving out something important.

If you discover that you still have some homework to do before sitting down to write your plan, here's where you can turn to for help with a particular business plan component:

- Company overview: Chapters 3, 5, 6
- Business environment: Chapter 4
- Company strategy: Chapter 5
- Company description: Chapters 6
- Financial review: Chapter 7
- Action plan: Chapters 2, 3, 5

And don't forget to make use of Chapter 8 if you're self-employed, Chapter 9 if you're planning a small business, Chapter 10 if you have your sights set on the Internet, and Chapter 11 if you're involved with a not-for-profit organization.

BUSINESS PLAN COMPONENTS CHECKLIST

☐ **Table of contents**

☐ **Executive summary**

☐ **Company overview**
- ○ Mission statement
- ○ Vision statement
- ○ Values statement
- ○ Listing of key products and/or services
- ○ Business model summary
- ○ Major business goals
- ○

☐ **Business environment**
- ○ Industry overview
- ○ Barriers to entry
- ○ Market segmentation
- ○ Ideal customer profile
- ○ Competitor analysis
- ○

☐ **Company strategy**
- ○ SWOT analysis
- ○ Business model
- ○ Business goals
- ○ Plans for growth
- ○ Exit strategy
- ○

☐ **Company description**
- ○ Introductory highlights
- ○ Products and/or services offered
- ○ Research and development
- ○ Operations
- ○ Sales and marketing
- ○ Distribution and delivery
- ○ Customer service
- ○ Management
- ○ Organization
- ○

Form 12-1: Business plan components checklist — page 1 of 2.

☐ **Financial review**
- ○ Income statement
- ○ Balance sheet
- ○ Cash flow statement
- ○ Financial forecasts
- ○ Master budget
- ○

☐ **Action plan**
- ○ Short-term goals
- ○ Immediate objectives
- ○ Next steps
- ○

☐ **Appendixes**
- ○
- ○
- ○

Form 12-1: Business plan components checklist — page 2 of 2.

Locating Additional Resources

Having the right resources at the right time can make the job of business planning easier and more successful. Fortunately, you can find more useful and useable business planning resources than ever before, from books and software to Internet Web sites and real, live experts. Of course, you may also find lots of stuff that's not worth looking at — much less paying for. And you can't always judge a book (or software program) by its cover.

As you begin to put together your business plan, you may discover that you need some additional tools — a book devoted to marketing, for example, or business-planning software that can help you create and maintain your written document. The following sections give you some advice on where to go and what to look for.

Your local bookstore

We think you've already selected one of the best hands-on business-planning books around. (For additional background on general business planning issues, you may also want to pick up a copy of *Business Plans For Dummies* by Paul Tiffany and Steven Peterson — published by Hungry Minds, Inc.) We're the first to admit, however, that other useful business-planning books are out there — particularly books that concentrate on specific areas, such as marketing or financial planning, and books that focus on particular kinds of businesses, such as not-for-profits or sole proprietorships.

You can find out a lot about a book by reading through its table of contents. It's also not a bad idea to dip into the first chapter. If you're browsing on the Web, booksellers like Amazon often include a detailed table of contents along with the first chapter right online. Readers' reviews and ratings can also help steer you toward other books that are particularly useful.

The basic principles of business planning may be timeless, but certain subjects — Internet marketing, for example — change rapidly, and a book that's more than a few years old may represent ancient history. (Not long ago we came across a year-old book praising the management team of an e-business site that had gone belly up the week before. Talk about Internet time!) If you're trying to find timely information — details about tax considerations for a small business, for example — be sure to check when the book was published.

Magazines, newspapers and journals offer a terrific way to keep up on what's happening in the world of business in general — and your industry in particular. The business press also provides an efficient way to routinely scan the business environment for trends or new developments that may affect your business plan. We suggest that you identify several titles of interest and subscribe to them.

The Web

Another useful place to search for additional planning tools is on the Internet. Today, hundreds of Web sites offer information on business planning. Some are free; others tease you with a sample of what they have to offer, and then charge you for more details. In our experience, some of the freebies can be just as helpful as the subscription sites, so we suggest that you check first to see what's free for the asking, before you plunk down your hard-earned cash. In particular, the federal government offers heaps of solid information on planning, starting, and operating your own business through its Small Business Administration site (`www.sba.gov`). Even the IRS has some helpful planning tips in its handbooks, which are also available on the Web (`www.irs.gov`).

Hot lists of top business-related Web sites have a way of going out of date as quickly as today's newspaper. Your best bet is to take a couple of hours and prowl around the Internet yourself, looking for useful resources. The keywords *business* and *plan* will lead you to plenty of generic business planning information. (Be prepared to slog through an awful lot of junk, however.) In addition, tailor your search by using keywords specific to your business area (*not-for-profit*, *retail*, *travel*, *financial services*, and so on.) And make sure to bookmark any promising Web sites so that you can return to explore them later on in more detail.

Internet links

The Internet contains a treasure trove of business-planning information and resources. To help you sort through all the riches, we've put together a list of popular sites that provide useful and reliable tips, tools, and examples — including dozens of real-life business plans.

- **www.sba.gov:** The Small Business Administration (SBA) site is far and away the best source of information about planning, funding, starting, and running a small business. You'll find useful FAQs, as well as counseling help and shareware software programs.
- **www.irs.gov/smallbiz:** This is a great site if you run a small business or are self-employed. The IRS provides all kinds of useful industry and profession-specific information. The site also includes links to other helpful non-IRS business resources on the Web.
- **www.nfib.com:** The National Federation of Independent Business (NFIB) calls itself the largest advocacy organization to represent small and independent businesses in the U.S. Its Web site features a frequently updated set of tools and tips that small business owners may find useful.
- **www.ncnb.org:** The National Center for Nonprofit Boards (NCNB) offers a bunch of useful information on its site, including a comprehensive checklist for forming a not-for-profit organization and tips on legal issues. For a subscription fee, you can get even more resources, along with discounts on workshops and books.
- **www.nonprofits.org:** The Internet Nonprofit Center is one of the best resources we've found for online information about every aspect of planning, starting, and operating a not-for-profit organization. Check out its extensive FAQ for information on dozens of topics.
- **www.score.org:** The Service Corps of Retired Executives (SCORE) offers free consulting to start-up businesses. Along with a way to contact SCORE, their Web site includes updated success stories from a variety of small- and medium-sized businesses. Also useful: SCORE's list of business-related links.
- **www.nolo.com:** You can't find a better place to turn for basic information on the legal aspects of virtually any kind of business than Nolo. Their Web site also offers free advice, including info on insuring your home business, independent contractor arrangements, trademarks and copyrights, debts, bankruptcies, and employment law.
- **www.bplans.com:** This Palo Alto Software Web site includes over 50 sample business plans from a wide variety of businesses. The site also includes useful articles on a wide range of business-related topics.
- **www.brs-inc.com:** Business Resource Software's Web site offers a useful set of sample business plans, including the winners of the MOOT CORP competition, sponsored by the University of Texas at Austin. Click on Sample Business Plans.
- **www.toolkit.cch.com:** The Business Owner's Toolkit Web site includes business plan examples for three different kinds of businesses: Manufacturing, service, and retail. On the homepage, click on Business Tools, scroll to Marketing, and click Sample Business Plans.

Beyond sharing some basic business-planning tools, the Internet is also a great place to turn for the latest information about competitors, markets, business trends, and new technologies — all the things you need to know to put together a complete picture of your business environment. We're constantly amazed at how much information can be found in corporate press releases, company home pages, executive bios, online business magazine articles, SEC registrations, and thousands of other online documents.

The Internet may be a gold mine of business information, but plenty of it is nothing more than fool's gold. Unlike magazine articles, which are typically checked and rechecked for accuracy, much of the stuff that goes up on the Web hasn't been validated or confirmed by anyone. More often than not, in fact, the Web site that's providing the information is also in the business of selling you something. So follow three simple rules when you use the Web for business research:

- **Make sure the material is current.** One of the biggest problems with online information is that many Web documents aren't dated, so you may not know whether what you're reading is the latest scoop or ancient history. Look for a date. And if you can't find one, dig a little further to make sure that the information is still relevant.
- **Know your sources.** In the wild, wild world of the World Wide Web, you may be hard-pressed to say exactly where the stuff you read is coming from. Needless to say, that's a critically important piece of information. If you read a rave review of a new business-software program, and the review comes from a respected business magazine, you can put your faith in it. If it appears without a source, however, on the software company's own Web site, be suspicious.
- **Double check key facts and statistics.** If you're using specific pieces of information — about business trends, markets, competitors, technology, or whatever — as the central building blocks of your business plan, make darn sure that they're correct. If your financial projections are built on the fact that the market for online lingerie is growing at 40 percent a year, for example, be certain that it's a fact and not some online press agent's private fantasy.

Business software

We think that business planning software can be helpful — so helpful, in fact, that we've included trial versions on the CD-ROM of some of the best business-planning software you can buy. We've also included really good freeware that you can try out, well, for free. See the Appendix for details.

Software programs are useful because they allow you to automatically assemble all the components of a business plan, turning them into a spiffy-looking document that's ready to print. The best programs also make easier work of the financial parts of business planning — creating income statements and cash flow statements, for example, or making financial projections. And software programs typically allow you to add graphics, such as tables and charts, into your plan, providing an easy way for your audience to see at a glance what you're describing in the written document. One of the programs we've included on the CD-ROM even allows you to publish your business plan over the Internet on a password-protected site. (See Business Plan Pro 4.0 on the CD-ROM.)

As useful as they are, business-planning software programs can sometimes make the job of business planning seem a bit too easy. With all the software bells and whistles, they can inadvertently cause newcomers to skip the serious (that is, difficult) work of creating and writing an effective plan. Remember, the best software-planning tools guide you through the important aspects of business planning and then keep track of your words, sentences, and paragraphs — they don't think for you. You still have to do the serious mental work yourself.

Something else to keep in mind: Investors and bankers who make a living reviewing and funding business plans are all too familiar with the look and feel of the most popular software-generated business-planning documents. So if you use one of these programs, make sure you customize your own plan to make it unique. The last thing you want is for your business plan to look exactly like a hundred others that cross a venture capitalist's desk every month.

Expert advice

No one knows the ins and outs of planning and running a business better than people who have done it before. And most business people are more than happy to share their experience and expertise. Many are even willing to mentor first-time entrepreneurs. So if you run into questions you can't answer — or you run out of ideas on ways to get your business off the ground — don't be afraid to turn to an expert for advice.

How do you find one? Of course the first place to look is in your own address book. You'll probably have an easier time getting help from someone you already know on a personal or business basis. If that doesn't pan out, ask your friends and colleagues for suggestions. Other good places to look for help are the Chamber of Commerce and the business section of your local newspaper. Of course, you may end up paying for some of this advice. But when you really need help, it can be well worth it.

The person you choose must have experience in a business similar to the one you're planning. After you identify this person, decide exactly what kind of assistance you need. You can't ask someone to plan your whole business for you, after all. But you can ask them to fine-tune your marketing strategy, for example, or review and critique your financial projections.

One rich — and underused — source of expertise can be found in the community of retired business people. By definition, they have more experience than almost anyone else, and they are often looking for ways to use what they've learned to help others. Think about contacting the Service Corps of Retired Executives, or SCORE, a nationwide organization that works with the Small Business Administration (SBA) to provide help to business owners. SCORE has a free online newsletter and provides free e-mail counseling. The group also has local chapters around the country, with retired business people ready and willing to help. For more information, check out their Web site at `www.score.org`.

A retired schoolteacher we know came up with a business idea that promised to keep her busy and help out some of the hardest working people in town. She wanted to start an agency that would represent the dozens of women who were working on their own cleaning houses in the area. She figured that she would be able to help these women find more work than they could get on their own. She could also help them organize their schedules, communicate with clients, and do the bookkeeping. And over time, she hoped to offer them benefits such as health insurance. In return, she would take a small percentage of the money they earned.

But how much of a percentage? And how much money would she need to get her business going? She tried to put together a plan on her own but quickly felt overwhelmed by questions that she didn't know how to answer. Then she happened to read about a local businessman who was retiring from a high-tech business he'd started. On a whim, she wrote to him, describing her idea and asking if he had time to help her put together a plan. He called back immediately, they met a few times, and within a month she had a solid business plan in place. Not only that, she was able to get a small business loan for the start-up money she needed. Now her business is growing, and the retired businessman continues to serve as her advisor.

Self help

Many local communities have organizations of business people who get together to share ideas, exchange contacts, help each other out — and just plain socialize. Some of these groups are focused on women, Hispanics, gay people, or freelancers, for example, while others are wide open, made up of local people across the business spectrum. Thanks to the Internet, you can also find virtual business groups that regularly schedule online meetings to support one another.

For more than three years, the Lakeland Area Chamber of Commerce has been running a small-business mentoring program in Lakeland, Florida. Companies asking for guidance have included a day-care center, a software company, and a professional cleaning firm. Most of the mentors are senior executives in established businesses who review the problems faced by these small businesses and then work with their protégés to find solutions. For example, the owner of a small day-care center asked for help when she began to experience serious business cash flow problems. Her mentor, the retired chief financial officer of a local tile company, helped her develop a business plan along with a complete set of financials. The owner credits the assistance she received with saving her day-care business — and inspiring her to think about expanding.

Business networking organizations are an invaluable resource for help in planning and running your business. For information about what's available in your own community, check with your local Chamber of Commerce. Ask if they have or intend to start a mentoring program. Because Internet Web sites are changing so fast, the best way to find a networking organization online is to surf the Web.

Putting Your Planning Team Together

Chances are you've already enlisted a fair amount of help as you've analyzed your industry (see Chapter 4), thought long and hard about your customers and competitors (see Chapter 4), worked on a business strategy (see Chapter 5), and reviewed your finances (see Chapter 7). But the team we're referring to in this section is the team that will actually create your written business plan, boiling down all the research, brainstorming, and analysis you've done into a coherent, persuasive, and readable document. The size of this team depends on the size and structure of your company — and on the complexity of the business plan itself.

If your business is small, you won't need to worry too much about who's in charge of which piece of your written plan. Lucky you: You get to be in charge of it all! But that doesn't mean you have to go it entirely alone. Bounce your thoughts around with someone who's willing to serve as a sounding board. And ask someone you trust to read and critique your final business plan.

If your business is medium-sized or bigger, the process of creating your written plan requires a certain amount of organization. So before you sit down at the computer and fire up your planning software or your word processor, consider the following sections as you get ready to assemble the pieces of you plan.

Delegating responsibilities

If your company is large enough to boast a management team, it's probably a good idea to divvy up the work involved in putting together your written business plan — and not simply because it makes your job easier. After all, different people bring different perspectives to your plan. And with a team in place, you have a group of people ready to read and review drafts, offer suggestions, and fine-tune the document so that it's as good as you can possibly make it.

Because every business is different, we can't give you a simple formula for putting together your team. We can't even tell you the ideal number of people to choose — that depends on the size of your company and how big and complicated your plan is. But we can give you a few tips to help you create a team that's both efficient and effective:

- **Keep your team lean and mean.** Too many planners — just like too many cooks — can spoil the recipe for successful planning. A bloated team can mean endless meetings and too many points of view. So involve only the number of people you think you really need to get the job done.
- **Appoint people who want the job.** There's no point in assigning a planning task to someone who really doesn't want to do it. And while you may have trouble finding volunteers who are jumping up and down at the chance to work on a business plan, make sure that whomever you choose is at least willing and able to complete the task. To help win your team over, take time at the beginning to explain why creating a written business plan is so important.
- **Organize your team around the plan.** This may sound like a no-brainer, but by organizing your team around the major components of your business plan, you make sure that everyone knows exactly what their task is, and how their work fits into the larger picture. Some of the assignments are pretty straightforward. Your financial person should take charge of the financial review. Your marketing head should put together the business environment section. If certain pieces of the plan are more complex than others, think about assigning a small group to work on them.
- **Put one person in charge.** Every team needs a leader, and that's particularly true when you're putting together your business plan. Keeping track of the whole process can be a job in itself, especially if you have a larger team or a complicated plan. So name one person as project director. Make sure everyone on the team understands that he or she has ultimate authority.
- **Appoint a wordsmith.** If you're lucky, someone on your team actually enjoys writing. Well, okay, maybe not *enjoys,* but at least you have someone who's pretty good at putting words down on paper. This person should be put in charge of writing key sections of your plan, such as the executive summary. He or she should also serve as senior plan editor, checking grammar and spelling and making sure that the writing style is clear and consistent throughout the plan.

Setting the ground rules

Putting together a business plan isn't all that different from other kinds of projects that involve teamwork, whether you're building a house or running a relay race. The clearer the ground rules, the smoother the process — and the happier your team. So as soon as you've selected your team, establish procedures that spell out exactly how the work is to be carried out. Make sure that your ground rules address the three following points:

- **Identify key steps.** Typically, the process of writing a business plan document includes five distinct steps: research, first draft, review, revised draft, and final review. You can specify as many or as few of these steps as you think you need, given your own situation. Just make sure you spell them out upfront.
- **Clearly assign duties.** Make sure that everyone involved knows exactly what's expected of them. You can use the key steps you've identified to create a set of tasks to be completed. Then assign each task to a member (or members) of your team.
- **Establish a schedule.** The process of writing a business plan doesn't have to be a long and drawn-out affair. In fact, it shouldn't be. We're not talking about a history of the world, after all. And a business plan has to be timely, responding to the business environment as it is — not the way it looked six months ago. After the preliminary research is complete, the rest of the steps should be fairly straightforward. To keep your project on track, set due dates for each component of the plan and each step in the process. Give the members of your team as much time as they reasonably need — but no more.

Putting first things last

Issues of timing are bound to come up as you try to put your plan down on paper. How can you put together the executive summary, for example, before you have the rest of the business plan pretty well in place? And don't you need the company strategy written up before you can tackle the action plan?

Without a doubt, each component of your written business plan has to be in sync with the sections around it. If you talk about the need to increase the subscriber base for your investment newsletter in the company strategy section, for example, and your action plan doesn't say a word about specific ways to do that, anyone reading your plan is going to wonder if you really know what you're doing.

So how do you make sure that everyone is working off the same page? The best approach, we've found, is to sit down with your team and hammer out an outline containing the key points to be addressed in each section of the plan. Refer to the checklist in Form 12-1 as a guide. You may need more than one meeting to create your outline, but it's time well spent. With your outline in place, each person on the team knows what his or her section should include — and how it relates to the other plan components. A detailed outline of your written business plan also allows your team to spot discrepancies or omissions early on.

And what about that executive summary? Well, there aren't many times when you should put something off until the last minute — but it's a good idea to do exactly that when it comes to the opening section of your business plan. You can't very well summarize a plan you haven't written yet, after all. Now that may seem obvious, but we can't tell you how many business planners have anguished over the executive summary simply because they tried to write it first. Save yourself the agony. The executive summary may come first in the finished plan, but it should be the last thing you write — usually after the second draft of each of the other components has been completed and reviewed.

Don't worry about repeating yourself in the executive summary. The whole point of the opening section is to capsulate the key points of the plan — using the same language you use in the plan. Don't grab a thesaurus, in other words, hoping to find some colorful new way to express your mission or your strategy — you'll only confuse everyone. Say it the same way, only shorter.

Keeping track of it all

If you're feeling a little overwhelmed at this point, take a deep breath and relax. Putting the written document together doesn't have to be complicated. We've found that two simple tools can go a long way toward streamlining the process for you — and keeping everyone involved smiling. One is a simple tracking sheet showing at a glance where every part of the process is at any given time. The other is nothing more complicated than a loose-leaf notebook. In fact, it is a loose-leaf notebook.

The master tracker

Especially if your plan is a bit complicated — or at least has a large number of sections and appendixes — having a master tracking sheet is essential. Done right, this powerful little form can track every piece of the plan, who's in charge of it, the key steps involved in completing it, and where it stands at any given moment. You can create your master tracking sheet online, on a blackboard, or on paper. Whatever you choose, make sure it's easily available to every member of your planning team — and that you update it regularly.

Because no two plans are precisely the same, tailor your master tracking sheet for your own purposes. To help you get started, we include a typical tracking sheet in Form 12-2 as a useful guide.

MASTER PLAN TRACKING SHEET							
Plan Components *(Fill in due dates)*	**Research**	**Outline**	**Draft I**	**Review**	**Draft II**	**Final**	**Done**
Executive summary							☐
Company overview							
Mission statement							☐
Vision statement							☐
Values statement							☐
Listing of key products and/or services							☐
Business model summary							☐
Major business goals							☐
							☐
Business environment							
Industry overview							☐
Barriers to entry							☐
Market segmentation							☐
Ideal customer profile							☐
Competitor analysis							☐
							☐
Company strategy							
SWOT analysis							☐
Business model							☐
Business goals							☐
Plans for growth							☐
Exit strategy							☐
							☐
Company description							
Introductory highlights							☐
Products and/or services offered							☐
Research and development							☐
Operations							☐
Sales and marketing							☐

Form 12-2: Master plan tracking sheet — page 1 of 2.

Distribution and delivery							☐
Customer service							☐
Management							☐
Organization							☐
							☐
Financial review							
Income statement							☐
Balance sheet							☐
Cash flow statement							☐
Financial forecasts							☐
Master budget							☐
							☐
Action plan							
Short-term goals							☐
Immediate objectives							☐
Next steps							☐
							☐
Appendixes							
							☐
							☐
							☐

Form 12-2: Master plan tracking sheet — page 2 of 2.

An old-fashioned loose-leaf notebook

Forget for a moment all those razzle-dazzle online resources and state-of-the-art software tools. Sure they're useful. But we still believe that the single most valuable tool for getting an effective business plan down on paper is — that's right — a good old-fashioned loose-leaf notebook. As you put together your business plan, you're going to be juggling a lot of information — versions of your mission and vision statements, biographies of your key managers, financial statements, charts and graphs, product specifications, and more. In our experience, a loose-leaf notebook is the simplest and most efficient way to keep track of it all. As you revise and reorganize, you can easily slip an old section out and pop a new one in.

A loose-leaf notebook is also one of the best — and most cost-effective — technologies around for capturing the big picture behind your overall plan. (Just try making sense of a long, complicated document as you scroll through it up-and-down on your computer screen!) And one of the reasons for putting together a formal document in the first place is to make sure that all the pieces of your plan support and complement one another.

If your planning effort involves several people, a single loose-leaf notebook can serve you well as the master working document. But make sure that the notebook is easily accessible to everyone on your team and be clear that changes or additions must be approved by the team leader before they go into the master document.

Targeting Your Plan to Key Audiences

Whether you're writing your business plan on your own or doing it by committee, keep in mind who will be reading the written document. A business plan is meant to communicate your vision and strategy — what you plan to do and how you intend to do it. The only way to do that successfully is to know exactly who you're addressing. You wouldn't speak French to someone who only speaks Italian, right? For the same reason, you don't want to fill your written business plan with all kinds of technojargon if your audience is made up of people who don't know the first thing about the new-fangled technology you're working on.

What if your whole business idea is based on something brand new? Don't you need to describe it in detail? Sure you do. But you can address different audiences, even within the same document. For example, your plan may include an overview of the new technology that can be understood by anyone who happens to read it, while the technical nitty-gritty can go into an appendix. Before you can really think about how to speak to different audiences, however, you have to know who your readers are going to be.

Identifying your stakeholders

Chances are, you'll come in contact with all kinds of people in the course of doing business. Your own employees and customers are on the list, of course. And you'll probably have contact with suppliers, outside consultants, lenders, shareholders, regulators, competitors, and other interested parties.

Just for the sake of simplicity, we refer to this motley crew as your *stakeholders* — as in everyone who has a possible stake in your company, what it does, or how it operates. Some of these people may have direct stakes: you owe them money, for example, or they own a piece of your business. Others may have less tangible interests: suppliers who want to continue selling to you, or civic organizations who want to make sure that you remain a good corporate citizen. Whatever the interest group, your business plan is one of the most important tools you have to communicate with them.

Here's the catch: Not all of your stakeholders are likely to share the same interests or values. In fact, certain groups may be in open conflict with each other. Someone who owns shares in your company, for example, is probably most interested in whether and when you plan to grow bigger. A local environmental group, on the other hand, may not want to see you grow at all; what they want to know is whether you're following all the necessary environmental regulations.

For their part, bankers look at your plan in order to decide whether to loan you money, so they're interested in your company's long-term prospects — in short, how good a risk you are when it comes to paying back the loan. Not surprisingly, they tend to focus on things like cash flow, your business assets, and the prospects for solid, stable growth in your industry. Investors, on the other hand, are interested in the factors that predict growth — especially rapid growth. So they are likely to keep a sharp eye out for a real business opportunity, a strong management team, and a well-defined plan of action.

How do you communicate with all these potential stakeholders in a single business plan? Well, it's not as difficult as it may seem. The first step: Consider each group of stakeholders you intend to address and think about the issues that really matter to them. To help out, we've put together a set of target audience guidelines in Form 12-3. The guidelines list the typical stakeholders in a company along with the parts of the business plan and specific issues that are of special importance to them.

After you've had a chance to look over the guidelines in Form 12-3, put a check beside the groups of stakeholders you intend to address in your plan and circle the issues that you feel concern them the most. As you're putting your business plan together, you can use the target audience guidelines to make sure you've addressed all the key topics.

Addressing more than one audience

How can one business plan possibly address so many audiences and focus on so many different sets of issues all at once? By making full use of the way your business plan is put together, you can allow different readers to read things differently.

BUSINESS PLAN TARGET AUDIENCE GUIDELINES			
Intended Audience	**Key Plan Components**	**Issues to Emphasize**	**Ideal Length**
☐ **Bankers**	• Executive summary • Company strategy • Financial review	• Cash flow • Assets • Solid growth	10-20 pages
☐ **Investors**	• Executive summary • Business environment • Company strategy • Company description • Financial review • Action plan	• Assets • Business opportunity • Management team	10-20 pages
☐ **Strategic partners**	• Company overview • Business environment • Company description • Financial review • Action plan	• Synergy • Proprietary products • Management	20-40 pages
☐ **Customers**	• Executive summary • Company overview	• Stability • Service • Management team	5-10 pages
☐ **Employees**	• Executive summary • Company overview • Company strategy • Action plan	• Security • Business opportunity • Clear strategy • Goals and objectives	5-10 pages
☐ **Shareholders**	• Executive summary • Company overview • Company strategy • Financial review • Action plan	• Financial growth • Strategic opportunity • Management team	10-20 pages
☐ **General Public**	• Executive summary • Company overview	• Mission and vision • Values	3-5 pages

Form 12-3: Business plan target audience guidelines.

- **Table of contents:** At first glance, the table of contents may not seem like a part of your business plan to spend serious time on. But a well-designed table of contents can offer a clear road map of the written document you're putting together, enabling your audience to quickly locate the specific sections of your plan that most interest them.

  If you're putting together a business plan that's over ten pages long, consider including a table of contents that lists both sections and subsections. And don't forget to include page numbers, so that you and your readers can quickly locate specific sections in the plan.

- **Executive summary:** A solid, well-written executive summary gives your audience a clear and concise description of your company and the key issues that will be described fully in the main body of your business plan. Some of your readers may learn all they need to know in this summary. Others may decide whether to read the rest of your plan, based on what they see in the executive summary. Either way, it's a critical piece of your written plan.

  How do you decide what should go into the executive summary? One way to make the first cut is to go back through the revised draft of your plan and highlight all the critical points you want made. Be ruthless here. Choose only the one or two elements in each section that are absolutely essential. Remember, the executive summary is meant to give a very quick overview — the rest of your plan fills in the details. After you highlight these critical points, organize them into a rough draft of the executive summary. Try to express major ideas using the same words that you use in the plan itself.

  Another strategy is based on the old elevator conversation trick. Imagine that you suddenly find yourself in an elevator with one of your stakeholders — a banker, a potential investor, or someone else who's critical to your plans. You have exactly one minute — the time it takes the elevator to go from the lobby to the 25th floor — to describe your business idea, your strategy, and how you intend to carry it out. What do you say? Without giving it another thought, sit down and write out your elevator pitch on a sheet of paper. (If you have a tape recorder handy, start talking.) Chances are you'll instinctively hit all the key points. Make sure that your executive summary also hits those same important points.

  Ideally, keep the executive summary of your business plan down to a single page. Longer than that is too long. This is a summary, after all. If you still need to get your own summary down to one page, try tightening up the language or pruning away the least essential points.

- **The appendixes:** Unlike your own appendix, which sits in your body and does nothing, the appendixes in your business plan can be useful and absolutely essential — especially if you want to address several

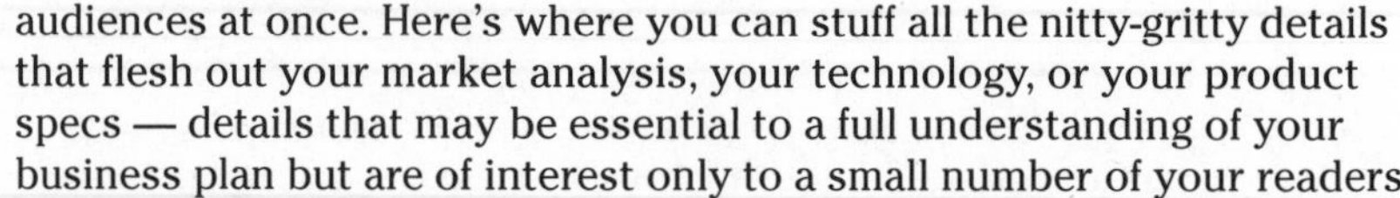

audiences at once. Here's where you can stuff all the nitty-gritty details that flesh out your market analysis, your technology, or your product specs — details that may be essential to a full understanding of your business plan but are of interest only to a small number of your readers.

Don't fill your appendixes with absolutely everything you know just to make your plan look heftier. Business plans aren't judged by the pound, after all. The material here should relate directly to your business plan and should provide important details about your markets, your strategy, your management team, your technology, or other key aspects of your business.

In fact, make sure you refer to all the documents that appear in the appendixes at some appropriate place within the main body of your plan. Here are two examples to show you how:

- Our advanced Internet platform offers many competitive advantages over existing software, including higher speed, lower cost, and greater reliability. (For technical details, see the "Technical Specifications of ISP Version 6.1" in Appendix 2.)
- Our market analysis shows that many IT professionals are concerned about the speed and bandwidth of existing Internet software platforms, and they're willing to pay more for next generation technology. Their chief concern is reliability. (For details, see the "Market Data Analysis Summary" in Appendix 3.)

References like these alert readers that they can find additional information in an appendix. By putting supporting documents at the end, you ensure that the main body of your written business plan doesn't become bogged down in the details.

Creating alternate versions of your plan

Sometimes it's just not possible to create a single written plan that effectively addresses every reader — especially if you have a wide variety of stakeholders that you absolutely need to communicate with. Don't worry. There's no law against having more than one business plan. In fact, many companies have several versions of their plan, each targeted at a different audience — one aimed at employees, for example, another toward potential lenders or investors, and a third for the general public.

Developing several versions of your business plan is pretty straightforward. First you need to create a complete and comprehensive master plan — one that includes everything that's likely to be important to any and all of your stakeholders. Using this master plan, you then decide which parts are important and which aren't relevant to a specific target audience. (If you need a reminder, refer to Form 12-3.) After that, putting together an alternate version

Nine lives

When the founders of Save Our Strays (SOS) first wrote a business plan for their not-for-profit organization, they never imagined that it would have more lives than a cat. Concerned about the growing number of feral felines in their community, the group put together its first plan in order to raise grant money to spay and neuter cats and to provide medical care and homes to cats abandoned on the street.

After SOS was up and running, the organization soon discovered that individual donors were also interested in contributing small sums to help out. Instead of printing up a glossy brochure, SOS decided to create a streamlined version of its business plan — one that included its mission and vision, of course, as well as the organization overview and action plan — but leaving out entire sections, such as the financial review.

As the group's efforts gained widespread attention, they began to receive press inquiries — including several television stations that wanted to produce stories on the problem of strays and what was being done to solve it. Once again, SOS turned to its business plan, this time creating a fact-sheet version of the document that contained all the essential points in a short, informal, easy-to-read format.

The media coverage soon led to interest from other communities that hoped to use the group's approach as a model to address their own problems with stray cats. To explain how SOS worked, the group returned once again to its business plan, cutting and pasting key information about fund-raising strategies and day-to-day operations into a new document. Organizations in other communities around the country have now used this new document as a template to create their own business plans. SOS figures that its original business plan has had more than nine lives — and it's still alive and well today.

is as simple as cutting and pasting the relevant parts of the master plan together.

If you decide to create several versions of your plan, make sure that they conform to one another. In other words, don't write one mission statement for one audience and another for a second group of readers. And whatever you do, don't create different sets of goals and objectives for different stakeholders. At the very least, you'll confuse everyone — yourself included. At worst, you'll anger one group or another. The job of creating a targeted version of your business plan is really one of deciding which parts of the master plan to include and which to leave out. The wording should remain the same in all versions.

Making Sure All the Pieces Fit

After you have a working draft of your written plan in place, step back and take a look at the entire document to make sure that all the pieces really fit together. Your mission statement should be reflected in your company overview, for example. Your assessment of the business environment should be in sync with your business strategy.

Looking over the document as a whole is particularly important if your plan is being assembled by a team. Sometimes the right hand doesn't know exactly what the left hand is doing, even when you have a solid outline for everyone to work from. This initial read-through can be done by the members of your planning team.

Later on in the review process, however, enlist the help of others who haven't been involved along the way. Outside readers will see the document with fresh eyes and are more likely to catch discrepancies or places where the language isn't crystal clear. Enlist the help of people who aren't afraid to tell it like it is — even if that means giving you a thumbs down on parts of your plan. Be clear from the start that the plan is a working draft, and that you welcome any and all comments, positive or negative.

To help you speed up the review process, we've put together a working draft checklist in Form 12-4. The checklist covers key questions to ask yourself as you review your written business plan. Consider asking your outside readers to also use this form as a guide when they give you feedback on your draft plan.

Don't panic if your reviewers come back with all sorts of suggestions or criticisms. This just means they're doing their jobs. The reason for looking over the plan at this stage, after all, is to identify problems and fix them. A little criticism never hurt anyone. And it has helped to make a lot of business plans much more effective. If you've done your homework, most of the fixes are likely to be fairly simple ones. And even if they require a little extra work on your part, it's probably well worth the effort.

WORKING DRAFT CHECKLIST
☐ Is our executive summary clear and compelling?
☐ Do the major pieces of the company overview – our mission statement, values and vision, and major business goals and objectives – work together to explain who we are and what we believe in?
☐ Does the overview provide a strong sense of the nature of our business and the products and services we plan to offer?
☐ Do our goals and objectives match the company's mission?
☐ Does the plan offer a convincing analysis of the market we intend to enter?
☐ Does the plan give a clear description of who our primary customers will be?
☐ Does the plan adequately and objectively assess our strengths and weaknesses?
☐ Does the company's strategy make sense in light of our analysis of the business environment?
☐ Does our action plan match up with our strategic direction, as outlined in the plan?
☐ Does the plan's financial review reflect our business strategy and action plan?
☐ Does our action plan include enough specifics to create a road map for the near-term?
☐ Is the plan clearly written and easy to understand?
☐ Is there anything missing from the plan that should be added?
☐ Is there anything that should be cut from the plan?
☐ Are there other changes that would strengthen our written plan?

Form 12-4: Working draft checklist.

Forms on the CD-ROM

Take a look at the following forms on the CD-ROM to help you put your written business plan together:

Form 12-1	**Business Plan Components Checklist**	A checklist of the major components of a business plan, along with the important items to consider including in each component
Form 12-2	**Master Plan Tracking Sheet**	A tracking sheet to help you see at a glance where you are in the process of writing your business plan document
Form 12-3	**Business Plan Target Audience Guidelines**	Guidelines to help you tailor your business plan so that you can better reach different target audiences
Form 12-4	**Working Draft Checklist**	A checklist of the questions to ask yourself as you review the working draft of your business plan

Chapter 13

Putting Your Plan to Work

In This Chapter

- Using the plan to organize your company
- Getting the best out of your employees
- Planning when trouble strikes
- Reviewing and revising your plan

Let us be the first to congratulate you! You've done the brainstorming, the research, and the analysis. You've come up with a solid business strategy, financial model, and a detailed plan of action. And you've pulled all this information together into a written business plan. So pat yourself on the back — and then roll up your sleeves. It's time to start the equally important job of putting your plan to work.

One of the biggest mistakes a new business can make is not taking full advantage of the business plan they've already worked so hard on. Time and again, we've watched as companies use their plans to raise money and assemble topnotch management teams — only to tuck their plans away and forget about them. Six months later, the managers wonder why their businesses are foundering. We've watched entrepreneurs with great ideas and sound business strategy never get their companies off the ground because they failed to follow through with their own plans.

If you ask successful entrepreneurs how they made it, they'll usually list two things. Number one: They had a solid business plan in place. Number two: They stuck to it.

In this chapter, we help you make the most of your own business plan. First, we talk about how to use your plan as a blueprint to organize your business. We look at how to choose the best organizational structure and the most effective procedures for getting the job done. Then we give you tips on how to use your plan to get the most out of your most important resource: your people. And because even the best-planned enterprise can run into trouble, we show you how to use your business plan to steer a course through rough times. Finally, we offer ways to keep your business plan fresh and vital.

Organizing Your Company around the Business Plan

The leap from writing a business plan to actually creating a business is a lot like the leap from drawing a blueprint to actually constructing a house. Suddenly, you have to build the dang thing. Blueprints tell a contractor exactly where everything is supposed to go, down to a fraction of an inch. A business plan isn't quite that specific, so when you begin to create your organization, you still have a fair amount of flexibility. But your business plan should serve as your primary guide. In fact, if you don't organize your business around your plan, we can almost guarantee that you'll have a tough time turning your plan into reality.

Form meets function

Your business plan should see its reflection in virtually every part of your company's organization, from the structure of your management team to the procedures you put in place to make your business work. In particular, three parts of your plan are likely to play leading roles in shaping your organization:

- **Company description:** Particularly the assessment of your company's capabilities and resources
- **Company strategy:** Including how you plan to reach, serve, and satisfy your customers
- **Action plan:** Including all the steps you need to take to carry out the rest of your business plan

These parts cover a lot of territory. What's the best way to think about organizing your business to address all the issues? One approach is to look at other companies and how they're organized. Of course no two companies are exactly alike, but most are built around one of four common organizational models. (Flip to Chapter 6 for details.) The organizational models include the following:

- **The pack,** in which one person runs the show and everyone else is an equal member of, well, the pack.
- **By function,** in which people are divided into groups depending on the functions they perform in the company.
- **By division,** in which distinct parts of the company's business are divided into separate divisions, each with its own management structure.
- **The matrix,** in which employees are allowed to wear more than one hat and report to more than one supervisor, encouraging team members to share talent, expertise, and experience.

The most effective organizational format for your business depends on the kind of company you're putting together — big, small, formal, informal, online, manufacturing, retail, service, and a dozen other considerations. But most of all, it depends on your business plan.

To help you shape the organizational structure that's best for you, think about the following questions as you look over your business plan. We've included a few pointers, depending on the answers you come up with:

- Is a single individual responsible for your company's vision and strategic direction? If so, you may want to model your company on the pack, with one leader and a team of pack members.
- Is employee creativity crucial to the success of your company? If so, you may want to consider a loose organizational structure with relatively few management levels, giving your staff the freedom to be creative.
- Are speed and flexibility crucial to your company remaining competitive? If so, think about a flat organizational structure with as few management levels as possible.
- Will your company consist of several distinct functions, each with its own culture and kinds of employees? If so, consider a functional organization.
- Does your company work much of the time on a project basis, moving people and resources from one job to another? If so, a matrix organization may work best for you.

You can always change the structure of your company at some point down the road. In fact, you may want do exactly that, especially if your business is growing rapidly, for example, or your business environment has changed significantly.

Duties and responsibilities

After you consider your organization and its structure, your next task is to assign duties and responsibilities to your key people. You've probably done some of the work already, at least for your top management team. (If not, check out Chapter 6.)

What's important here is to make sure that the duties and responsibilities you assign are closely aligned with the major goals and objectives you've laid out in your business plan. After all, if the work your key employees do isn't directly tied to the company's business goals, those goals are never going to get accomplished.

Take a look at Word for Word, a secretarial services company, to see how it aligns the duties and responsibilities assigned to key employees with the company's business goals and objectives. (For more details on this company, take a look at Chapter 3 and Figure 3-2). Figure 13-1 shows how the company used a simple chart to match up the goals and objectives identified in their business plan with members of their management team.

GOALS AND OBJECTIVES ASSIGNMENT CHART		
GOAL • OBJECTIVE	**WHO'S RESPONSIBLE**	**NOTES**
Enhance staff expertise	Director, H.R.	Must work closely with Director of Sales to determine key skills required by clients
• Schedule regular training seminars (by 5-1)	Training manager/ outside training consultant	
• Have all staff certified (by 12-15)	Director, H.R.	
Increase brand awareness	Marketing/Sales VP	Must work closely with direct reports to shape marketing strategy
• Create customer referral bonus program (by 6-15)	Director, Sales	
• Begin monthly newsletter (by 8-1)	Director, Marketing Communications/ outside contractor	Consult with Information Technology to determine feasibility of an online version
Improve customer service	Marketing/Sales VP	High priority–should involve input from all senior management
• Hire two new employees (by 7-15)	Director, H.R.	Consult with marketing
• Install new job-tracking software (by 9-15)	Operations VP/ outside consultant	Work closely with marketing staff to determine requirements

Figure 13-1: Use an assignment chart to make sure management duties and responsibilities align with major business goals and objectives.

By assigning responsibility for their major goals and objectives, Word for Word significantly improved the chances that its action plan will be carried out. What's more, the assignment chart confirmed that senior managers will have to work closely together to accomplish the plan — supporting the company's decision to adopt a relatively flat, flexible management structure. Finally, the company found that the chart provided useful guidelines when it created more detailed job descriptions for the management team.

Set aside some time to fill out an assignment chart for the key people in your own organization. Form 13-1, which you'll find on the CD-ROM, provides a handy template designed to ensure that your major business goals and objectives stay on track.

Systems and procedures

Another question to consider, and it's a biggie: How will your business operate on a day-to-day basis? In other words, what sorts of systems and procedures do you need to establish in order to accomplish everything from product development to sales and customer service? Okay, we're the first to admit that talk about systems and procedures can easily put almost anyone to sleep. But having them in place can mean the difference between success or failure.

When online publishing exploded onto the Internet a few years back, many of the early startups had little experience in the traditional publishing world. The truth is, most of them didn't have a clue about what's involved in developing editorial content — whether for a newspaper, a magazine, a brochure, or a Web site. As a result, all sorts of stuff began to show up on the Web — good, bad, and the truly awful.

If these clueless online publishers had taken the time to talk traditional magazine publishers, for example, they would have discovered a time-tested set of procedures already in place, designed to shepherd articles or stories along from first idea to finished draft. Here's how the process works: A story editor assigns the piece to a writer and edits the piece when it's submitted; a copy editor edits the piece for grammar and style; a top editor reviews the piece to make sure it's clear and readable. Magazines also have fact-checkers, who verify the key facts and details of a piece before it goes to print.

It wasn't long, in fact, before a few online publishers got smart and began to hire people with experience in traditional publishing. The reason: These old hands knew how to put procedures and systems in place that would guarantee an efficient operation and the highest quality control.

The lesson here, even if you aren't starting an online magazine, is that a rational set of procedures and well-defined systems can ensure efficiency and maintain quality control in any kind of business. These procedures and systems help you keep your employees productive and your customers satisfied. And in the end, they protect your bottom line.

The specific procedures you will need to develop depend on what your company plans to do. Your first step: Look back over your company description, strategy, and your action plan. Then jot down all the systems and procedures you think you need to get the job done.

You don't have to reinvent the wheel here. Instead, check with industry groups and ask about standard operating procedures or basic business systems that may already be well documented. Read trade publications and investigate third party providers who may offer software or other packaged solutions that meet your operational requirements.

To make sure you don't leave anything out, we've put together a checklist of the most common business systems and procedures in Form 13-2. We've left a few open slots for you to fill in procedures that may be specific to your own company.

After you complete the checklist, circle the two or three procedures that are most critical to your business strategy and plan. Break down each of them into the series of steps that are involved. The exercise can help you identify potential gaps in your planning before they cause problems.

Making the Most of Your People

Business buzzwords tend to have a lot in common with the hula hoop or pet rocks: wildly popular one day, clichés the next. But one buzzword has never gone out of fashion, and that's teamwork. Whenever more than one person is involved in a business — from small shop to sprawling multinational — teamwork is critical to long-term success.

Without the strong sense of being part of a team, employees often have little incentive to work hard and work together. In fact, they often end up working against each other. Teamwork, however, can change a basic business equation. One plus one can actually equal three, because team players often produce results that are greater than the sum of the individual contributions. And because teams are inherently strong, a business culture that encourages teamwork can help carry you and your employees through the bad times as well as the good.

COMMON SYSTEMS AND PROCEDURES CHECKLIST
☐ **Research and development** ○ New product/service design ○ Existing product/service modification ○ Product testing and certification ○ Product specifications, manuals, users guides ○ ○
☐ **Operations** ○ Facilities management ○ Supplies and raw materials procurement ○ Manufacturing processes ○ Quality control ○ Packaging ○ ○
☐ **Sales and marketing** ○ Advertising and promotions ○ Public relations ○ Sales force management ○ Customer contact management ○ Customer order tracking ○ ○
☐ **Distribution and delivery** ○ Distributor relationships ○ Delivery systems ○ Inventory management ○ ○
☐ **Customer service** ○ Help-desk procedures ○ Warrantee and service fulfillment ○ Customer complaints and returns ○ ○

Form 13-2: Common systems and procedures checklist — page 1 of 2.

☐ **Management**

- ○ Business planning
- ○ Goal setting
- ○ Industry and market analysis
- ○ Strategy and tactics
- ○ Investor relations
- ○ Budgeting
- ○
- ○

☐ **Organization**

- ○ Employee recruitment
- ○ Salary, wages, and benefits setting
- ○ Employee training and development
- ○ Job descriptions and performance review
- ○ Employee complaints and terminations
- ○
- ○

☐ **Finance**

- ○ Business asset control
- ○ Cash flow tracking
- ○ Customer billing
- ○ Accounts payable and receivable
- ○ Payroll management
- ○ Financial reporting
- ○ Tax accounting
- ○
- ○

Form 13-2: Common systems and procedures checklist — page 2 of 2.

Distributing your plan

What do people have to do with your business plan? Plenty, of course. Your plan lays out your company's mission, vision, and values. It also sets down the rules of the game and exactly how you plan to win. So if you want to create a winning team, make darn sure that everyone is familiar with your plan, knows the rules, and understands exactly what has to be done to be successful.

To put your own business plan to work, make sure that the members of your management team all have copies and have read them. Even better, distribute the most important parts of your plan — at meetings, in a newsletter, on your intranet — to everyone in the company, from entry level assistants all the way to the top. The following are just a few reasons why we think distributing your plan is so critical:

- **To promote teamwork:** If you want your company to work efficiently and effectively, you have to make sure your employees are working together to make your business plan work. And that means that they have to know what's in it. We don't necessarily mean that every employee needs to review every last detail, but each of your employees should know your company's mission, basic strategy, major goals, and plan of action.
- **To create a sense of ownership:** Your business plan serves as a blueprint for what you want your company to become. By sharing this information with employees, you allow them to see how their personal involvement contributes to making the plan a reality. There's no better way to create a sense of ownership. And that, in turn, goes a long way toward motivating everyone around you.
- **To link individual and company performance together:** Linking individual and company performance is a way of acknowledging that your organization's success depends on the hard work of every employee. Too often, employee performance reviews can seem disconnected and rather arbitrary. By evaluating your people in relation to key goals and objectives in the business plan, you underscore why their performance really matters.
- **To generate feedback and new ideas:** Your employees can be a great resource, whether you need an infusion of new ideas or simply a reality check. After all, many of them are at ground zero as far as your business is concerned. To make full use of this resource, however, you have to make sure that your people are familiar with what you plan to do.

We're not suggesting that you give a pop quiz to test everybody's knowledge of the business plan. (Although it may be fun to spring one on your top managers: "In 25 words or less, describe our ideal customer. Which of the following best describes our action plan?") But we do think it's crucial to give the plan to employees and encourage them to read it. If your plan is more than ten pages long, consider creating a shorter version to accompany the employee handbook.

Whenever you revise your business plan, make sure that copies are distributed to everyone on staff. In fact, we even suggest going one step further and informing employees directly about key changes that have been made. If your company has an internal newsletter, publish a piece describing the revised plan and its features. If you have an intranet, use it to publish the new plan along with an FAQ (frequently asked questions) that discusses the changes that have been made — and why.

Starting at the top

Effective teams demand strong leaders. Leadership, after all, is built on the ability to influence others and make things happen. Solid management skills play an important role, of course, but good managers are not guaranteed to be good leaders. We're talking about the capacity to inspire people, for example, and the ability to cut to the chase, focusing in on the most critical issues.

The best leaders turn out to be those people who know how to adapt their approach to specific situations. They can lay down the law when they have to. But they also know how to elicit help and ask for advice. They move easily among three different leadership styles:

- **The boss,** who tells employees what to do, when to do it, and how to do it.
- **The advisor,** who gives people a fair amount of independence and responsibility while remaining available to help or advise as necessary.
- **The colleague,** who sits down with employees for a free exchange of ideas in which everyone is treated with equal respect and mutual decisions are made.

Do leaders come from Mars or Venus?

Men are from Mars, women are from Venus, as a runaway bestseller has taught you. But what about great leaders? Of course, we know that men and women are equally adept at heading up successful companies. But research out of Purdue University suggests that men and women tend to have different leadership styles, and that employees respond differently to these styles, depending on whether they are men or women.

The Purdue team found that men typically adopt a more traditional, transactional style of leadership, which depends on rewards and punishments to influence employees. *Transactional* leaders tend to be hands-off unless something goes wrong. Women, on the other hand, more typically use a *transformational* style, one that employs encouragement and individual attention to influence employee behavior. Transformational leaders tend to relate to employees on an emotional level.

Now here's the real surprise: Men in the survey said they appreciated the considerate attention they received from female managers who used the transformational style. But female employees weren't impressed at all by the extra attention. They tended to respond best to the traditional approach.

What's a manager to do? The researchers concluded that effective managers should employ different leadership styles, depending on whom they're managing. Of course, that's something good leaders have known for a long time.

Beyond that, the most effective leadership style for you really depends on the kind of business you're in. If you're running a design or advertising agency, for example, the ability to give people plenty of freedom to be creative is an absolute must. If you're starting a local courier service, however, the ability to give orders, direct people, and keep everyone on schedule is essential.

Review your business plan to get an overall sense of the management skills and leadership traits that will prove most effective for you. Check off the skills and traits listed in Form 13-3 that most clearly apply to your own situation. These may prove particularly helpful as you put your plan to work.

CHECKLIST OF MANAGEMENT AND LEADERSHIP TRAITS	
☐ Inspires people	☐ Promotes loyalty
☐ Wins trust	☐ Encourages creativity
☐ Communicates well	☐ Adapts to changing conditions
☐ Makes quick, confident decisions	☐ Delegates responsibilities
☐ Manages diverse projects	☐ Solves problems
☐ Sets specific goals and objectives	☐ Moves projects along on deadline
☐ Manages a tight budget	☐ Offers criticism without alienating
☐ Cultivates leadership in others	☐ Resolves conflicts
☐ Leads by example	☐
☐	☐

Form 13-3: Checklist of management and leadership traits.

Look for opportunities to practice the skills and traits you think you'll need to be an effective manager and a strong leader. If tight deadlines are a fact of life in your business, develop ways to make everyone aware of each deadline and comfortable meeting it. If creativity is the hallmark of your business, sit down with your colleagues to get their thoughts on the best ways to encourage it.

Creating the vision thing

Your business plan represents the vision of what you want your company to become, right down to the last market initiative and financial projection. Vision is all important when creating a sense of shared commitment and direction, and your business plan is a terrific way to communicate your vision to everyone who has a stake in your company. Wanting to share this vision doesn't necessarily mean that everybody has to read and reread your business plan on a monthly basis. You can use other methods to make your plan a living, breathing document and keep your vision, mission, and business goals front and center. The following are some examples:

- Reproduce your mission and vision statements in company newsletters, the employee handbook, even on the back side of business cards.
- Refer to the business plan whenever appropriate — during marketing strategy meetings or new product development forums, for example.
- Use the plan as a standard yardstick to evaluate all programs and initiatives.
- Use your business goals and objectives as a primary guide when conducting employee performance evaluations.
- Actively enlist feedback from everyone in the company when you're preparing to reassess and revise your business plan.

Leading from within

You may be the supreme leader of the company pack right now. But if your vision for the business has anything to do with growth — especially rapid growth — now's the time to think about who's going to support you and perhaps one day step in to fill your shoes.

Don't worry: We're not planning your retirement party quite yet. But as companies grow bigger, they inevitably reach a point when the person at the top can't do everything. Even if you already have a management team in place, a time will likely come when you have to expand — and loosen up on the reins. That's what growing a company is all about. How well you manage the growing pains often determines how successful your company ultimately becomes.

Passing on the leadership mantle represents one of the most difficult transitions a company can make. That's hardly surprising. Many leaders have a tough time relinquishing control at the top. And too many entrepreneurs fail to take the time to cultivate leaders from within. The issue of succession can be particularly tricky for family-run firms, because it brings up both business and personal considerations. Some family members may not want to become involved with the family's company; others may want to play a role but lack the training or experience. That's why planning is so important. Family members who will eventually take over key roles in the business must be prepared and groomed, just like any other employees.

When facing the leadership issue head-on, most people ask: "How do I identify the rising stars in my organization who are most likely to become leaders?" It's an important question, of course. But the first question should really be: "Where is our business likely to need strong leadership in the future?" And that's where your business plan comes in. Reviewing your business goals and objectives should provide some insight into this second question. Your action plan will also suggest areas where strong leadership is essential. But the best guide you have is likely to be your SWOT analysis (if that doesn't sound familiar, check Chapter 5 for details). A SWOT analysis is a nifty way to assess your company's strengths and weaknesses in relation to the opportunities and threats you're likely to face.

Consider the situation facing a West Coast mail-order company specializing in travel-related merchandise. The company's biggest strength is its efficient Internet operation, which boasts a 24-hour turnaround on customer orders. Largely because of this quick turnaround, customer satisfaction has remained consistently high. But the business has grown dramatically over the last year, and the company has begun to experience periodic breakdowns in its order-fulfillment operations. And while the boom in travel has expanded the market, it has also brought in a slew of competitors. Unfortunately, the company's marketing capabilities are only so-so. And one of its continuing weaknesses has been its inability to differentiate its catalog and Web site from the rest of the pack.

After a complete SWOT analysis and review, the company has now identified three key areas where leadership will be crucial over the coming year:

- Order fulfillment and quality control
- Marketing and branding
- Web site development

Take some time to review your own SWOT analysis and identify important areas where leadership may be particularly critical to your future. Check these areas against the business goals and objectives you've set to make sure they're also represented. After you identify the key areas, begin to consider people around you who can be cultivated to take on future leadership roles.

Encouraging pride of ownership

People who own businesses usually work long hours, put up with lots of stress — and typically love every minute of it. They're building something of their very own, a business that reflects their talents and inspirations. In other words, they're motivated by a strong pride of ownership. As a leader, you have to find ways to motivate your employees so that they feel the same way.

Of course the most obvious way to instill this pride of ownership in your employees is literally to give them a piece of the company, using stock-purchase plans that can be tied to individual or team performance. You can also pay out bonuses at the end of the year that are based on how well the company is doing. Both of these methods motivate employees, no doubt about it.

But you can also instill a sense of employee pride in ways that go beyond dollars and cents. You can foster a real entrepreneurial spirit, for example, by giving employees the sense that they "own" the success of the projects or departments they're in charge of. You do this by making clear that they have full control and responsibility for particular programs — including the freedom to make key decisions. Then follow up by rewarding them for jobs well done.

We're talking more than money here. Although a performance bonus is always nice, try to recognize contributions in other ways, as well. You may consider things like an "employee of the month" award, write-ups in the company newsletter, a round of applause at the next company-wide meeting, or simply a heartfelt pat on the back. In fact, these simple morale boosters are often more effective than money in motivating employees.

A major health-related Web site recently reorganized its writers and editors to create small editorial teams, each in charge of a specific content area or "channel" — men's health, diet and nutrition, children's health, fitness, and other health subjects. What's more, each team was explicitly given creative freedom to shape the channel and develop new features. The company then set up monthly meetings to review channel performance and recognize important achievements, such as award-winning stories. By virtually every measure, the quality of the Web site improved dramatically over the next six months.

Then the company tried to go one step further. To create real competition among the channels, they started tracking the number of *hits* (people logging on to the Web site) each channel received during the month. Of course, fostering competition among teams can be a potent motivator, but the approach can also backfire, creating resentment and hard feelings. In this case, the number of hits had less to do with the quality of a particular channel and more to do with the Web site's users, who tended to be women in their 30s and 40s. As a result, the men's health channel was always less popular than the women's health channel, regardless of the quality of stories or its special features. The result: Instead of motivating employees, the use of hits as a measure created a sense of frustration and unfairness among the teams. Fortunately, the competition was quickly abandoned in favor of data reflecting the popularity of the entire Web site.

If you plan to use competition among teams or departments as a motivating tool, make sure everyone is playing on a level field. Whatever measure you choose to compare your internal "competitors" — profits, unit sales, or Web site hits — make sure they reflect the work of the teams, not external factors over which team members have little control.

Investing in skills

No matter what kind of company you're putting together, your success in making your business plan a reality depends to a large extent on the quality of the people you can attract and keep. And as you begin to grow, expanding the skills of your existing workforce can be just as important as finding qualified employees to hire in the first place, especially in tight labor markets. It's a win-win situation. Your employees get the opportunity to take on more responsibility, and you gain an increasingly qualified (and loyal) staff.

Talk the talk and walk the walk

In 1994, United Airlines became one of the largest employee-owned companies in the world, with its pilots, mechanics, and other employees owning over 50 percent of the company. Many analysts thought that a new pride of ownership would improve employee morale and motivation — and help turn the ailing airline around.

Unfortunately, it hasn't quite worked out that way. Lately, the friendly skies of United have been clouded with work slowdowns and threats of union strikes. Management has even taken United's machinists to court, charging them with conducting illegal job actions. What went wrong? Although the airline made a big deal about calling its workers "owners," they never really treated them like owners. They talked the talk, in other words, but they never really walked the walk. And as for the employees, they never really felt as if they had any role in shaping the company or its future. United's CEO was quoted as saying: "One of the greatest opportunities we did not take advantage of was sitting down and agreeing on a joint vision of where we wanted to go."

Employee ownership can create a strategic advantage for a company. Just ask any one of the 11,000 employee-owned businesses in the United States, most of them doing very well. But in order for it to work, employees must feel as if they really are owners — and that they have a place at the management table and a voice in shaping the company's future.

To make the most of your investment in training, target the capabilities your company absolutely has to have in order to meet your goals and objectives. Take the time to review your business plan in order to identify specific skills your employees will need, focusing on your company strategy and action plan. And don't forget to include general abilities, such as the ability to manage information, think independently, work in teams, and deal with change.

After you have your critical skills list in hand, explore education and training opportunities that are best suited to your needs and your pocketbook. To help you get started, Form 13-4 offers a checklist of some of the most common training options available. Check off the ones that seem most promising, given your situation.

EMPLOYEE TRAINING RESOURCE CHECKLIST
☐ Adult-education degrees
☐ Outside training courses
☐ In-house training programs
☐ Certification programs
☐ Internet-based education
☐ CD-ROM training
☐ Self-help business books and instructional guides
☐ Mentoring programs

Form 13-4: Employee training resource checklist.

A word about *mentoring,* which is a process in which more experienced employees take on new hires or junior members of your team and shepherd them along in their careers. This can be one of the most cost-effective ways to enhance the skills of your employees. And it has the added pay off of encouraging both teamwork and company loyalty. If you decide to institute a mentoring program, remember that mentoring takes time and hard work. So make sure that you reward employees who serve as mentors. And free up their schedules in order to give them the extra time they need. Pick up a copy of *Coaching & Mentoring For Dummies* by Marty Brounstein (Hungry Minds, Inc.) for the lowdown on mentoring.

While we're at it, we'll put in a plug for some other terrific and under-used training resources: self-help business books, instructional guides, educational Web sites, and CD-ROMs. You can find plenty of terrific products on subjects ranging from accounting and marketing to computer programming and customer service. Your company may want to encourage continuous employee training by maintaining a library of appropriate titles in-house.

Whatever training resources you decide upon, don't forget to encourage employees to take advantage of them by offering appropriate incentives — job promotions, salary increases, bonuses, or other rewards.

Using Your Plan in Times of Trouble

Bad things can happen even to the very best companies. Suddenly the economy goes south. Or a big client decides to take its business somewhere else. A product that looks really good on paper isn't as attractive in real life. Or some regulatory ruling abruptly alters the competitive landscape, leaving the strategic plan in tatters.

What can you do when things go wrong? Unfortunately, way too many companies simply abandon their business plans and begin swimming in circles. And that's almost always a big mistake.

If you happen to find yourself in this situation, don't panic. Sure, you probably have flaws in parts of your business plan. Maybe your business model isn't quite what it was cracked up to be. And maybe those financial projections are a wee bit too hopeful. But that doesn't mean the entire business plan is worthless. By carefully reviewing a business plan, in fact, a company in trouble can often pinpoint what went wrong and begin planning a way to turn things around.

Recognizing the warning signs

If your company finds itself in trouble, your first step should be to discover the source of the problem. In some cases, that may be easy. A new competitor has entered the market, for example, and gobbled up half your business. Or the economy has taken a nosedive just as you've opened your doors, and initial sales are down 50 percent from projections. Ouch.

But in other situations, the problems you face may not be so clearly defined. Perhaps your manufacturing costs have inched up gradually, for example, at a time when your competitors are cutting their prices. Maybe you're also having trouble filling a key marketing position, which means you can't hammer together an effective strategy to deal with the changing competitive environment.

Diagnosing your problems

Most companies don't find themselves in hot water overnight. The warning signs are slight at first and appear months or even years before someone at the top finally says, "Uh-oh." So how do you know if your business may be headed for trouble down the road? In Form 13-5, we've put together a checklist of some of the early warning signs to be aware of. If you see some items that strike close to home, check them off. If not, keep the list handy and return to it from time to time, just to be on the safe side.

What if you *have* checked off some of the warning signs in Form 13-5? Well, if you've checked three or more items on the list, step back and take a long, hard look at your business, and try to figure out why your best-laid plans haven't worked out quite the way you expected them to. Review your business plan and the assumptions behind it. Suppose, for example, that your problem is with customers: They're not flocking to that new location the way you thought they would. If that's the case, review your original market analysis and customer profiling. What assumptions did you make? What's different? Do you have new competitors? Have your customers wants and needs changed?

Whatever you do, don't start playing the blame game when things go sour. Companies in trouble immediately begin to look for scapegoats — as if the sacrifice will somehow solve the problem. In fact, you may eventually need to — how can we put this delicately? — make some personnel changes in order to get the business back on its feet. But the most important first step you can take is to understand not who's to blame, but what has gone wrong.

Getting a second opinion

Ever hear of *turnaround professionals?* They're a whole new breed of management consultants. Heck, there's even a Turnaround Management Association filled with these people, who are more than willing to tell you what's wrong with your company and how to fix it. For a price, of course.

CHECKLIST OF COMMON WARNING SIGNS
☐ Key goals and objectives have gone unmet
☐ Sales are lagging in a growing market
☐ Key customers have gone over to the competition
☐ Quality and service complaints are on the increase
☐ Employees are coming in late and leaving early
☐ An unusual number of employees have left for good
☐ Morale and motivation are down across the company
☐ Personality conflicts are on the rise among the staff
☐ Relationships between employees and managers are strained
☐ Revenues are down, expenses are up
☐ Projects are coming in over budget
☐ Payments to vendors are falling behind
☐ Customers aren't paying on time
☐ Cash reserves continue to fall
☐ Management meetings are cancelled at the last minute

Form 13-5: Checklist of common warning signs.

Are they worth it? In some cases — absolutely. You may have a tough time finding people on the inside of an organization who see critical issues objectively. All sorts of vested interests, assumptions, and emotions can get in the way. Outside consultants don't bring along all the excess baggage. The best of them take a clear-eyed and unemotional look at the business, pinpoint what's wrong, and come up with a solution — even if it's a painful one.

The best of them don't come cheap, however, so don't rush out and ask for help right off the bat. In fact, you can gain all sorts of benefits by bringing your own management team together to assess the damage and attempt to find a solution from the inside. Done right, it's an opportunity to create a stronger sense of teamwork and inspire the troops. You may find yourself coming up with more creative solutions than an outside consultant can suggest.

Analyzing your current situation

If your company is in trouble, chances are you're not where you expected to be six months or a year ago. If you want to begin shaping a plan to get back on course, you first have to know exactly where you stand right now. And we mean *exactly.* You won't do yourself any favors by whitewashing your situation or clinging to overly optimistic projections. Now's the time for harsh, black-and-white reality.

Focus on three parts of business planning when your company is in trouble:

- **Financial review:** At some point or another, troubles in the business are bound to boil down to a simple, painful fact: Money is flowing out faster than it's coming in. Maybe revenues are too low, expenses are too high, or your money in the bank just isn't enough to cover what you planned to do. In any case, there's no time like the present to face the music and assess your current financial picture, with a particular focus on cash flow and revised financial projections. (Check out Chapter 7 for details.)
- **SWOT analysis:** The opportunities and threats your business faces today may look a little different now that your company is struggling a bit. Even your own relative strengths and weaknesses may have changed. So this is an opportune time to revisit your SWOT analysis. Look at both the long and the short terms. And depending on what you find, direct your immediate attention to the strategic issues that are most likely to have an immediate impact on your situation. (Refer to Chapter 5 if you need help.)
- **Business model:** A shaky business model is very likely to be at least part of your problem. Even if it's not, this is still a good time to take another look at the assumptions you built into your model in the first place. Revisit your notions about how your company expects to make money. Spend some time thinking about creative ways a revised or expanded model could help turn your business around. (For more background info, take a look at Chapter 5.)

Back to basics

For years, Moe's Music rented and sold musical instruments. And the small, California-based business did modestly well. Then in the early 1990s, the company decided to expand into music education. The plan made sense on paper: Many junior highs and high schools were dropping their music education programs in California, and Moe's Music hoped to pick up the slack.

The company's plan's soon hit a sour note, however. First, Moe's had trouble recruiting and retaining qualified music teachers, and they struggled unsuccessfully to find ways of controlling the quality of music instruction. Finally, the expense of expanding their facilities to accommodate practice and rehearsal rooms proved more costly than they had projected.

Within two years, the company was singing the blues. Fortunately, the management team moved quickly to refocus Moe's strategy on the core business of renting and selling musical instruments. Moe's used the extra space they'd added to enlarge their inventory of instruments and to create audition rooms for customers to try out instruments. It took another full year, but by returning to the company's core business, Moe's was able to return to profitability.

The moral of Moe's: When trouble hits, companies often find their way back on track by returning to what they do best. They refocus on their core business — the single, essential thing they do, above everything else, that offers real value to their customers.

Charting your turnaround

After you diagnose the problems facing your company, create a revised business plan that reflects the new realities out there and sets out a step-by-step action plan to address them.

We're not suggesting that you go through the whole process of business planning all over again. Far from it. More than likely, your mission and vision statements are still intact. Your company overview probably hasn't changed all that much, either. And we're guessing that your industry hasn't gone through a top-to-bottom upheaval. In fact, you can probably focus your immediate attention on just four areas of your plan. (The rest you can tend to later, after the heat is off.) These include the following:

- Modified goals and objectives
- Revised company strategy
- Updated financial review
- Revised action plan

The steps to take are pretty much the same ones you took to create your business plan in the first place. (For a refresher, look through the chapters in

Part II.) Only this time around, make sure to keep the most urgent issues front and center. Focus your goals and objectives on resolving your direct threats first and getting your company back on an even keel. The same goes for your revised strategy and action plan: Make sure that they specifically address the immediate problems you face and that the solutions you propose can be achieved within the time frames you set down.

Desperate times sometimes call for desperate measures. If you're awash in red ink or burning through resources faster than you can say "venture capital," you have to take bold action. Like slashing expenses. Or letting people go. Or shaking up your management team. We're not going to tell you that it's easy or pleasant. But if you don't think that you can do it, remember this: If you can't, your investors will find someone who can. In fact, when turnaround managers are brought in from the outside, one of the first steps they take is to order a change at the top.

Keeping an eye on the clock

All good business plans are built around time frames. When you're creating a turnaround plan, time is especially critical — and not only because your money may be running out. When times get rough, employees grow restless. Morale begins to slide. And your company's reputation — both inside and out — begins to suffer. Over time, your relationships with suppliers, distributors, bankers, even clients can be damaged.

The faster you can turn things around, the smaller the impact this rocky period will have on your business and its future. So when you draft your revised goals and objectives, keep one eye on the clock. Set precise deadlines for when specific steps must be completed, and make sure that everyone knows them by heart.

While time is certainly of the essence, you won't be doing anyone a favor by setting unreasonable time frames for when tasks need to be done. More than anything else, your number one goal must be to reassure everyone around you that your company can make good on its word — and that means making only promises you can keep. So meet with all the people who will actually be doing the work and talk through exactly what it's going to take. After you have everyone's input, agree on times and dates that make sense. Then get ironclad commitments all around.

Focusing on what's do-able

When your company's in trouble, you're looking for bare bones, no nonsense planning. You have to focus on what you can do, not what you'd like to do. Don't make the mistake of turning your goals and objectives into a wish list. Sure, developing a new technology to streamline your manufacturing would be nice, for example, as would expanding into international markets. And maybe someday you will. But when times are tough, focus on what's do-able within the time you have.

Making sure everyone's in the loop

If your business gets into trouble, you're likely to find yourself spending your time talking to a lot of unhappy people: unhappy investors, unhappy vendors, unhappy employees, and unhappy customers. We can't help you put smiles on their faces. (That will come when the company's back in the black again.) But we can offer a piece of good advice: Whatever you do, keep on talking. Keep everybody informed all the time of exactly what's going on.

Not long ago, a leading turnaround professional put together his list of the steps involved in successfully turning a company around. The following is what he included:

- Meet with your management team
- Meet with your senior advisors
- Meet with your employees
- Meet with your customers
- Meet with your suppliers
- Contact the tax authorities
- Contact your bank

In other words, be in close communication with everyone who has any stake in your business and the turnaround you're trying to accomplish. And don't pretend business is better than it is. Be honest with everybody about what they can expect and exactly when they can expect it. The more straightforward you are, the better the odds that you'll keep people on your side. And especially when your company is experiencing hard times, people are often the biggest asset you have.

Using your plan to communicate

You won't find a better way to convince people that you can change the fortunes of your company than by putting together a solid turnaround plan. In fact, make your revised plan the basis for communicating with all your stakeholders. Your investors and lenders will probably insist on seeing the plan. (In some cases, they may even have played a role in shaping it.) Your suppliers aren't likely to clamor for it, but fill them in on the details, anyway, especially if you can't pay them on time. At least you can give them the confidence that your good intentions are supported by a solid plan.

Make sure that you also share your turnaround plan with employees — every last one of them. Teamwork is always important, but never more so than when a company is in trouble. If you make everyone a part of the plan, you enlist everyone's support along with their loyalty. And you make it clear that everyone's on the same team. Nothing goes quite as far to boost morale at a time when people are asked to work harder, often under difficult circumstances.

Keeping Your Plan Fresh

If you enjoyed the process of creating your business plan — everything from the first brainstorm to the written document — you're in luck. Why? Because business planning is never really done, and your business plan will always remain a work in progress. The reason is quite simple: The only constant in business is change. Markets evolve. New technologies emerge. Even your company is bound to change.

Of course the pace of change varies depending on the kind of industry you're in. If you're in the business of making high-speed telecom switches, for example, times are changing fast. If you run the corner hardware store, change may come more slowly. But don't ever make the mistake of thinking that you're in the one business that's immune to all this. The truth is, we can't think of a single company that isn't vulnerable to change at some level.

Take the medical profession as a prime example. For years, doctors were in one of the most secure (and lucrative) businesses around. Everyone gets sick, after all, and doctors thought they had a well-defined market for their services. Then along came managed care, and the business of doctoring changed dramatically — and some would say for the worse.

Or consider the family farm. Of course, farmers have always been at the mercy of the weather, but for generations, farming remained a pretty steady and predictable business in all other ways. Enter big agribusiness and new, sophisticated agricultural technologies — and the business of farming has been altered forever from top to bottom.

Change isn't all bad, by any means. After all, change creates new opportunities. And chances are, you wouldn't be starting a new business if markets, customers, and competitors weren't evolving in one way or another. But change also poses threats. Taken together, these changing opportunities and threats are a big part of the reason you need to make business planning an ongoing process.

Through a business plan, you create your company's future. And the more successful you are, the more your plan must evolve to reflect that future and the future beyond it. Your business goals and objectives are based on time frames that, once met, have to be reassessed and redefined. It's all about moving forward.

Reviewing the situation

What's the best way to make business planning an ongoing process? Many companies schedule a review of their entire business plans once a year, and that's great. But consider checking in with certain parts of your plan on a more frequent basis. Precisely which parts you review depends on which aspects of your business are changing most rapidly. If new competitors are popping up everywhere, you have to keep close tabs on your competitor analysis and possibly your customer profiling. If sales are falling short of expectations, monitor your sales and marketing plans more closely.

Even if your company is buzzing along precisely as planned, however, review the following parts of your plan on a semi-annual or even a quarterly basis:

- SWOT analysis
- Company strategy
- Financial projections
- Goals and objectives
- Action plan

If you already have a planning team in place, consider asking the team members to take on the ongoing task of reviewing — and possibly revising — key parts of your business plan during the course of the year. If you're on your own, create a schedule at the beginning of the year that sets out which parts of the plan to look over and when.

When you find yourself caught up in day-to-day business demands, you may be tempted to put off the important work of reviewing and revising your business plan. Especially when your company is under pressure — from competitors, finances, and operational deadlines — you may want to postpone any kind of planning until things cool off and settle down. Don't. Working your plan is most critical at times like these. Indeed, it can sometimes make the difference between pulling through and being pulled under.

Encouraging feedback

How do you know whether your business plan is working? The most obvious answer is by looking at the bottom line. If the company is making money, the plan must be working, right? Well, yes, in a way. The bottom line is critical. But it's not a foolproof gauge of success. Equally important is hearing what your employees have to say about the company and its strategic direction. By listening to the people who are actually carrying out your plans — from top managers to entry-level hires — you can find out a lot more about what's working and what's not. And you tap into a rich vein of ideas about how to revise and refine your business plan to make it even more effective.

Granted, not all the ideas you hear will be do-able, and some of them may be downright wacky. But others are likely to be terrific. Employees working on the front lines may be aware of marketplace trends even before you are. They may tip you off to customers worth pursuing or competitors worth watching.

And employees behind the scenes may have some useful insights into better processes. Heck, your staff may even have something valuable to say about your company's strategic direction.

The best way we've found to encourage feedback is to establish regular procedures for your employees to offer their comments and suggestions. The procedures don't have to be complex or sophisticated. Some companies use a good old-fashioned suggestion box. Others turn to their intranets, creating virtual suggestion boxes, chat rooms, and online Q&A areas.

When the time comes to review and revise your business plan, actively solicit suggestions and ideas throughout the company using memos, company-wide meetings, and employee questionnaires. In addition, you may want to invite employees to talk about the business plan during their performance reviews. Whatever methods you come up with, consider asking for answers to the following ten questions:

- Is the company doing enough to communicate its vision, mission, and strategic plan to employees? If not, how would you suggest we do a better job?
- Are the business goals and objectives outlined in the plan clear and appropriate?
- Do your own duties and responsibilities help support the company's goals and strategic direction?
- Can you suggest specific changes in the way your work is done that will help the company better meet its goals?
- Can you suggest ways to improve the company's overall operations?
- Do company procedures get in the way of your doing your best job? If so, how do you suggest changing them?
- Are you aware of changes in the industry — including our customers and our competitors — that should be addressed in our business plan?
- Can you suggest ways we can enhance the value we offer our customers?
- Can you think of additional ways to market our products and services?
- If you were in charge of revising the business plan, what other changes would you make?

By soliciting suggestions and ideas from people at every level of your company, you do more than bring in constructive information. You also encourage a strong sense of teamwork and a shared mission. And that, in turn, goes a long way toward making your business plan work and your business a long-term success.

Forms on the CD-ROM

Check out the following forms on the CD-ROM to help you put your business plan to work:

Form 13-1	**Goals and Objectives Assignment Chart**	An assignment chart designed to help you align management duties and responsibilities with major business goals and objectives
Form 13-2	**Common Systems and Procedures Checklist**	A checklist of business systems and procedures that are common to many companies
Form 13-3	**Checklist of Management and Leadership Traits**	A checklist of traits to help you develop management skills and leadership traits that are best suited to your business needs
Form 13-4	**Employee Training Resource Checklist**	A checklist of the most common training resources that can help you discover the best ways to develop your employees
Form 13-5	**Checklist of Common Warning Signs**	A checklist of common danger signals that may mean your company is headed for trouble

Part V

The Part of Tens

"I appreciate your sharing your dreams and wishes for starting your own pool and spa business, but maybe I should explain more fully what we at the Make-A-Wish Foundation are all about."

In this part . . .

This is the fun part, where we get to feature our own personal favorite top tens. First, we list ten ways to evaluate a new business idea — a checklist that can help you polish your own idea to really make it shine. To convince you that all the hard work of business planning is well worth the effort, we also list ten real benefits of having a written business plan. Next up, a list of ten ways to get your plan funded. And finally, because the work of business planning is never done, we point out ten possible signs that your business plan needs an overhaul.

Chapter 14

Ten Ways to Evaluate a New Business Idea

In This Chapter

- Making sure your business idea is the right one for you
- Testing whether your idea stands a good chance of success

Every business venture starts with an idea. The idea may be as simple as opening a shop that features local arts and crafts or as complex as creating a company that offers space-flight vacations. Either way, the success of the business depends, to a large degree, on the strength of the original idea and how well it fits your temperament and the resources you have at your disposal.

While we can't give you a foolproof way to guarantee that your new business idea will make it in the marketplace, we can offer ten questions that you absolutely, positively need to ask about your business idea before you take the big plunge.

Is This Something I Really Want to Do?

Starting a business is more than just a job. For most successful entrepreneurs, it's a full-time passion. In our experience, the people most likely to succeed are the ones who really believe in their idea, care about the product or service they offer, and love what they do — even when the going gets tough. So take a moment to think through your own idea. What would it be like to turn the idea into a business? Is this something you care about? And is it really how you want to spend your time? If the answers are all an enthusiastic yes, read on. If not, maybe it's time to go back to brainstorming (see Chapter 1).

Is This Something I am Capable of Doing?

Thomas Edison called genius "one percent inspiration, ninety-nine percent perspiration." You've had your stroke of inspiration. But do you have what it takes to sweat out the details and do the hard work required to turn your inspiration into reality? You may have the desire to do it, but that's not quite enough. We really mean *can* you do it? Do you have the resources, connections, skills, and experience to do it? And if you don't have everything required to do the job well, do you know how to assemble a team that does?

Does This Tap My Personal Strengths?

Not everyone is cut out to run a high-tech business — or a local gift shop, for that matter. Everyone brings his or her strengths and weaknesses to work. Successful entrepreneurs are lucky enough — or smart enough — to devote themselves to businesses that leverage their own strengths and allow them to work around their personal weaknesses. How do your own strengths and weaknesses match up to the business idea you're considering? If the business requires lots of personal contact, for example, are you good with people? If the business requires you to move rapidly to seize an opportunity, are you prepared for long, sometimes stressful days?

Can I Describe it in 25 Words or Less?

If your business idea is so complex that it takes half an hour and 20 flip-charts to explain, chances are it's too complicated. Almost every great business idea we can think of can be described in under 25 words. Consider a few examples:

- A combination electronic organizer and wireless Internet device (eight words).
- A gift certificate that you can redeem online to contribute to the charity of your choice (16 words).
- A catering service that delivers meals based on The Zone, Atkin's, or Weight Watchers diets (15 words).

As you evaluate your own idea, try paring it down to its essentials by describing it as simply and concisely as you can. A simple, polished phrase may make your idea shine — or may reveal a fatal flaw. Either way, you're better off knowing that now.

What's the Closest Thing to This in the Marketplace?

As the saying goes, there's nothing new under the sun. Most business ideas, in fact, are really refinements or recombinations of existing ideas. Here's a TV, there's the Web — hey, how about WebTV? Cool! To judge how good your idea really is, think about similar products or services that are already out there in the marketplace. Then ask yourself a tough question: How is my idea better?

Does it Solve a Customer Problem or Meet a Real Need?

Most customers don't plunk down their hard-earned cash just because they love spending money. They do it because they're buying something that solves a real problem (ring around the collar) or meets a real need (staying warm in the winter or cool in the summer). Your business idea may sound good to you on paper. But will customers agree?

Does it Take Advantage of a New Opportunity?

What makes a great leader? Well, greatness requires both internal resources and the opportunity to prove them. The same goes for a great business idea. Many ideas turn out well because they come along at just the right time and place to take advantage of a new opportunity. The rise of the Internet — and American's passion for collecting — were the twin opportunities that made the booming auction site eBay into a household word. And the nation's growing waistline was the opportunity that turned Weight Watchers into a multimillion-dollar success story.

What's its Biggest Drawback or Limitation?

If you're convinced that your idea is foolproof, think again. Every great business idea has its drawbacks and limitations. Maybe your idea is something that's very easy for would-be competitors to copy, for example. Or maybe it's something that requires a real change in some ingrained customer behavior. Perhaps it requires a long research and development phase or poses difficult marketing challenges. By thinking long and hard about the potential drawbacks of your idea, you help put the plus side in perspective. If all the pluses far outweigh the worst things you can say about your business idea, chances are your idea is a pretty good one.

Will it Make Money — and How Fast?

Oddly enough, this simple question is the one mostly likely to go unasked by wannabe entrepreneurs. Maybe that's because it's one of the toughest questions to face up to. It's not as simple as asking whether customers will be willing to pay for your product or service. We mean: Do you think your business idea can be profitable over time? And how much time can you afford to take? Perhaps you can't answer these questions in detail just yet. But give them some thought upfront. Ultimately, of course, money is going to be how you spell success.

Am I Willing to Re-mortgage my House?

Don't worry: We're not *really* suggesting that you have to take out a second mortgage to fund your new business venture. But ask yourself — if all else fails — would you be willing to do it. If not — if you're not willing to take on some real financial risk — you may not be cut out for the business you're thinking about going into. You may have trouble convincing investors that they should take on the risk for you. And you must stop and think hard before taking out a business loan that you absolutely have to repay.

Chapter 15

Ten Things a Business Plan Does for You

In This Chapter

- Identifying reasons why a plan is a must
- Getting the most out of your business plan

You may be amazed at how many would-be entrepreneurs set out to start a business without a plan. Maybe they figure that a great idea is all they need. Or maybe they feel that they just don't have the time. They're wrong. In fact, not having a solid business plan in place is the number one reason why businesses fail. The bottom line: A new business can't afford *not* to have a plan. If you still need more convincing, here are ten essential things a business plan will do for you:

Put Your Business Idea to the Test

So you think you have the hottest new business idea since sticky-backed notes, huh? Well, we sure hope you're right. But before you plunge in, remember: The best way to test whether your idea is as good as it sounds is to create a business plan. The planning process forces you to think about who's going to buy your product or service, who your competitors are likely to be, and how much time and money you need to get your company going. Chances are you'll find yourself refining or even retooling your idea as you go through the process of planning, and that's good, too. The more fine-tuning you do upfront, the better your odds of success down the road.

Turn a Good Idea into a Viable Business

The heart of business planning involves taking a good idea and turning it into a working enterprise — laying out exactly where and how the money is going to be made. If you can't figure out where your revenues will come from, for example, it's back to the drawing board. Not-for-profits don't have to worry about making money, of course, but they do have to make sure there are contributors out there willing to support a worthy cause — and clients to serve. In either case, a business plan helps you come up with a way to make your business work.

Show You What You're Up Against

You're probably not the first kid on the block to dream of striking it rich by offering pet rocks, virtual pets, doggy daycare, or whatever your very cool new product or service happens to be. And that means you better have a really good idea of who your competitors are before you get started. Putting together a business plan gives you the chance to analyze your market and scope out the competition, gathering critical data that will allow you to prepare upfront and avoid pitfalls later. It also requires that you create a detailed action plan describing exactly what you need to do to keep one competitive step ahead.

Specify What You Need to Start Your Business . . .

Beginning entrepreneurs often underestimate how much they need — in terms of time, equipment, personnel, and sheer determination — to get a business up and running. A business plan helps you develop a no-nonsense list of the equipment you need and the chores to do to get your business off the ground. In addition, your plan's goals and objectives, along with an action plan, provide a timetable for when you need to finish the items on your to-do list.

. . . and How Much it's Likely to Cost

Something else that wannabe entrepreneurs often underestimate: How much getting a business going costs. When you take the time to create a detailed business plan, you provide yourself with financial guidelines. In addition, your plan's financial review increases the likelihood that you'll have the cash available when you need it.

Help Get You Get Funding

If you need money to get your business started, you need a business plan. Period. Oh sure, you may have heard of times in the past — the recent past — when investors wrote out million dollar checks on a handshake and a promising idea, but those days are gone. To persuade a venture capitalist or your local banker to put up cash today, you have to convince him or her that you not only have a solid idea, but also that you know exactly how you're going to turn it into a successful business. A strong and convincing business plan can do just that.

Tell the World Who You Are

A big part of marketing your new business involves telling anyone and everyone who's interested exactly who you are and what you do. Your business plan provides a great resource here. In fact, your mission and vision statements, along with the company overview, form the basis for your entire business identity — the way you describe yourself and your company to the world. Your business plan also serves as the basis for communicating directly with your stakeholders, everyone from investors and shareholders to regulators and the business press.

Inspire Your Employees

A business plan with a compelling mission statement, vision, and values tells your employees not only what your company is but what it stands for. Just as important, a business plan describes exactly how the company will accomplish its mission through specific goals and objectives. By sharing your business plan with employees at all levels — and better yet, making them part of the planning process — you create a strong sense of team work and *esprit de corps*. If you're putting together a business completely on your own, a business plan can still inspire, convincing you that you have what it takes to make it work.

Gauge Your Progress

A good business plan provides reliable benchmarks to measure your progress over time. Part of your plan contains a description of where you are right now. Part of it describes where you'd like to be at the end of six months, a year, or even farther down the road. After you reach these milestones, you can look back at your plan to assess how your business has performed. And if you don't reach them? By having a business plan in place, you know exactly where — and why — you've fallen short.

Prepare You for the Unexpected

We'll be thrilled if your path to a successful business is smooth and free of obstacles. But the real world seldom works out that way, so chances are good you'll hit a few potholes along the road. You may even find yourself on a dead-end street, trying to figure out how in the world you got there. Never fear. A good business plan helps you find your bearings if you lose your way. The best business plans include contingencies to provide direction, just in case things go wrong.

Chapter 16

Ten Ways to Fund Your Business Plan

In This Chapter

- Finding the cash you need to start your business
- Weighing the pros and cons of different support

A great business idea may be the spark that gets most successful companies going, but money is the fuel that keeps them running. Even if you're setting up a freelance business all on your own, chances are you're going to need some cash to get started. If you're starting a high-tech company, you'll probably need lots of it. This chapter shares ten places to go to look for the money you need.

Your Own Pocket

Using your own funds has its advantages and disadvantages. If you can get your business up and running using only your own bucks, you maintain 100 percent ownership and 100 percent control. But you also take on all the risk. If the business goes under, your money goes down the drain. Even if you take out a loan or get investment capital to fund your business, by the way, chances are you're going to end up putting some of your own money into the pot. In fact, many venture capitalists insist that entrepreneurs ante up some of their own cash (as proof of commitment) before they'll add their own.

Friends and Family

Turning to friends or family members for help is a time-honored tradition when starting a small business. Some people borrow money in return for a simple I.O.U., to be paid back in full when the company starts making a profit. Others set up a more formal loan, to be paid back with interest on a specific schedule. Whatever arrangement you choose, make sure that everyone involved understands the terms and knows what to expect and when. To be on the safe side, put the terms of your financial help in writing and ask all parties to sign the documents, because disagreements over money can spoil even the closest relationship.

Bank Loan

Local branches of most banks are more than willing to lend money to local businesses, provided they have a solid business plan in place. The simplest arrangement: a standard commercial loan. In this case, the bank loans you the money and you pay it back, usually in monthly installments and with interest. But you can find all sorts of variations on this theme, from real estate loans on commercial property to loans secured by your inventory or accounts receivable. If the loans are secured by business assets, you usually pay a lower interest rate. The advantage of a bank loan: You get to keep all the equity in your company. The disadvantage: You have to pay the money back, even if your business runs into hard times.

Commercial Line of Credit

If you don't intend to use all the money all at once, consider applying for a commercial line of credit. A credit line allows you to draw on the funds whenever you happen to need the cash. Banks don't usually require collateral to secure small lines of credit, but larger lines (and some banks loan up to $10 million or more) are typically secured against the business's accounts receivable, inventory, machinery and equipment, or real estate.

Equipment Leasing

Another way to borrow money from banks takes the form of an equipment lease, which can be used to acquire anything from computers, printers, and copiers to manufacturing equipment, tractors, and trucks. Financial arrangements include lease-to-buy options, equipment upgrade options, and master leases designed to cover a bunch of your equipment at once.

An SBA Loan

Bravo to the Small Business Administration (SBA): This government agency is dedicated to handing out money to small businesses that may otherwise have a tough time securing financing from commercial banks. The SBA has more than a dozen separate loan programs. The primary one is called the 7(a) Loan Guaranty Program, which arranges loans through private lenders which are then guaranteed by the SBA. The micro-loan program is another useful one to know about, because it provides very small loans to start-ups and established small businesses alike. For information, check out `www.sba.gov`.

Deep-Pocket Partners

It sounds like a marriage made in heaven: Entrepreneur with great business idea but no money seeks like-minded entrepreneur with money who's looking for a great idea. In fact, many such partnerships do end happily ever after. But if you're thinking about forming one as a way to get the cash you need, establish up front how much control your partner or partners will exercise over business strategy, planning, and day-to-day operations. Make certain you all agree on the details of the business partnership. And make sure you get along. It may sound obvious, but a good working relationship with a business partner can help get you over the inevitable bumps along the road to success.

Venture Capital

Do you need more money than a bank is willing to lend you? Are you nervous about taking on all the risk of repaying a big loan? You may want to knock on the venture capital door. When venture capitalists like a business concept and are confident that the management team has what it takes, they're willing to fork over sizeable sums. The catch: they want something back in return (surprise, surprise). Usually that something is a big piece of the action — and a major chunk of your company. To learn more about how to go after venture capital, check out Chapter 10.

Angel Money

Talk about pennies from heaven! *Angels,* in the world of high finance, are wealthy individuals who agree to invest their money in a start-up business in the hopes that their bet will pay off down the road when your company makes it big. Like venture capitalists, angels usually want a piece of the equity pie. But they're less likely to interfere in the day-to-day operations of your business. And they're usually a little more patient about getting their rewards.

Prospective Customers

The success of your business ultimately depends on loyal, paying customers — so why not turn to your customers upfront, asking them to ante up to help you get your business off the ground? Sound crazy? In fact, a variety of businesses do just that. Community supported agriculture programs, for example, pair up local farmers with consumers in the community who are willing to pay a set fee in advance in return for a weekly load of produce during the summer growing season. And condominium projects often sell all their units to prospective owners before any ground is ever broken.

You may even considering getting the companies who supply you with goods and services to help fund your plan. In many cases, after all, those companies stand to make more money if you succeed in growing bigger.

Chapter 17

Ten Possible Signs That Your Plan Needs an Overhaul

In This Chapter

- Recognizing the warning signs that your business plan needs updating
- Revising your plan to reflect new business realities

Once a year, most companies revise their business plans — or at least they give it the old college try. That's not a bad schedule under most circumstances. But at times, your company may need to complete an unscheduled review of your business plan — and those times are usually associated with big changes inside or outside your company. This chapter gives you ten possible warning signs that your business plan needs an immediate overhaul. We could come up with dozens of other signs, so use these as examples of what to watch for as you continue to monitor your business situation.

Costs Rise, Revenues Fall

The clearest sign that a company is in trouble is when costs go up and revenues go down — but you may be amazed at how many business owners ignore it. Why? Because things don't usually go wrong overnight. Costs rise very gradually; revenues slowly drift downward. By the time the warning bells go off, it's often too late for a simple fix. Our advice: At the first signs of a profit squeeze, revisit your business plan — especially your financial projections.

Sales Figures Head South

If your sales projections for that new product or service don't meet your expectations — or if you see an unexpected drop in your current sales figures — move quickly to diagnose the problem. There may be a mismatch between the features you offer and the benefits customers want, a problem with quality control, or a breakdown in customer service. Or perhaps the competition is simply tougher than you expected. Your mission: to identify the reason and revise the appropriate parts of your business plan — product design, operations, marketing strategy — accordingly.

Employee Morale Sags

The morale of the people who work for you isn't easy to measure, but it's absolutely critical to your success. If you sense that morale and motivation are on the skids, don't sit on your hands. Talk to key people around you and find out exactly what's wrong. Perhaps your planned goals and objectives are unreasonable, creating frustration instead of motivation. Or maybe you have a mismatch between the company's stated mission and your plan of action, creating confusion and indirection. In these cases, you can't wait for the annual business plan review: You have to fix the plan now.

Key Projects Fall Behind

A serious business plan has specific timelines in place to show what needs to happen when. Deadlines are one of the engines that keep your business moving forward. If your company begins to miss them, and important projects start to fall behind schedule, sit down with your staff and figure out why. Identify the source of the problem, including aspects of your current business plan that may not be playing out as expected. With the help of your team, brainstorm solutions that will get you back on schedule. If you can't catch up, revise your timelines so that employees don't become frustrated.

Financials Fall Short

Predicting the financial future of your company is an art, not a science. Plenty of things can come along to knock even the most conservative financial projections out of whack. If yours are beginning to look a little wobbly, don't wait until they crash. Take the time to review all the assumptions that went into your original projections and make a detailed list of the things that may change your forecasts. Then work up a revised set of financial statements based on the new reality. Don't forget to revise your action plan, if necessary.

New Competitors Appear

Competitor analysis is one of the foundations of an effective business strategy. So if a big, predatory fish comes swimming into your little pond, revisit your competitor analysis and adjust your business plan accordingly. Keep in mind: Competition isn't always a bad thing. It usually forces you to focus on what you do best and develop ways to do it as efficiently as possible.

Technology Shakes Up Your World

Technological innovation can change everything: what your customers want, how your business operates, and even who your competitors are. A shift in technology can make existing products obsolete and create a market for new products or services almost overnight. So when a new technology that may affect your industry appears on the horizon, reassess your business plan. Fast. Ask yourself how this new technology may change the way you do business or the customers you serve. Then lay out plans for how you can use it to your advantage.

Important Customers Defect

It's not all that unusual for a good customer to find a new supplier. But if you start to notice a trend in customer defections, something's probably wrong. Your competitors may be stronger than you think, your own efforts may be falling short, or the market itself could be changing. The defection of important customers is an alarm signal you can't afford to ignore for long. When appropriate, ask departing customers why they're making the change, talk to your own salespeople for further insights, and then retool your business plan.

Business Strategy Does a 180

Slight course adjustments in your strategy are a normal part of doing business. But if your company is suddenly doing 180-degree shifts, something's very wrong. Rather than swinging wildly from one direction to another, sit down with your management team and your business plan to figure out why your original strategic direction isn't working. Take the time you need to do a complete diagnostic. Then plan a rational course change that will address the problems you've identified.

You're Growing too Fast

Entrepreneurs don't usually complain when business is booming. But companies can grow *too* fast — and that can mean trouble if they're not prepared. Customer service can suffer, for example, or manufacturing may not be able to keep up with demand. Some companies even find that their basic organizational structure no longer fits their new dimensions. If you're experiencing similar growing pains, look at your business plan to identify the parts that need to change in order to accommodate the good news — and your increasing size.

Appendix

About the CD

In This Appendix

- System requirements
- Using the CD with Windows and Mac
- What you'll find on the CD
- Troubleshooting

System Requirements

Make sure that your computer meets the minimum system requirements shown in the following list. If your computer doesn't match up to most of these requirements, you may have problems using the software and files on the CD.

- A PC with a Pentium or faster processor; or a Mac OS computer with a 68040 or faster processor
- Microsoft Windows 95 or later; or Mac OS system software 7.6.1 or later
- At least 32MB of total RAM installed on your computer; for best performance, we recommend at least 64MB
- A CD-ROM drive

If you need more information on the basics, check out these books published by Hungry Minds, Inc.: *PCs For Dummies* by Dan Gookin; *Macs For Dummies* by David Pogue; *iMacs For Dummies* by David Pogue; *Windows 95 For Dummies, Windows 98 For Dummies, Windows 2000 Professional For Dummies, Microsoft Windows Me Millennium Edition For Dummies* — all by Andy Rathbone.

Using the CD with Microsoft Windows

To install items from the CD to your hard drive, follow these steps:

1. **Insert the CD into your computer's CD-ROM drive.**

   A window appears with the following options: HTML Interface, Browse CD, and Exit.

2. **Choose one of the options, as follows:**

   - **HTML Interface:** Click this button to view the contents of the CD in standard Dummies presentation. It'll look like a Web page.
   - **Browse CD:** Click this button to skip the fancy presentation and simply view the CD contents from the directory structure. This means you'll just see a list of folders — plain and simple.
   - **Exit:** Well, what can we say? Click this button to quit.

Note: If you do not have autorun enabled or if the autorun window does not appear, follow these steps to access the CD:

1. **Insert the CD into your computer's CD-ROM drive.**
2. **Click the Start button and choose Run from the menu.**
3. **In the dialog box that appears, type** d:\start.htm**.**

   Replace *d* with the proper drive letter for your CD-ROM if it uses a different letter. (If you don't know the letter, double-click My Computer on your desktop and see what letter is listed for your CD-ROM drive.)

   Your browser opens, and the license agreement is displayed. If you don't have a browser, Microsoft Internet Explorer and Netscape Communicator are included on the CD.

4. **Read through the license agreement, nod your head, and click the Agree button if you want to use the CD.**

   After you click Agree, you're taken to the Main menu, where you can browse through the contents of the CD.

5. **To navigate within the interface, click a topic of interest to take you to an explanation of the files on the CD and how to use or install them.**
6. **To install software from the CD, simply click the software name.**

   You'll see two options: run or open the file from the current location or to save the file to your hard drive. Choose to run or open the file from its current location, and the installation procedure continues. When you finish using the interface, close your browser as usual.

Note: We have included an "easy install" in these HTML pages. If your browser supports installations from within it, go ahead and click the links of the program names you see. You'll see two options: Run the File from the Current Location and Save the File to Your Hard Drive. Choose to Run the File from the Current Location and the installation procedure will continue. A Security Warning dialog box appears. Click Yes to continue the installation.

To run some of the programs on the CD, you may need to keep the disc inside your CD-ROM drive. This is a good thing. Otherwise, a very large chunk of the program would be installed to your hard drive, consuming valuable hard drive space and possibly keeping you from installing other software.

Using the CD with Mac OS

To install items from the CD to your hard drive, follow these steps:

1. **Insert the CD into your computer's CD-ROM drive.**

   In a moment, an icon representing the CD you just inserted appears on your Mac desktop. Chances are, the icon looks like a CD-ROM.

2. **Double-click the CD icon to show the CD's contents.**

3. **Double-click** `start.htm` **to open your browser and display the license agreement.**

   If your browser doesn't open automatically, open it as you normally would by choosing File⇨Open File (in Internet Explorer) or File⇨Open⇨Location in Netscape (in Netscape Communicator) and select *Biz Plans Kit FD*. The license agreement appears.

4. **Read through the license agreement, nod your head, and click the Accept button if you want to use the CD.**

   After you click Accept, you're taken to the Main menu. This is where you can browse through the contents of the CD.

5. **To navigate within the interface, click any topic of interest, and you're taken you to an explanation of the files on the CD and how to use or install them.**

6. **To install software from the CD, simply click the software name.**

What You'll Find on the CD

The following sections are arranged by category and provide a summary of the software and other goodies you'll find on the CD. If you need help with installing the items provided on the CD, refer to the installation instructions in the preceding section.

Shareware programs are fully functional, free, trial versions of copyrighted programs. If you like particular programs, register the software for a nominal fee and receive licenses, enhanced versions, and technical support. *Freeware programs* are free, copyrighted games, applications, and utilities. You can copy them to as many PCs as you like — for free — but the companies or individuals behind them offer no technical support. *GNU software* is governed by its own license, which is included inside the folder of the GNU software. There are no restrictions on distribution of GNU software. See the GNU license at the root of the CD for more details. *Trial, demo,* or *evaluation* versions of software are usually limited either by time or functionality (such as not letting you save a project after you create it).

Business plan forms

All the business plan forms we refer to in the book are included on the CD-ROM in the Author directory. The form files come in three distinct flavors:

- **Word for Windows files:** Use this version if you use Microsoft Word 95 or later as your word processor. These forms all have a .doc extension and are found in the Author\DocForms directory.
- **Rich Text Format files:** Use this version if you use an earlier version of Microsoft Word, prior to Word 95, or if you use another word processor such as WordPerfect, WordPro, or WordPad. These forms all have a .rtf extension and are found in the Author\RTFForms directory.
- **Adobe Acrobat (PDF) files:** You must install the Adobe Acrobat Reader program before you can view files in this format. A version of the program is included on the CD-ROM. You can't modify the forms in this format, but you can print them out. These forms all have a .pdf extension and are found in the Author\PDFForms directory.

The form files are organized by chapter. We've given them names that correspond to their references in the book. So, for example, if you want to work with the Microsoft Word version of Form 4-7 that appears in Chapter 4, you would go to the file located and named:
Author\DocForms\Chapter04\Form0407.doc.

Table A-1 gives you a list of the forms you'll find on the CD-ROM.

Table A-1 Forms at a Glance

Form Number	*Form Name*
Form 1-1	The Idea Blender — Your Personal Traits and Interests
Form 1-2	The Idea Blender — Mixing and Matching Your Interests
Form 1-3	The Idea Blender — Your Business Ideas
Form 1-4	Business Opportunity Evaluation Questionnaire
Form 1-5	Business Opportunity Framework
Form 1-6	Personal Strengths and Weaknesses Survey
Form 1-7	Personal Strengths and Weaknesses Grid
Form 2-1	Typical Business-Planning Situations
Form 2-2	Checklist of Common Business Plan Audiences
Form 2-3	Business Plan Target Audiences and Key Messages
Form 2-4	Major Components in a Typical Business Plan
Form 2-5	Business Plan Time Frame Questionnaire
Form 2-6	Business Plan Tracker
Form 3-1	Your Mission Statement Questionnaire
Form 3-2	Your Mission Statement Framework
Form 3-3	Examples of Real-World Mission Statements
Form 3-4	Our Mission Statement
Form 3-5	Goals and Objectives Flowchart
Form 3-6	Goals and Objectives Based on ACES
Form 3-7	Checklist of Common Business Goals
Form 3-8	Our Major Business Goals
Form 3-9	Values Questionnaire
Form 3-10	Our Values Statement
Form 3-11	Examples of Real-World Vision Statements
Form 3-12	Our Vision Statement
Form 4-1	Basic Business Definition Framework
Form 4-2	Industry Analysis Questionnaire

(continued)

Table A-1 *(continued)*

Form Number	*Form Name*
Form 4-3	Barriers to Entry Checklist
Form 4-4	Good Customer/Bad Customer Comparison
Form 4-5	Ideal Customer Questionnaire
Form 4-6	Ideal Customer Snapshot
Form 4-7	Business Customer Profile
Form 4-8	Customer Intelligence Checklist
Form 4-9	Basic Market Segmentation Framework
Form 4-10	Our Biggest Competitors
Form 4-11	Potential Stealth Competitors Questionnaire
Form 4-12	Potential Competitors We Need to Watch
Form 4-13	Competitive Intelligence Checklist
Form 4-14	Our Biggest Competitors and Their Likely Moves
Form 5-1	Company Strengths and Weaknesses Survey
Form 5-2	Company Strengths and Weaknesses Grid
Form 5-3	Company Opportunities and Threats
Form 5-4	Company SWOT Analysis grid
Form 5-5	Business Model Questionnaire
Form 5-6	Quick Financial Projection Worksheet
Form 5-7	Resources for Growth Checklist
Form 5-8	Planning for Growth Questionnaire
Form 5-9	Checklist of Common Exit Strategies
Form 6-1	Product/Service Description Checklist
Form 6-2	Operations Planning Survey (Location)
Form 6-3	Operations Planning Survey (Equipment)
Form 6-4	Operations Planning Survey (Labor)
Form 6-5	Operations Planning Survey (Process)
Form 6-6	Customer Communications Strategy Checklist
Form 6-7	Distribution and Delivery Survey

Form Number	*Form Name*
Form 6-8	Customer Service Checklist
Form 6-9	Management Team Member Profile
Form 7-1	Company Income Statement
Form 7-2	Company Balance Sheet
Form 7-3	Company Cash-Flow Statement
Form 8-1	Is Self-Employment Right For You?
Form 8-2	Checklist of Business Networking Resources
Form 8-3	Tasks and Time Survey
Form 8-4	Self-Employed Expense Checklist
Form 8-5	Evaluating Your Home Office Options
Form 9-1	Start-up Costs Worksheet For Small Business
Form 9-2	Job Description Profile
Form 9-3	Job Recruiting Checklist
Form 9-4	Employee Retention Checklist
Form 9-5	Tips on Promoting Teamwork
Form 9-6	Ways to Promote Your Small Business
Form 10-1	Checklist of Key Steps in Planning an e-Business
Form 10-2	Online Customer Profile
Form 10-3	E-Business Value Proposition Worksheet
Form 10-4	E-Business Model Construction Worksheet
Form 11-1	Not-for-Profit Planning Worksheet
Form 11-2	Examples of Real-World Not-for-Profit Mission Statements
Form 11-3	Ideal Individual Donor Questionnaire
Form 11-4	Checklist of Responsibilities For a Not-for-Profit Board
Form 11-5	Checklist of Typical Grant Proposal Sections
Form 12-1	Business Plan Components Checklist
Form 12-2	Master Plan Tracking Sheet
Form 12-3	Business Plan Target Audience Guidelines

(continued)

Table A-1 *(continued)*

Form Number	*Form Name*
Form 12-4	Working Draft Checklist
Form 13-1	Goals and Objectives Assignment Chart
Form 13-2	Common Systems and Procedures Checklist
Form 13-3	Checklist of Management and Leadership Traits
Form 13-4	Employee Training Resource Checklist
Form 13-5	Checklist of Common Warning Signs

Business plan software

The business plan software we've included on the CD ranges from trial versions of commercial programs to freeware programs that are, well, free to use. Some of the tools are standalone programs; others make use of Microsoft Word and Excel. We encourage you to try out any and all of them before you decide which one best suits your working style, company situation, and the requirements of your business plan.

- **Business Plan Pro:** *Trial version. For Windows.* The latest version of this full-featured program comes compete with audio files, tutorials, and sample business plans. Useful features include a 16-step Plan Wizard and a Resources Tab that offers immediate access to additional help and online references. The Task Manager helps you keep track of the business plan components you've completed, and you can click on the Plan Outline to jump to specific topics. After you've finished your plan, Palo Alto Software even offers to securely publish it to the Web, with hosting on their own servers free for the first three months. For more information, visit `www.paloalto.com`.
- **Exl-Plan Free:** *Freeware version.* Limited to six-month financial projections. *For Windows and MS Excel and Word 95 or higher.* This freeware program produces a fully-integrated set of financial reports and projections — including an income statement, cash-flow statement, and balance sheet. While the software focuses on the financial aspects of business planning, you'll also find extensive online help and a 30-page Word-based business plan guide and template. If you like the program, but need a longer planning horizon, you can upgrade to one of company's shareware programs. For more information, visit `www.planware.org`.

- **PlanMagic Business:** *Demo.* Some of the forms are restricted. *For Windows, IE and MS Office 95, 97, 2000 including Word and Excel.* This program uses a clear Web browser interface along with a detailed set of Microsoft Office templates to help you create your business plan. The browser view describes each of 18 business plan components. Read the description and then click on the appropriate link to launch MS Word or Excel. After you enter your data and text into the template, you'll see the information consistently presented throughout the formatted and organized business plan document. For more information, visit `http://planmagic.com`.
- **Plan Write For Business:** *Trial version. For Windows.* This program comes complete with its own word processor, business plan outliner, and an integrated spreadsheet-charting module. Other helpful features include a business term glossary and context-sensitive advice on various planning topics. The software will generate a Web version of your business plan, and you can make use of the company's Web site to collaborate with your planning team. This second feature requires a subscription. For more information, visit `www.businessplansoftware.org`.
- **Quick Insight:** *Trial version. For Windows.* You may not like what this program has to say about your brand-new business idea — but that's the point. By answering about sixty questions and then reviewing the resulting analysis, you'll gain a detailed understanding of the potential strengths and likely problems you are likely to face — everything from your market situation and competitive potential to the odds of making a profit. It takes about 90 minutes to go through the program. Upon completion, you can print out a 55 page evaluation of your business idea. For more information, visit `www.businessplansoftware.org`.

Other software

We've included two more software packages that can help you view and use the other elements of this CD:

- **Adobe Acrobat Reader:** *Evaluation version. For Windows and Mac OS.* The program lets you view and print Portable Document Format (PDF) files. To find out more about using Acrobat Reader, choose the Reader Online Guide from the Help menu or view the Acrobat.pdf file installed in the same folder as the program. For additional information, visit `www.adobe.com`.
- **Internet Explorer:** *Commercial product. For Windows and Mac OS.* This browser from Microsoft enables you to view Web pages and perform a host of other Internet functions, including e-mail, newsgroups, and word processing. For additional information and program updates, visit `www.microsoft.com`.

Troubleshooting

We tried our best to compile programs that work on most computers with the minimum system requirements. Your computer may differ, however, and some programs may not want to work properly for one reason or another.

The two most likely problems are that you don't have enough memory (RAM) for the programs you want to use, or that you have other programs running that are affecting installation or running of a program. If you get an error message such as `Not enough memory` or `Setup cannot continue`, try one or more of the following suggestions and then try using the software again:

- **Turn off any antivirus software running on your computer.** Installation programs sometimes mimic virus activity and may make your computer incorrectly believe that it's being infected by a virus.
- **Close all running programs.** The more programs you have running, the less memory is available to other programs. Installation programs typically update files and programs; so if you keep other programs running, installation may not work properly. This may include closing the CD interface and running a product's installation program directly from Windows Explorer.
- **Have your local computer store add more RAM to your computer.** This is, admittedly, a drastic and somewhat expensive step. However, if you have a Windows 95 PC or a Mac OS computer with a PowerPC chip, adding more memory can help the speed of your computer and allow more programs to run at the same time.

If you still have trouble installing the items from the CD, please call the Hungry Minds, Inc. Customer Service phone number at 800-762-2974 (outside the U.S.: 317-572-3993) or send email to `techsupdum@hungryminds.com`.

Index

• Numbers •

504 program, SBA, 194
7(A) program, SBA, 194

• A •

accounts payable, 157
accounts receivable, 154
accrued expenses payable, 157
accumulated depreciation, 155
accumulated retained earnings, 158
ACES (Achieve, Conserve, Eliminate, Steer clear), 57–58, 69
action plan, 34
  form meets function style and, 262
  self-employed persons, 182
  small businesses, 196
administration, Web site development, 216
advertising
  customers and, 84
  growth and, 119
advisor leadership style, 270
alternate versions of plan, 257–258
angels, funding and, 302
appendixes, 34
  multiple audiences and, 256
assets, 152–156
audience for plan, 27–30, 44
  checklist of members, 31
  guideline sheet, 254, 260
  multiple, 255–257
  targeting, 32, 252–258

• B •

B2B (business to business), 85–88
  e-business, 208
balance sheet, 146, 171
  accounts receivable, 154
  accumulated retained earnings, 158
  assets, 152–154
  cash, 154
  creating, 151–159
  equity, 152
  estimated, forecasting and, 169
  example, 153, 160
  intangibles, 155–156
  inventories, 154
  invested capital, 158
  investment portfolio, 154
  liabilities, 152, 156–157
  long-term liabilities, 157
  owners' equity, 157–158
  prepaid expenses, 154
  statement of financial position (NPOs), 220
  total assets, 156
  total liabilities and equity, 158
  working capital, 157
bank loans, 300
barriers to entry, 78–81, 100
benchmarks, 27
BizPlanBuilder software, 314
Board of Directors, 31
Board of Directors, NPOs, 228, 234
Board of Trustees, NPOs, 228–230
bookstores, plan resources, 240–241
boss leadership style, 270
bplans.com Web site, 242

brainstorming, 8–11
mission statement writing, 50
sessions, assembling, 13–14
bridge financing, VCs, 217
brs-inc.com (Business Resource Software) Web site, 242
budgeting, master budget, 170–171
buildings and equipment, 155, 163
business capabilities, 131–132
customer service, 136–139
distribution/deliver, 135–136
management, 139
operations, 133–134
organization, 139–142
R&D, 132–133
sales/marketing, 134–135
business customer profile, 87–88
business environment, 33–34
e-business, 206
economic change, 206
self-employed persons, 179–181
business leagues (NPOs), 223
business model
analyzing troubled situations and, 280
creating, 117
defining, 112–113
e-business, 207, 212–214
exit strategy, 123–125
financial projection worksheet, 115
fixed costs, 114
questionnaire, 117, 118, 125
revenues, 113
timing, 115–116
variable costs, 114
business networking groups, 41, 190
self-employed persons, 180
business opportunities, 14–19, 24
Business Owner's Toolkit Web site, 242
Business Plan Pro software, 314
business plan software, 314–315
business plan tracker, 43
business plans. *See* plans
Business Plans For Dummies, 61
business revenues, 116
business schools, 40
business software, 243–244
business trends, changes in, 200

capabilities, 104, 131–132, 292
customer service, 136–139
distribution/delivery, 135–136
growth and, 134
management, 139
operations, 133–134
organization, 139–142
R&D, 132–133
sales and marketing, 134–135
capital, 297, 299–302
working capital, 157
cash, 154
changes in, 164
NPOs, 232–233
cash flow statement, 146, 171
creating, 159–167
example, 161, 166
liquid assets, changes, 164–165
net change in cash position, 164, 165
projections, 169–170
total funds in/out, 162–164
CD bundle
contents, 309–315
freeware programs, 310
idea-generating forms, 24
Mac OS, 309
shareware programs, 310
system requirements, 307
troubleshooting, 316
Chamber of Commerce, 41
charitable organizations (NPOs), 223
clients, 31
NPOs, 220
cloak-and-dagger methods of competition analysis, 95–98

Coaching & Mentoring For Dummies, 277
colleague leadership style, 270
commercial lines of credit, 300
communications, Web site development, 216
company description, 34, 127, 292–293
  capabilities, 131–142
  form meets function style and, 262
  introduction, 128–130
  NPOs, 227–230
  products or services, 129–130
  self-employed persons, 181
  small businesses, 195
  what you do best, 142–144
company overview, 33, 179
competition analysis, 93–94
  cloak-and-dagger methods, 95–98
  staying a step ahead, 98–100
  stealth competitors, 94–95
  updating plan and, 305
competitive intelligence, 97–98
computer hardware, Web site development, 216
consumables, 113
content, Web site development, 216
contents of plan, 33–37
contributors, message and, 31
corporations, NPOs, 223
cost of goods acquired, 163
cost of goods sold, 148
costs, 27
creativity, 8–14. *See also* ideas
credit, commercial lines of credit, 300
CRM (customer-relationship management), 136
cultural change, 200
current assets, 152–154
current liabilities, 156–157
customer analysis, 81
  bad customers, 81
  business customer profile, 87–88
  businesses as customer (B2B), 85–88
  customer intelligence checklist, 91
  good customers, 81
  grouping customers, 90–93
  ideal customers description, 81–86
  Internet resources, 90
  market research, 88–90
  market segments, 91–93
  observation, 89
  online profile, 208
  response cards, 90
customer service, 104, 142
  business capabilities and, 136–139
  sole proprietor, 108
customers, 31
  clients (NPOs), 220
  funding and, 302
  message and, 30
  potential, 26
  updating plan and, 305–306

• D •

day-to-day work goals, 58
decision making, 205–206
delegating writing responsibilities, 246–247
depreciation expenses, 149, 155
description of company. *See* company description
design, Web site development, 216
development goals, 58
diagnosing problems in times of trouble, 278
distributing plan, 268–269
distribution/delivery, 104
  business opportunities and, 14
  capabilities and, 135–136
  sole proprietor, 108
  survey, 137, 142
distributions to owners, 164
distributors, 31
divide and conquer style of organization, 141–142, 262

dividend and interest income, 162
donors (not-for-profits), 31
drawbacks, evaluation and, 294
duties and responsibilities, implementation and, 264

• E •

earnings report, 145
e-books, 208
e-business
abandoned shopping carts, 211
business model, 207, 212–214
customer profile, online, 208
decision making, 205–206
environment, 206
extensions of bricks and mortar businesses, 214–216
flexibility of plan, 207
mission statement, 205
online presence, 215
planning, 205–206
stand-alone Internet business, 208–209
start-up costs, 206–207
timeline, 207
value proposition worksheet, 210
Web site tips, 215
economic change, 199
business environment and, 206
Internet, 203–204
mission statement and, 205
planning importance, 205
speed and, 204
elevator talk, mission statement, 51–52
employees, 31
building team, 197
inspiration, 297–298
mentors, 277
morale, plan update and, 304
retention checklist (CD), 202
training resources checklist, 276, 287
employees' associations (NPOs), 224
entry barriers, 78–81, 100
environment, 33–34
small businesses, 193–194
equipment, 155
equipment leasing, 300
equity, 146, 152
owners' equity, 157–158
estimated balance sheet, forecasting and, 169
evaluating business opportunities, 17, 291–294
executive summary, 33
multiple audiences and, 255–256
exit strategy, 123–125
checklist, 124, 126
Exl-Plan Free software, 314
expenses
depreciation, 149
interest expenses, 163
prepaid, 154
self-employed persons (CD), 190
SG&A, 148
expert advice, 41–42
writing plans, 244–245

• F •

fact checking, Web site info, 242
favorite things, creativity and, 9
feedback
plan distribution and, 269
plan updating and, 285–286
final draft, 258–259
financial condition, 104
balance sheet, 146
cash flow statement, 146
earnings report, 145
equity, 146
evaluation and, 294
income statement, 145
liabilities, 146
net profit, 145

profit-and-loss statement, 145
small businesses, 196
sole proprietor, 108
updating plan and, 305
VCs and, 217
financial projection worksheet, 115
CD form, 126
financial review, 34
self-employed persons, 182
trouble situations and, 280
first-stage financing, VCs, 217
fixed assets, 154–155
accumulated depreciation, 155
buildings, 155
equipment, 155
land, 154
fixed costs, 114
flexibility, e-business plan, 207
flowchart, goals and objectives, 56–57
forecasting, 167–170
estimated balance sheet, 169
pro forma income statement, 168–169
projected cash flow, 169–170
form follows function style of organization, 141
implementation and, 262–263
forms, CD-ROM, 310–314
ACES goals/objects, 69
audience checklist, 44
balance sheet, 171
barriers to entry checklist, 100
biggest competitors, 101
board responsibilities, NPOs, 234
business customer profile, 100
business definition framework, 100
business model questionnaire, 125
business networking, 190
cash flow statement, 171
communications strategies, 142
competitive intelligence checklist, 101
competitors checklist, 101
competitors to watch, 101
components of plan, 44
customer comparison, 100
customer intelligence checklist, 100
customer profile, 218
customer service checklist, 142
distribution and delivery, 142
e-business model, 218
e-business planning checklist, 218
employee retention checklist, 202
employee training resource checklist, 287
exit strategies checklist, 126
financial projection worksheet, 126
goals and objectives assignment chart, 287
goals checklist, 69
goals/objectives flow chart, 68
grant proposal system checklist, 234
growth planning questionnaire, 126
growth resources checklist, 126
home office options, 190
idea-generating, 24
ideal customer questionnaire, 100
ideal customer snapshot, 100
ideal donor questionnaire (NPOs), 234
income statement, 171
industry analysis questionnaire, 100
job description profile, 202
job recruiting checklist, 202
key messages, 44
management and leadership traits, 287
management team profile, 142
market segmentation, 101
marketing, 202
master plan tracking sheet, 260
mission statement examples, 68
mission statement framework, 68
mission statement questionnaire, 68
mission statements, NPOs, 234
not-for-profit planning worksheet, 234
online customer profile, 218
operations planning, 142

forms, CD-ROM *(continued)*
- opportunities/threats, 125
- plan components checklist, 260
- product/service checklist, 142
- self-employed expense checklist, 190
- self-employment assessment, 190
- start-up costs worksheet, 202
- stealth competitors questionnaire, 101
- strengths/weaknesses grid, 125
- strengths/weaknesses survey, 125
- SWOT analysis grid, 125
- systems and procedures checklist, 287
- target audience guidelines, 260
- target audiences, 44
- tasks and time survey, 190
- teamwork promotion, 202
- time frame questionnaire, 45
- tracker, 45
- typical situations, 44
- value proposition worksheet, 218
- values questionnaire, 69
- values statement, 69
- vision statement, 69
- vision statement examples, 69
- warning signs checklist, 287

framing mission statement, 50
fraternal organizations (NPOs), 223
freeware programs (CD), 310
frequency of planning, e-business and, 206
friends/family, funding and, 299–300
function style of organization, 262
funders (NPOs), 220, 231–232, 234
funding, 297, 299–302
fundraising (NPOs), 229

• G •

goal setting, 55–56
- ACES, 57–58
- final decision, 59–60
- flowchart, 56–57
- mission statement and, 56–57
- NPOs, 224–226
- objectives, 55

goals, 26
- ACES, 59
- checklist, 60, 69
- day-to-day work goals, 58
- development, 58
- flowchart (CD), 68
- innovation, 58
- problem-solving, 58

goals and objectives assignment sheet, 264, 287
goodwill, 156
government affairs, change and, 200
grant money (NPOs), 230
- proposals (CD), 234

gross profit, income statement, 148
gross revenue, income statement, 147
ground rules for writing plan, 248
grouping customers, 90–93
growing small businesses, 197
- change and, 199–200
- marketing, 198

growth, 117
- advertising, 119
- capabilities and, 134
- expanded products/services, 119
- new markets, 119
- planning for, 120–122, 126
- resources checklist, 121, 126
- updating plan and, 306

• H •

handbook, 27
hardware servicing, Web site development, 216
hardware upgrades, Web site development, 216
hiring, self-employed persons, 177
home office options, CD form, 190

hourly charges, self-employed persons, 183–184
hype in mission statement, 51

• I •

idea blender, 8
business ideas (CD), 24
mixing and matching interests (CD), 24
personal traits and interests form (CD), 24
ideal customer description, 81–85
ideas, 8–14
CD-ROM forms, 24
excitement level, 16
LCS (likes, concerns, suggestions), 13
questions to ask, 15
reality check, 19–24
responsiveness, 13
selecting best, 16–19
unrealized, 16
where people get them, 12
words that kill, 12
implementation, 261
duties and responsibilities, 263–265
form follows function style of organization, 262–263
goals and objectives assignment sheet, 264
leadership and, 270–272
plan distribution, 268–269
skills investment, 275–277
systems and procedures, 265–266
teamwork and, 266–268
vision and, 272
in the black, revenues, 113–114
income statement, 145
CD form, 171
creating, 146–151
depreciation expenses, 149
example, 151
gross profit, 148
gross revenue, 147
net profit, 149–150
operating profit, 148–149
personal version, 150–151
pro forma income statement (forecasting), 168–169
profit before taxes, 149
time frame, 146
independent contractors, 31. *See also* self-employed persons
definition, 178
industry analysis, 26, 74–75
big picture outlook, 76–78
business definition framework, 75
questionnaire, 77–78, 100
industry experience, small businesses and, 192
industry symposiums, 40
informal not-for-profits, 223
information resources, 40–41
information verification, Web sites, 242
innovation goals, 58
intangibles, 155–156
interest expenses, 163
Internet, economy and, 203–204
Internet resources, 40
competition analysis, 97
customer analysis, 90
introducing company, 128–129
inventories, 154
invested capital
balance sheet, 158
cash flow statement, 162
investment portfolio, assets, 154, 164
investors, 31
funders (NPOs), 220
message and, 30
IRS Web site, 242

• J •

job description (CD), 202
job recruiting checklist (CD), 202

• L •

labor and agricultural organizations (NPOs), 223
land, 154
language of mission statement, 51
LCS (likes, concerns, suggestions), 13
leadership, 270–272
  leading from within, 272–273
  traits checklist, 271, 287
  transactional style, 270
  transformational style, 270
lenders, 31
length of plan, 37
liabilities, 146, 152
  current liabilities, 156–157
  long-term, 157
libraries, 40
limitations, evaluation and, 294
lines of credit, commercial, 300
liquidity, assets, 152, 164–165
loans
  bank, 300
  SBA, 301
  self-employed persons, 177
  small businesses, 192
long-term debt reduction, 163
long-term liabilities, 157
loose-leaf notebook for tracking, 251–252

• M •

Macintosh, CD bundle and, 309
male/female leadership styles, 270
management, 31, 104
  business capabilities and, 139
  delegating writing responsibilities through team, 246–247
  NPOs, 228–230
  sole proprietor, 108
  team member profile, 140, 142
  traits checklist, 271, 287
market research, 293
  customers, 88–90
  needs assessment (NPOs), 220
  response cards, 90
market segments, 91–93
  CD form, 101
marketing strategies, 26
  CD form, 202
  self-employed persons, 177
  small businesses, 198
master budget, 170–171
matching interests, idea blender, 10–11
matrix style of organization, 142, 262
mentors
  employees, 277
  reality check and, 19–20
message, 30–32, 44
mezzanine financing, VCs, 217
micro loan program, SBA, 194
mileposts, objectives, 57
milestones, 38–39
minivans versus SUVs, 89
mission statement, 26, 48, 68
  brainstorming, 50
  crafting, 50–52
  e-business, 205
  economic change and, 205
  elevator talk, 51–52
  examples, 53–54
  framework, 51
  framing, 50
  goal setting, 56–57
  hype in, 51
  items to include, 51
  language, 51
  NPOs, 221–223, 234
  questionnaire, 49
  questions to ask while writing, 48–50
  reasons to use, 48

reviewing others, 52
specificity, 51
workability, 52–54
writing, 50–52

• N •

NCNB (National Center for Nonprofit Boards) Web site, 242
needs assessment (NPOs), 220
net change in cash position, 164, 165
net profit, 145, 149–150
networking groups, 41
new hires, 31
newspapers, 40
NEXUS/LEXUS, 40
NFIB (National Federation of Independent Business) Web site, 242
Nolo Web site, 242
not-for-profit organizations (NPOs), 219
accountability, 233–234
benefits, 226
Board of Directors, 228
Board of Trustees, 228–230
cash, 232–233
company description, 227–230
corporations, 223
financial organization, 231–234
funders, 231–232
fundraising, 229
goal setting, 224–226
grant money, 230
informal, 223
management, 228–230
mission statement, 221–223, 234
nonprofits.org Web site, 242
objectives, 224–226
operations, 227–228
organization, 228
overhead, 232
planning worksheet (CD), 234
purpose, 222
qualified, 224
R&D, 230–231
running like business, 220–226
structure, 223
tax-exempt, 223–224
vision, 221–223

• O •

objectives, 26
ACES, 59
goal setting and, 55
mileposts, 57
NPOs, 224–226
observation, customers, 89
obstacles to entering business, 78–81
online presence, 215
operating profit, income statement, 148–149
operations, 104
business capabilities and, 133–134
NPOs, 227–228
planning surveys (CD), 142
sole proprietor, 108
opportunities (SWOT), 109–110, 125
opportunities/threats grid, 110
organization, 104
business capabilities and, 139–142
division organization, 262
duties and responsibilities, 263–265
function organization, 262
goals and objectives assignment sheet, 264
matrix organization, 262
NPOs, 228
organizing around plan, 262–266
pack organization, 262
sole proprietor, 108
systems and procedures, 265–266
outside opinions, 42–44
outsourcing, self-employed persons, 181
overhead, 148, 163
NPOs, 232

owners' equity, 157–158
accumulated retained earnings, 158
invested capital, 158
total owner's equity, 158
ownership feeling, plan distribution and, 269

• P •

pack style of organization, 141, 262
partners, funding and, 301
payment methods, 116
self-employed persons, 188–189
performance, plan distribution and, 269
personal assessment
creativity and, 9
strengths/weaknesses, 21–24
personal strengths, 292
pictures in plan, 130
Plan Write For Business software, 315
PlanMagic Business software, 315
planning
economic change and, 205
frequency, e-business, 206
typical situations, 28–30
planning ability, small businesses and, 192
plans. *See also* implementation; written plans
alternate versions, 257–258
audience, 27–32, 252–258
components (CD), 44, 260
compressing, 212
contents, 33–37
distributing, 268–269
final draft, 258–259
importance in small businesses, 192
importance of, 25–26
initial idea, 7–8
keeping fresh, 284–286
length, 37
message, 30–32
organizing around, 262–266
purpose, 295–298
purpose, self-employed persons and, 177–178
results, 295–298
trouble and, 277–283
political organizations (NPOs), 224
potential customers, 26
prepaid expenses, 154
pricing strategies, 26
self-employed persons, 182–190
pride of ownership, implementation and, 274–275
pro forma income statement, 168–169
problem-solving goals, 58
products. *See also* services
business opportunities and, 14
checklist, 130, 142
company description and, 129–130
programs (NPOs), 220
professional groups, 41
profit, 27, 148
before taxes, 149
net profit, 149–150
profit-and-loss statement, 145
statement of financial activities (NPOs), 220
programs (NPOs), 220
progress, plans and, 298
project charges, self-employed persons, 183–184
projected cash flow, forecasting and, 169–170

qualified NPOs, 224
questionnaires
business model, 117, 118, 125
business opportunities evaluation, 17
growth planning, 122, 126
ideal customer, 83–84

industry analysis, 77–78, 100
mission statement, 49, 68
personal strengths/weaknesses, 22–23
stealth competitors, 96
time frame, 39, 45
values, 64–66
Quick Insight software, 315

• R •

R&D (research and development), 104
business capabilities and, 132–133
NPOs, 230–231
sole proprietor, 108
raises, self-employed persons, 189
reality check, 19–24
receipts on sales, 162
recoverers from catastrophes, 62
red ink, revenues, 114
REDF (Roberts Enterprise Development Fund), 226
regulators, 31
research companies, 40
resources, 40–41
small businesses, 192
response cards, customer analysis, 90
résumé, 27
return policies, customer service and, 137
revenues, 27, 113, 147
consumables, 113
financial projection worksheet, 115
in the black, 113–114
red ink, 114
updating plan and, 303
variable costs, 114
reviewing other mission statements, 52
reviewing situation, updating plan and, 284–286
Rolls-Royce, value proposition, 209

• S •

sales/marketing, 104
capabilities and, 134–135
sole proprietor, 108
updating plan and, 304
savings, self-employed persons, 189
SBA (Small Business Administration), 40. *See also* small businesses
definition of small business, 191
expert advice, 245
loans, 301
programs, 194
Web site, 242
SBIC (Small Business Investment Company), 194
SBUs (strategic business units), 141
SCORE (Service Corps of Retired Executives)
expert advice, 245
Web site, 242
search and research companies, 40
seasonal customers, 116
second-stage financing, VCs, 217
seed financing, VCs, 217
self-employed persons, 175. *See also* independent contractors
action plan, 182
billable hours, 185
business environment, 179–181
business networking, 180
company description, 181
company overview, 179
expenses checklist, 187
financial review, 182
get-rich-quick schemes, 188
hourly charges, 183–184
outsourcing, 181
payment, 188–189
plan purpose, 177–178
pricing, 182–188

self-employed persons *(continued)*
  project charges, 183–184
  pros/cons, 176
  raises, 189
  saving money, 189
  scams, 188
  written plan benefits, 175–177
self-reliance, 20–21
senior management, 31
services. *See also* products
  business opportunities and, 14
  checklist, 130, 142
  NPOs, 220
setting goals, 55–56
  flowchart, 56–57
  mission statement, 56–57
  objectives, 55
SG&A (sales, general, and administration) expenses, 148
  cash flow statement, 163
shareware programs (CD), 310
shopping carts, e-business, 211
small business. *See also* SBA (Small Business Administration)
  action plan, 196
  business environment, 193–194
  change and, 199–200
  company description, 195
  financial needs, 193
  financial review, 196
  growing, 197–201
  marketing, 198
  plan focus, 192–193
  plan importance, 192
  strategies, 195
social clubs (NPOs), 223
social return on investment (SROI), 226
social welfare organizations (NPOs), 223
software
  business plan, 314–315
  business software, 243–244
  upgrades, Web site development, 216
sole proprietor, strategies and, 108
SOS (Save Our Strays), 257
sound management, small businesses and, 192
sources, Web sites, 242
special groups, 245
specificity in mission statement, 51
speed, new economy and, 204
SROI (social return on investment), 226
stakeholders, target audience and, 252–255
stand-alone Internet business, 208–212
start-up costs
  e-business, 206–207
  worksheet (CD), 202
start-up financing, VCs, 217
statement of financial activities (NPOs), 220
statement of financial position (NPOs), 220
statement of vision, 66–68
stealth competitors, 94–95
strategies, 34
  form meets function style and, 262
  small businesses, 192, 195
  SWOT, 103–104
  updating plan and, 306
strengths/weaknesses, 125
  grid, 106–108
  survey, 105
  SWOT, 104–109
structure, NPOs, 223
suppliers, 31
support system, 42–44
SUV/minivan comparison, 89
SWOT (strengths, weaknesses, opportunities, and threats), 104
  analysis, 110–112
  analyzing troubled situations and, 280
  opportunities, 109–110
  strengths, 104–109

threats, 109–110
weaknesses, 104–109
systems and procedures, organization and, 265–266
CD form, 287
checklist, 267–268
systems installation, Web site development, 216

• T •

table of contents, 33
multiple audiences and, 255
tapas bars, 15
target market
audience guidelines (CD), 260
capabilities and, 134–135
guideline sheet, 254
multiple audiences, 255–257
stakeholder identification, 252–255
tasks and time survey, self-employed pricing, 184, 190
taxes, 163
profit before taxes, 149
tax-exempt NPOs, 223–224
team building to write plan, 246–252
teamwork promotion
CD form, 202
plan distribution and, 269
technical support, small businesses and, 192
technology, changes in, 199
updating plan and, 305
testing idea, 295
threats (SWOT), 109–110, 125
time frame, 37–39
income statement, 146
questionnaire, 39, 45
troubled situation turnaround, 282
writing plan, 248–249
timeline, 39
e-business, 207
timing, revenues and, 115–116
toolkit.cch.com (Business Owner's Toolkit) Web site, 242
total assets, 156
total funds in, cash flow statement, 162
total funds out, cash flow statement, 163–164
total liabilities and equity, 158
total owner's equity, 158
tracker, 43
writing plan, 249–252
tracking sheet for master plan, 250–251, 260
trade journals, 40
trade shows, 40
training resources checklist, 276
transaction style of leadership, 270
transformational style of leadership, 270
Travelocity.com, value proposition, 209
trend tracking, self-employed persons, 180
troubled situations
analyzing situation, 280–281
diagnosing problems, 278
turnaround, charting, 281–283
turnaround professionals, 278, 280
turnaround time frame, 282
warning signs, 278–280
troubleshooting CD, 316
turnaround professionals, 278, 280
typical business-planning situations, 28–30

• U •

U.S. Small Business Administration, 40
United Airlines, employee ownership and, 275
updating plan
business strategy and, 306
competition and, 305
costs and, 303

updating plan *(continued)*
employee morale and, 304
feedback and, 285–286
financial condition and, 305
growth and, 306
projects and, 304
revenues and, 303
reviewing situation, 284–285
sales figures and, 304
technology changes and, 305
upgrades, Web site development, 216

• V •

value proposition
NPOs, 226
stand-alone Internet business, 209–212
values, 26
importance of, 61–62
questionnaire, 64–66, 69
uncovering, 63
values statement, 61, 63–66
variable costs, revenues, 114
VCs (venture capitalists), 217
vendors, 31
venture capital, 301
veterans' organizations (NPOs), 223
vision for business, 26
implementation and, 272
NPOs, 221–223
vision statement, 61, 69
examples, 67–68
writing, 66–68

• W •

Wal-Mart, value proposition, 209
warning signs of trouble, 278–280, 287
weaknesses (SWOT), 104–109
Web sites, 242
development, 215–216
economic change and, 206
fact checking, 242
information verification, 242
maintenance costs, 216
resources for writing plan, 241–243
retail, 215
searches for business plan information, 241
sources, 242
Windows, CD bundle and, 308–309
winery example, 131
working capital, 157
written plans
alternate versions, 257–258
audience, targeting, 252–258
benefits, self-employed person and, 175–177
bookstore resources, 240–241
business software, 243–244
component checklist, 238–240, 260
delegating responsibilities, 246–247
expert advice sources, 244–245
final draft, 258
ground rules for writing, 248
readiness, 237–238
special groups, 245
team, 246–252
time frame for writing, 248–249
tracking, 249–252
Web site resources, 241–242

Notes

Notes

Notes

Hungry Minds, Inc., End-User License Agreement

READ THIS. You should carefully read these terms and conditions before opening the software packet(s) included with this book ("Book"). This is a license agreement ("Agreement") between you and Hungry Minds, Inc. ("HM"). By opening the accompanying software packet(s), you acknowledge that you have read and accept the following terms and conditions. If you do not agree and do not want to be bound by such terms and conditions, promptly return the Book and the unopened software packet(s) to the place you obtained them for a full refund.

1. **License Grant.** HM grants to you (either an individual or entity) a nonexclusive license to use one copy of the enclosed software program(s) (collectively, the "Software") solely for your own personal or business purposes on a single computer (whether a standard computer or a workstation component of a multiuser network). The Software is in use on a computer when it is loaded into temporary memory (RAM) or installed into permanent memory (hard disk, CD-ROM, or other storage device). HM reserves all rights not expressly granted herein.

2. **Ownership.** HM is the owner of all right, title, and interest, including copyright, in and to the compilation of the Software recorded on the disk(s) or CD-ROM ("Software Media"). Copyright to the individual programs recorded on the Software Media is owned by the author or other authorized copyright owner of each program. Ownership of the Software and all proprietary rights relating thereto remain with HM and its licensers.

3. **Restrictions on Use and Transfer.**

   (a) You may only (i) make one copy of the Software for backup or archival purposes, or (ii) transfer the Software to a single hard disk, provided that you keep the original for backup or archival purposes. You may not (i) rent or lease the Software, (ii) copy or reproduce the Software through a LAN or other network system or through any computer subscriber system or bulletin-board system, or (iii) modify, adapt, or create derivative works based on the Software.

   (b) You may not reverse engineer, decompile, or disassemble the Software. You may transfer the Software and user documentation on a permanent basis, provided that the transferee agrees to accept the terms and conditions of this Agreement and you retain no copies. If the Software is an update or has been updated, any transfer must include the most recent update and all prior versions.

4. **Restrictions on Use of Individual Programs.** You must follow the individual requirements and restrictions detailed for each individual program in the "About the CD" Appendix of this Book. These limitations are also contained in the individual license agreements recorded on the Software Media. These limitations may include a requirement that after using the program for a specified period of time, the user must pay a registration fee or discontinue use. By opening the Software packet(s), you will be agreeing to abide by the licenses and restrictions for these individual programs that are detailed in the "About the CD" Appendix and on the Software Media. None of the material on this Software Media or listed in this Book may ever be redistributed, in original or modified form, for commercial purposes.

5. **Limited Warranty.**

   (a) HM warrants that the Software and Software Media are free from defects in materials and workmanship under normal use for a period of sixty (60) days from the date of purchase of this Book. If HM receives notification within the warranty period of defects in materials or workmanship, HM will replace the defective Software Media.

   (b) **HM AND THE AUTHOR OF THE BOOK DISCLAIM ALL OTHER WARRANTIES, EXPRESS OR IMPLIED, INCLUDING WITHOUT LIMITATION IMPLIED WARRANTIES OF MERCHANTABILITY AND FITNESS FOR A PARTICULAR PURPOSE, WITH RESPECT TO THE SOFTWARE, THE PROGRAMS, THE SOURCE CODE CONTAINED THEREIN, AND/OR THE TECHNIQUES DESCRIBED IN THIS BOOK. HM DOES NOT WARRANT THAT THE FUNCTIONS CONTAINED IN THE SOFTWARE WILL MEET YOUR REQUIREMENTS OR THAT THE OPERATION OF THE SOFTWARE WILL BE ERROR FREE.**

   (c) This limited warranty gives you specific legal rights, and you may have other rights that vary from jurisdiction to jurisdiction.

6. **Remedies.**

   (a) HM's entire liability and your exclusive remedy for defects in materials and workmanship shall be limited to replacement of the Software Media, which may be returned to HM with a copy of your receipt at the following address: Software Media Fulfillment Department, Attn.: *Business Plans Kit For Dummies,* Hungry Minds, Inc., 10475 Crosspoint Blvd., Indianapolis, IN 46256, or call 800-762-2974. Please allow three to four weeks for delivery. This Limited Warranty is void if failure of the Software Media has resulted from accident, abuse, or misapplication. Any replacement Software Media will be warranted for the remainder of the original warranty period or thirty (30) days, whichever is longer.

   (b) In no event shall HM or the author be liable for any damages whatsoever (including without limitation damages for loss of business profits, business interruption, loss of business information, or any other pecuniary loss) arising from the use of or inability to use the Book or the Software, even if HM has been advised of the possibility of such damages.

   (c) Because some jurisdictions do not allow the exclusion or limitation of liability for consequential or incidental damages, the above limitation or exclusion may not apply to you.

7. **U.S. Government Restricted Rights.** Use, duplication, or disclosure of the Software by the U.S. Government is subject to restrictions stated in paragraph (c)(1)(ii) of the Rights in Technical Data and Computer Software clause of DFARS 252.227-7013, and in subparagraphs (a) through (d) of the Commercial Computer–Restricted Rights clause at FAR 52.227-19, and in similar clauses in the NASA FAR supplement, when applicable.

8. **General.** This Agreement constitutes the entire understanding of the parties and revokes and supersedes all prior agreements, oral or written, between them and may not be modified or amended except in a writing signed by both parties hereto that specifically refers to this Agreement. This Agreement shall take precedence over any other documents that may be in conflict herewith. If any one or more provisions contained in this Agreement are held by any court or tribunal to be invalid, illegal, or otherwise unenforceable, each and every other provision shall remain in full force and effect.

Installation Instructions

The *Business Plans Kit For Dummies* CD offers valuable information that you don't want to miss.

For Microsoft Windows users

To install items from the CD onto your hard drive, follow these steps:

1. **Insert the CD into your computer's CD-ROM drive.**
2. **Open your browser.**
3. **Select Start⇨Run.**
4. **In the dialog box that appears, type** D:\START.HTM.
5. **Read through the license agreement, nod your head, and click the Accept button if you want to use the CD.**

   After you click Accept, you jump to the Main Menu.
6. **To navigate within the interface, click on any topic of interest to take you to an explanation of the files on the CD and to instructions on how to use or install them.**
7. **To install the software from the CD, click on the software name.**

For more information, see the "About the CD" Appendix.

For Mac users

To install items from the CD onto your hard drive, follow these steps:

1. **Insert the CD into your computer's CD-ROM drive.**

   An icon representing the CD you inserted appears on your Mac desktop. Chances are, the icon looks like a CD-ROM.
2. **Double-click the CD icon to show the CD's contents.**
3. **Double-click** `start.htm` **to open your browser and display the license agreement.**

   If your browser doesn't open automatically, open it by choosing File⇨Open File (in Internet Explorer) or File⇨Open⇨Location in Netscape (in Netscape Communicator) and select *Biz Plans Kit FD*. The license agreement appears.

4. **Read through the license agreement, nod your head, and click the Accept button if you want to use the CD.**

   After you click Accept, you're taken to the Main menu. This is where you can browse through the contents of the CD.

5. **To navigate within the interface, click on any topic of interest to take you to an explanation of the files on the CD and to instructions on how to use or install them.**

6. **To install the software from the CD, click on the software name.**

For more information, see the "About the CD" Appendix.

Notes